Between Two Worlds

Structures of Early Christianity

Christoph Markschies

SCM PRESS

Translated by John Bowden from the German *Zwischen den Welten wandern. Strukturen des antiken Christentums.* Published 1997 by Fischer Taschenbuch Verlag GmbH, Frankfurt am Main.

0 334 02750 0

This edition first published 1999 by
SCM Press
9–17 St Albans Place London N1 0NX

SCM Press is a division of
SCM-Canterbury Press Ltd.

Typeset by Regent Typesetting, London
Printed in Great Britain by
Biddles Ltd, Guildford and King's Lynn

Contents

Introduction

This book could also have been entitled 'An Outline of a Structural History of the Early Church'. Anyway, I have attempted to write such an account, focussing on institutions and forms of life. Such a study has often been called for since the end of the nineteenth century – thus Adolf von Harnack (1851–1930) described the institutions as 'the skeleton of history' – but so far very few scholars have actually made it: for example Robert M.Grant,[1] or, in a very modified form as a 'history of ecclesiological types', Carl Andresen.[2] I want to talk of 'structures' in order to take into account not only the classical 'institutions' of Christian history (which might include marriage, the ordained ministry, the papacy, etc.), but also those historically relevant phenomena which have only been given the attention they deserve in recent decades: the piety of individual members of the community and whole groups, and also the various social forms of Christianity in the early Roman empire. The fact that this is a 'structural history' also means that here I shall not be presenting a history of early Christianity in the classical sense: the theme of 'church and state' is not discussed as a history of events (nor does the legal side of the persecutions of Christians become a separate topic). Finally, this is not a social history of early Christianity or a history of relations between the sexes in early Christianity; nor is it a history of theology or literature presented in embryo: early Christian authors, papyri, inscriptions and archaeological sources will be cited only if they can illuminate structures of early Christianity – in the sense described.

The title, *Between Two Worlds,* is meant to refer to a central theme of the book: the experience, fixed at a very early stage,[3] that the real home of Christians is in heaven, stamps the expressions of this religion throughout antiquity – despite the many modifications in almost all its variants. Here the starting point of the account was an observation of the history of the influence of Christianity: the Christian church of the time of the Roman empire and late antiquity had lasting significance for the development of European culture from the late Middle Ages on, above all in three spheres.

First of all it contributed to the replacement of the plurality of cults in the time of the emperors with a new unitary religion which had great power to shape society. This obligated its followers, in a hitherto unaccustomed way, to give their individual lives a quite specific form (e.g. the marriage ethic) and similarly produced hitherto unaccustomed forms of social responsibility (e.g. the care of widows).

Secondly – in quite the opposite direction – it so to speak 'undermined' the possibility of Christians making their home in their environment and identifying themselves with it, by summoning the community to the 'better morality of continence'. Here again it developed social forms of such a life as an escape from the world (e.g. colonies of hermits or monasteries).

Thirdly, the church of the time of the Empire and late antiquity was able to make use of a scholarly theology which in part flourished alongside the communities. This utilized the methods and thought-forms of ancient philosophy to explain the message of the New Testament and thus made Christianity attractive to the educated as well.

The background of this history of the influence of Christianity dictates the arrangement of this book. First an external framework is sketched out by an introduction to the geographical space and time within which Christianity appeared and developed. Here the most important stages of the Christianization of the Roman empire are presented, with a particular focus on social, political and legal aspects. Then follow three sections which are concerned with the individual, the forms of life which stand between individual and community, and finally the wider community. It has not been possible to give more than a brief account of a central aspect of the history of early Christianity, the reshaping of the Christian message by theologians with a scholarly training[4] – here phrases like 'the Hellenization of Christianity' are popular.

It is obvious that in less than three hundred pages only a sketch of the structures of early Christianity can be offered, and that some scholarly discussion or extended background evidence has had to be omitted. It has been important to allow space for quite lengthy quotation of ancient texts, in order to make the account more objective and vivid. The sometimes equally extensive references to the New Testament and to Jesus of Nazareth can be explained, among other things, by the fact that this book has been written by a Protestant church historian. I do not believe that the intentions of Jesus or the first Christians have been preserved, in principle or a priori, outside the majority church and among the so-called heretics who were separated from it. Rather, in both the so-called 'orthodoxies' and the 'heresies' we have highly complex processes of the transformation of a Jewish teaching related to the local conditions of Palestine into a distinctive religion for the whole Roman empire. Careful and unprejudiced examination of the history of early Christianity would show that in many cases – but of course by no means all – these processes of transformation and theological or ethical decisions by the majority church can claim greater plausibility than those of the minorities which once again are being energetically brought into the foreground.

One last word on the bibliography at the end of the book: this documents above all the sources and usable translations of these ancient texts. Only the most important titles of the secondary literature have been mentioned. However, the extensive debate which has been carried on above all over the past few decades about Walter Bauer's book *Orthodoxy and Heresy in Earliest Christianity*[5] and the theses contained in it has rightly drawn our attention to the plurality of early Christianity and helped to replace a monolithic picture of its development with more precise historical sketches. This book now seeks to draw attention to structures which despite sometimes very different theological options bound together the most different Christian communities. These structures, which shaped identity, allows us despite all the plurality to speak of *one* early Christianity.[6]

It is thanks to many friends and colleagues that this account, which for reasons of space is rather brief on some points, has not been even sparser: special mention must be made of Hanns Christof Brennecke and Georg Schöllgen. I also want to mention two of my professorial assistants, Ursula Reuter and Susanne Böhm. Some of the remarks on the ethical legal statements of the synods come from my first senior seminar at Jena. The last chapter goes back to lectures and discussions which Emma Brunner-Traut invited me to hold in Tübingen; the remarks on buildings in Syria and Jordan to a course given at the German Evangelical Institute for the Antiquities of the Holy Land in Jerusalem and Amman. Finally, work on the text was finished during a stimulating stay on Mount Zion in Jerusalem in spring 1996.

I am particularly pleased that only two years after its publication in Germany this text can now also appear in an English edition: I am grateful to John Bowden for his excellent translation.

One last word on the bibliography at the end of the book; this documents above all the sources and usable translations of these ancient texts. Only the most important titles of the secondary literature have been mentioned.

Christoph Markschies

Berlin,
Institute for Advanced Studies
Easter 1999

Early Christianity – Space and Time

The geographical sphere of early Christianity – influences and development

Geographical Setting

The geographical setting of the history of early Christianity was for many years almost exclusively identical with the Roman empire, and then with the states that succeeded it. Neighbouring empires – for example that of Persia – were only involved very partially, and in contrast to the European Middle Ages, the Christian church also carried out hardly any mission beyond the frontiers of the empire. Here world mission meant having reached the frontiers of the *imperium Romanum*, the Roman empire. We must not see anything specific to Christianity about this – on the contrary, in being thus limited the Christian community showed itself to be part of the ancient world, which alongside the empire usually recognized only a barbarian or desolate land. The *imperium* was the *oikoumene*, the whole of the inhabited world. *Orbis terrarum*, the circle of the earth, was identified with *orbis Romanus*. Where – as for example in Trier – a map of the world was painted on the wall of the corridor of an educational establishment,[7] those looking at it could also make this identification. Anyone who stood in the capital, Rome, before the mausoleum of the emperor Augustus, who died in AD 14, and read there (or in some of the other places in the empire where it had been put up) the account of his actions which the *imperator* had composed shortly before his death, was already reminded of these notions in the heading above that text: '[Report] of the actions of the divine Augustus, by which he subjected the earth to the authority of the Roman people.'

Thanks to such efforts on the part of Augustus, the title of this text – also called *monumentum Ancyranum*, after the best preserved copy in Ankara in Turkey – the *imperium* now embraced the whole inhabited world, the *oikoumene*. As long as the Roman empire existed, the Christian church only very rarely broke with this ideology and proclaimed its message beyond the frontiers of the state.

Nevertheless, the geographical sphere of the history of early Christianity is not simply identical with that of the Roman empire: its ideal centre lies elsewhere, and that shifts the emphases in every respect. As is well known, Rome, with its comparatively central geographical position, formed the heart and metropolis of the pagan empire – as *urbs* it was *the* city; other cities were called *oppidum*, to make the difference in category clear. The *imperium* was centred on Rome in every respect, and alongside it there were only a few great cities like Alexandria or Antioch. These cities were not viable, because of their sometimes monstrous concentration of population or the environs in which they were set. As well as the capital, many other metropolises (like Antioch, Athens and Ephesus, for example) were dependent on imports of food. These lay in the hands of private merchants, although they were controlled by the state.

But Christianity did not come into being there, in Rome or in the melting pot of cultures formed by the other larger cities. Rather, it began its triumphant progress through the ancient world from some small villages in northern Palestine. Even now one can conveniently cross in an afternoon the sphere in which Jesus of Nazareth was active, on the north shore of Lake Gennesaret: it is four kilometres walk from Capernaum, his home town (Matt. 9.1), to Chorazin, where he did many miracles, and just over five from Capernaum to Bethsaida, where Peter came from.[8] Jesus avoided towns by the lake; the places where this son of an ordinary craftsman without any theological training was active were the Galilean villages. So it is not surprising that an educated pagan like the Roman emperor Julian reminds the followers of Jesus of their simple origins and always calls them 'Galileans'. As the ruler polemically remarks, one can hardly regard a few healings in such villages as mighty acts.[9] Jerusalem proved more significant than these small localities, which soon became less important for a Christianity extending over the empire. Only after the fourth century was it visited again by a larger number of pilgrims.

Jerusalem

This Jewish capital, from the perspective of an educated Roman situated far away on the periphery of the empire in a relatively new and unruly province, became the location of the first larger community which formed in the year AD 30 after the execution of Jesus. The New Testament reports how Jesus' distressed followers were brought together again by appearances of the Risen Jesus and confessed him Messiah (*mashiach*, Greek *christos*) or Lord (Greek *kyrios*, e.g. Luke 24.13–34). Relatives of Jesus quickly came to dominate this group and, faithful to the biblical promises, people expected his imminent return on the hill of Zion in the middle of Jerusalem (thus also Paul, Rom. 11.26f.). In the first years of the history of Christianity, Jerusalem formed not only the ideal but also the geographical centre of this young community. Paul carried the gospel 'from Jerusalem' (Rom. 15.19) throughout the inhabited world and made a collection among those members of his mission communities which did not come from Judaism (so-called 'Gentile Christians') 'for the poor among the saints in Jerusalem'. Only when Jerusalem was razed to the ground by Roman troops in connection with two Jewish revolts in AD 70 and 132–135, and Jews were banned from entering the city, which was rebuilt as Aelia Capitolina, did the real significance of this ideal centre of Christianity for the moment retreat right into the background. Nevertheless, in many circles people continued to maintain that the eschatological return of Christ was to be expected on Mount Zion in Jerusalem. Thus Justin, who originally came from what is now Nablus and then taught in Rome, explained to his Jewish conversation partner around the middle of the second century that Jesus would appear in glory at the same place where he had once been dishonoured by his extremely shameful execution.[10]

Great Cities and Regions

After its destruction in AD 70, Jerusalem was replaced as the centre of early Christianity by a series of other centres. Significantly these include those three places which we describe – somewhat anachronistically – as ancient 'great cities': Antioch, Rome and Alexandria. Alongside them the communities which were in part founded by Paul on his missionary journeys in densely populated centres of the province of Asia (for example Ephesus, but also Smyrna) played some role, as later, towards the end of the second century, did the provincial capital of *Africa proconsularis*, Carthage. In the course of only a generation, Christianity had changed from a movement within the Jewish religion, originally at home in villages, to a distinctive religion primarily with an urban stamp. This very drastic alteration of the character of this community is a first and early phenomenon of acculturation. Beyond doubt it is closely – if not exclusively – connected with the activity of the missionary Sha'ul (Saul), who was born in Tarsus in Asia Minor. In three missionary journeys this theologian, better known under his

Paul

Latin name Paul, carried the Christian message into a great many places in the eastern Mediterranean, the Aegean and Asia Minor: to Cyprus, to Lycia and Pamphylia in southern Asia Minor, to Galatia in central Asia Minor, and to Ephesus and Miletus on the coast of Asia Minor. With his preaching he turned first to the Jewish synagogue communities; probably simply because travel there was easier, he preferred the cities in which there were such communities. Whereas his stay in Athens obviously did not produce any great results, he left flourishing Christian communities behind on the west coast of Asia Minor, in Corinth and on the coast of Macedonia (Thessaloniki and Philippi), having usually been thrown out of the synagogue relatively rapidly. Then on the way to his trial in Rome around AD 60/61, he came upon an already existing community there in which perhaps he lived and taught for a while (according to Acts 28.30 for at least two years in a rented house in the city), before he was executed in Rome. The whole of Paul's missionary practice shows how Roman was the thought of this Jew from Asia Minor. He by no means used his coveted citizenship simply as a mark of legal status: already before his last journey he turned his attention to the Roman community (Rom. 1.10) and wanted to carry on his mission as far as Latin-speaking Spain. The frontier territory of Parthia and Persia, the more northerly regions of the provinces of Germania or Dalmatia, were of no interest to him; similarly, he left out Alexandria, a rival, indeed an occasional enemy, of Rome. Nevertheless, already at the beginning of the second century, in this great cultural metropolis, as in Rome, there seem to have been Christians – in neither case do we now know the names of those who founded the communities. But in both places there were large Jewish communities which kept up intensive contacts with the mother country and especially with the temple in Jerusalem: Christianity may have spread in both cities by such contacts. Thus just as the geographical framework of Christianity changed as it became rooted in the great metropolises, so too the form of this religion changed: it now took part in the cultural climate of these cities, at the level of their education and institutions, and of course also in a range of social classes which was wider than that in the villages of northern Galilee.

Antioch

The first of these metropolises of the Roman empire which Christianity reached was Antioch, the third largest city of the empire after Rome and Alexandria. Even by present-day standards, given the size of the population (estimated as being 200,000 freemen at the beginning of the second century, though the information is very uncertain), Antioch could be called a great city. The city on the Orontes had been part of the Roman empire since 64 BC and functioned as capital of the province of Syria: its streets were thronged principally by descendants of the Greek and Macedonian colonists, Jews and Syrians from the neighbouring lands, and also Phoenicians, Arabs, Persians and Egyptians, indeed even Indians who had brought trade here. The confusion of languages, cultures and religions was similarly colourful. It was here that the groups which had presumably grown out of the Jewish community of those who confessed Jesus as Messiah first also attracted the attention of non-Jews as a trend separate from the synagogue. Its members were spoken of in the city as *Christiani* (Acts 11.26). As this kind of word-formation was also used officially to name parties, it could already have been an official designation: the group would then have been named by the authorities after its supposed founder (or, more precisely, after his title of Messiah, which was already treated as a proper name). Unfortunately, because of a lack of relevant information we do not know whether in Antioch Christianity had quickly also reached the more prominent and well-educated social classes: be this as it may, at the end of the second century Theophilus, a bishop of the Syrian provincial capital, demonstrated to a pagan friend how rational Christianity was and how ridiculous were the pagan religious mythologies. He displays his education on almost every page of this apology: 'Herodotus, Thucydides or even Xenophon'[11] are called upon, and copious poetical quotations are scattered through the work. Politically, too, Theophilus is not necessarily a rebel: he shows his respect to the emperor by praying for him. So an educated urban Christian, a child of his metropolis, is head of the Christian community of Antioch at the end of the second century, barely 150 years after its foundation. However, we first get really reliable information about the everyday life of wider circles of the community in the rich tradition of sermons by the pulpit star John Chrysostom (died 407), which he gave in the principal church between 386 and 397, clearly making a considerable impact on the public.

Alexandria

For want of reliable sources, the picture of Alexandria, also a new Hellenistic foundation with a very colourful mixed population and a large and significant Jewish community, is even more hazy. At around 300,000 freemen, the population of the city in the first century is thought to have been considerably greater than that of Antioch. However, since here not only the foundation of the Christian community but also its history in the second century is completely enigmatic at many points, modern scholars have constructed the research legend of a Christianity in the port which had been given a completely 'heretical' form, the memory of which was suppressed by the victorious 'catholic' church.[12] In truth, the Christian community may at first have consisted quite markedly of members of the Jewish population of the city;[13] even two of the five districts of the city have been described as 'Jewish'. After bloody persecutions and a rebellion in AD 115 this very heavily Hellenized Jewish community was reduced to a small remnant; it presumably perished completely in connection with another Jewish rebellion in AD 132–135. The heyday of the Christian community dawned only when with Clement (died before 215) and Origen (died 253/254), from the end of the second century two highly educated theologians fought for the synthesis of Christianity and Hellenistic culture or education. Neither of the two categories of 'heresy' and 'orthodoxy' (or 'catholicism') really do justice to the thought of these two great Alexandrians, which in many respects was experimental, nor are they appropriate descriptions of other theologians from that city. In the second century academic theology was still far too young and its form still too fluid to speak here of 'norm' and 'deviation'. Evidently at an early stage Christianity adapted to a specific characteristic of the city: since already by virtue of possessing two libraries, the Serapeion and the Museion (which were flourishing again despite the catastrophic fire of the year 48 BC), Alexandria can be described as the classical cultural metropolis of antiquity, it is not surprising that particularly well educated Christian teachers appeared here. For example, in his work *The Instructor,* Clement gave advice about how the converted educated pagan should live his everyday life as a Christian and compiled arguments in defence of the reasonable nature of Christian teaching against the most important Greek philosophies. Origen, one of the most productive writers of antiquity (his bibliography amounted to around 2000 works), was particularly influential through his scholarly biblical commentaries and series of sermons: in Caesarea in Palestine, to which he had moved in 230/231, a school gathered around him and his extensive library. It moulded theologians well into the fourth century and led to the triumphal course of an 'Origenistic' theology in the east of the empire. From the existence of this school and also from the different forms of school in Alexandria itself we can see the degree to which groups in this community had accepted forms of Hellenistic training, education and philosophy. Above all in philosophy since Plato's time, schools had gathered around famous teachers who stood in the succession *(diadoche)* of the master even after his death. The Alexandrian community established a school which in addition to elementary Christian instruction (explanation of the creed, liturgical information, introduction to the sacraments) also offered 'higher' theological education. However, we must not imagine this to have been a firmly organized college on a mediaeval or modern pattern.

Of course the Alexandrian community did not just consist of such highly educated Christians; in the 'social underground' of the city, in the Egyptian quarter of Rhakotis, there were also Christians of quite a different stamp. Unfortunately the community also shared in one characteristic of the urban populace which was already vigorously criticized in antiquity, the fury of mob anger. At the end of the second century the orator Dio Chrysostom from Asia Minor attributed peace in the inner city to the presence of Roman troops in Alexandria: 'How else could you keep people's hands off one another?'[14] One of the last excesses of this notorious potential for violence was the attack by Christian fanatics on the celebrated pagan Neoplatonic philosopher Hypatia in 415: she was thrown from her litter and stoned naked, and her body was dismembered and burned.[15]

Asia Minor

Probably originally as a result of missionary activities by Paul, a very old centre of ancient Christianity lay in Asia Minor – more precisely in cities of the regions of Asia, Lydia and Phrygia. Here – alongside Palestine – was the densest concentration of Christian communities, especially in and around the Meander valley, which served as the central trade route from the port of Miletus and Ephesus into the interior. Alongside these two cities mention should be made of Magnesia, Tralles, Hierapolis, Colossae, Laodicea and, further north, Smyrna, Sardes and Philadelphia. Again in the first phase theologians above all come into view as representatives of communities; they convey the picture of a very colourful Christianity, but still with a strong

Jewish stamp. Before 190 the bishop of Sardes, Melito, faithful to the synagogue tradition, preached on Passover night about the exodus of the Israelites from Egypt and the first celebration of the Passover, with the slaughtering of the Passover lamb (Ex. 12). He interpreted all this as a model (*typos*) provided by God for the suffering, death and resurrection of Christ: 'So now understand, beloved . . . how mortal and immortal it is, the mystery of the Passover . . . For in reality, the slaughter of the lamb and celebration of the Passover feast is contained in Christ . . . As Son he was born, as lamb led out, as sheep slaughtered, and as man buried; from the dead he arose as God, by nature God and man.'[16] In Hierapolis, a spa with baths famous for its hot springs, around AD 130 bishop Papias wrote five books of 'Interpretation of the Sayings of the Lord', a monumental collection of reports about Jesus of Nazareth from oral and written tradition; unfortunately these are lost. In the little Phrygian villages above Hierapolis a radical-conservative movement established itself around a prophet named Montanus and some prophetesses, which in the last century of the second century attempted to revive the theology (above all the expectation of an imminent return of Christ), ethics and structures of the primitive community; its influence spread as far as North Africa.

Rome

In view of the significance of the *urbs Roma* for the whole empire, it is not surprising that urban Roman Christianity also quickly made a name for itself. So much so, that the history of Christianity in antiquity could also be written as the history of the growing influence and final domination of this city over the Western church and theology. When Paul came to Rome (in AD 60 or 61), he already found a Christian community there. His letter to the Romans shows that urban Roman Christianity had already detached itself from the synagogue and, as in Antioch, soon was also perceived by its pagan environment as an independent entity. The young community gathered in the houses of more prosperous Christians; from the letters of Paul we even know some names, for example those of the tent-making(?) couple Prisca and Aquila (contrary to convention, the sources mention the name of the wife first; evidently she played an important role in the community). A Roman tradition locates the couple's house on the Aventine, though the tradition can be demonstrated only in late antiquity. Like Peter, Paul was presumably executed along with many members of the community during the Neronian persecution of Christians (in AD 64). From then on the urban community of Christians could appeal to a proud 'apostolic tradition' – one of the roots for the origin of a 'papal' claim from the third century on and its establishment at the end of the fourth. We have indications that very soon the Roman community contained people from all social strata. The Roman consul of the year 95, Titus Flavius Clemens, a close relative of the emperor Domitian (81–96), was executed possibly because he and his wife were Christians.[17] The accounts from the Roman community of the second century give above all the names of free teachers who – in a way comparable to the practice in Alexandria practice – gathered schools around them, and also of prominent women who were active in the community. Divergent theological views were tolerated, with characteristic exceptions. One of these exceptions was the teacher Marcion, who after his expulsion was given back the 200,000 sesterces which he had donated to the Roman community when he entered it.[18] Thus already in the second century Christianity was clearly a phenomenon widespread in the upper classes.

North Africa

Literary reports about Christianity in North Africa occur extremely late, for the first time in 180 CE. In this year twelve men and women from Scilli were taken before the governor of Carthage; six of them were executed. Scilli was evidently such a small place that so far it has not been possible to locate it. Minor references in later texts indicate that African Christianity was established by travellers both from Asia Minor and Syria and from Rome. The community seems to have been geographically, socially and institutionally quite widely scattered at the beginning of the third century, though it is impossible to quantify this information (for example along the lines of the traditional 'the majority in the lower classes').[19] In Carthage, Quintus Septimius Florens Tertullianus (died after 200) was the first Christian writer to write in Latin; his father had held high military rank in the city cohort of Carthage.[20] His first literary works, including an *Apology*, date from the years before the turn of the century. In 213 Tertullian finally broke with the majority church and joined the Montanist movement, which originally came from Phrygia. However, this movement had changed its character by comparison with its beginnings: the rigoristic ethic had come more strongly into the foreground.

Gaul

In Gaul, too, Christianity could already point to flourishing communities in the second century: one of the most important theologians from the second half of the second century, Irenaeus, who came from Asia Minor, held office first as presbyter and later as bishop in Lyons. There he wrote his most important work in five books, *Refutation of the Gnostic Heresy* (commonly known as '*Against the Heresies*'). After the middle of the fourth century the region became notable for a wealth of literature. Here the writers above all came from senatorial circles with a high level of education.

The expansion of Christianity

How could it come about that within a few hundred years Christianity had already expanded into the three great metropolises of the empire, into the cities on the west coast of Asia Minor, and of course into Palestine, although only the apostle Paul and his fellow-workers had carried out a comparatively planned mission for a brief period of around ten years? And how could the expansion continue in the second century in cities of North Africa, on the Rhone, Rhine and Moselle, and on the Black Sea coast? Of course it was not until the fourth century that a so to speak blanket Christianization began. We possibly have more or less chance reports of Christian communities even in very remote villages for the late first century: the church historian Hegesippus who comes from Syria reports in his *Memoirs* (written at the end of the second century) that the emperor Domitian had met great nephews of Jesus. These kinsfolk declared that they worked a field of thirty-nine measures of land with their own hands, without a large number of employees or day labourers.[21] However, it is difficult to decide whether Hegesippus is conveying a memory which has reliably been handed down over almost one hundred years, or whether this is an anecdote of no historical value. Reliable information comes from the third and fourth centuries. For example the Palestinian bishop Eusebius mentions a small village near the town of Madaba (in present-day Jordan) named Kariathaim and adds: 'now a completely Christian village'.[22] Of course we do not know why, by whom and how the village was Christianized. All we can infer from the context is that such a completely Christian village was still special at the time of the composition of the work (between AD 320 and 327). Many places emerge for the first time so to speak from nowhere as settlements with major Christian communities on a list which mentions those who took part in the first empire-wide council under Constantine (in AD 325, in the imperial summer residence of Nicaea). The around 220 bishops came above all from the regions of Bithynia, Asia, Lydia, Phrygia, Cappadocia, Lycia, Pamphylia, Pisidia, Lycaonia, Cappadocia and Cilicia in Asia Minor, and of course from the heartland of Syria, Phoenicia, Palestine and Arabia. Distances between the few episcopal sees on the Nile, on the coast of North Africa and in Macedonia, Greek and Pontus were often more than one hundred kilometres, sometimes more than three hundred. As virtually no Western participants attended the synod, we still do not have a complete inventory of the cities with major Christian communities even at the beginning of the fourth century. There are further references to places where communities existed in the accounts of Christian martyrs. On the basis of these sources it is also difficult to say whether the number of five million Christians which Ramsay MacMullen arrived at for the beginning of the fourth century is right or is far too high.[23] Basically the reports are very sparse and mostly connected with legendary reports about individuals. One example makes this clear. The Life of Origen's pupil Gregory, called the Miracle Worker – though this was only composed in the 380s by Gregory of Nyssa – tells how in the middle of the third century this learned man suddenly abandoned his solitude and accepted the bishopric in Amasea, Pontus, a city 'which hitherto had been so entangled in the madness of idolatry that among the countless inhabitants of the city itself and in the neighbouring region there were no more than seventeen who had accepted the word of faith'.[24] Because it was raining, Gregory entered a pagan temple, cried out the name of Christ, 'purified' with the sign of the cross the air laden with the smell of burnt sacrificial animals, and spent the whole night praying in the temple, whereupon the next morning the pagan priest promptly 'failed' with his prayer, because the spirits had gone out of the temple. The Life also reports that this priest was finally convinced by Gregory – they made a kind of bargain. Gregory gave him a letter to the temple spirits and commanded them to appear once again for a short while.

A few points in this legend are relevant to the history of mission. We learn that the extraordinarily small diocese of Amasea grew strongly through the activity of the Origenist teacher. A reference to a house initially put at Gregory's disposal by a prominent person and the accounts of his activity as a kind of arbitrator are important information. We can surmise that the rich estate of the family facilitated missionary activity in the land, so that a more non-urban Christianity became established in Pontus. Nevertheless we are a long way from extensive and reliable information.

The military

Evidently, although the Christian community did not have a systematic mission strategy for the Roman empire, it was so mobile that it kept reaching ever larger groups. The extent of this mobility is impressive: in his famous history of mission alone, Adolf von Harnack collected twenty-six names of Christian theologians who travelled to Rome from every possible corner of the empire during the second and early third centuries[25] – in view of the fact that at most ten per cent of the relevant Christian literature is still extant, this may be said to be the tip of an iceberg. These people, who as teachers were so to speak missionaries by profession, are a clear sign of the considerable mobility of Christianity, but not the only one. In the ancient world, changes of location and journeys in times of peace took place almost exclusively for economic reasons or in the course of an official or military career (not to mention the quite considerable cultural tourism among the upper classes). So it is not surprising that Christianity was in part also disseminated by soldiers and by merchants (but not by slaves). In excavations of the Roman military settlement of Dura Europos on the central Euphrates near the Persian frontier, remains were found of the building of a Christian community, which of course essentially consisted of soldiers. And as some detachments of troops had been posted to Dura Europos from already Christianized cities (like e.g. parts of the *Legio III Cyrenaica*, possibly also the *X Fretensis*, which were active in Egypt, Palestine and Syria), Christianity might have been introduced here by soldiers. However, the decoration of the room for the Mithras cult in Dura, which is of essentially better quality, shows that this mystery religion was a classical cult introduced by soldiers,[26] whereas the interest of soldiers in Christianity and their acceptance by the religion (see 121 below) was far from being the norm throughout the empire. However, as units of the same legions were also to be found in other places in Syria (for example the *III Cyrenaica* in Jerash/Gerasa, present-day Jordan), the significance of the soldiers in missionizing should not be either underestimated or overestimated.

Merchants

As well as the military, merchants travelled through the empire, and they too may have been of decisive importance for the expansion of Christianity. For example, an Egyptian papyrus has preserved for us the greetings of an Irenaeus to a business friend;[27] the letter was written in Rome where the sender had gone after unloading his delivery of grain in Puteoli or Ostia. The phrases he uses show that the Christian from Fayyum in Egypt had turned to his Christian sisters and brothers in the capital: 'The place has welcomed us as God willed' (cf. the allusion to Paul: I Cor. 12.18). So Christianity and business could be combined. At the same time we see clearly a decisive internal presupposition of Christian mission: it was made possible by the great importance attached to hospitality, which already played a central role for faith in the person of Jesus (Matt. 25.35–40). The comparatively late chronicles of

Edessa and Arbela also show that in these cities of Mesopotamia, Christianity was partly disseminated also by merchants. And as there are very few Jewish names among Christians in the written sources for this region,[28] here the converted Jews did not lay the foundation stone for Christian communities – as they did in Alexandria or Rome. What is true of the soldiers is also true of the state officials, who as a result of their various postings right across the empire almost automatically disseminated Christianity to the most varied regions of the empire. Near to the entrance to the park of the Villa Borghese today there stands the very splendid sarcophagus of an imperial freeman named Marcus Aurelius Prosenes (plate 1). Two winged and striding cupids are holding an inscribed tablet from which the life and the impressive career of the official can be reconstructed. Whether the inscription is Christian has indeed been disputed time and again, but a detail in its formulation makes that quite certain. Prosenes was born a slave, but freed by his patrons, the emperors Marcus Aurelius and Commodus, some time between 177 and 180. That made him a Roman citizen, obligated to show respect and obedience to his patrons. He rose from being administrator of state wine supplies to administrator of the imperial gladiatorial games, after which he became administrator of the emperor's private property and then of the imperial treasury. At the end of his career he was serving as chamberlain to the emperor; he died in 217, and his valuable sarcophagus was given by people whom he had freed in his turn. Prosenes is an example of how success in mission was accelerated not only by geographical mobility but also by social mobility in imperial society. The impressive martyrdoms probably won over more people to the cause than they deterred – on this see in more detail below, 103–9.

State officials

We can also describe the mission history of early Christianity by 'patterns of movement'[29] and integrate countless further individuals and destinies into such patterns. For example, at the end of the second century an Abercius from Hierapolis reported (he was then seventy-two years old) a series of journeys in his famous epitaph which attest great mobility: he came 'to Rome to see the capital . . . and I saw Syria's plains and all the cities, (as far as) Nisibis, after I had crossed the Euphrates; and everywhere I found companions in the faith'. However, Abercius, like almost all the Christian mission in antiquity, limited himself to the empire. Nisibis, since AD 162 again in Roman hands, and since 195 the provincial capital of Mesopotamia, marked the limit of his travels, which were probably missionary activity at the same time. A reference to his travel reading shows that we have a Christian here: 'I had Paul in the carriage.'[30]

Pax romana

The Christian mission made use of the excellent travel facilities and the close economic and political relationships within the empire – in other words what even today we can still describe as *pax Romana*, a term which appears for the first time in Seneca (died AD 40, father of the better known politician, philosopher and poet of the same name). A state of political and military peace and economic prosperity prevailed in the Roman empire above all during the first half of the second century. The senior Roman officer and scholar Pliny the Elder describes – around twenty years after the death of Paul – as a high point of 'Roman peace' that it had 'made the people of different lands and peoples known to one another'.[31] We can interpret the Christian mission and above all the comparatively rapid expansion of the movement as a specifically religious side of this process. 'Peace, harmony and friendship'[32] prevailed between Rome and the different regions or cities that had been conquered: these three qualities are matched on the Christian side by the close relationship between the different local churches, which is dealt with in more detail elsewhere (172–81). However, in part it has become customary to interpret such positive ancient testimony about the *pax Romana* as 'the cynicism of the rulers' and in a critical comparison to contrast with it a system of oppression, 'accompanied by streams of blood and tears of unimaginable proportions': 'the system of slavery'.[33] Of course if we measure the *pax Romana* by the criteria of modern European notions of a just constitutional, economic and social order, it comes off badly. But this verdict must not conceal the fact that in the perspective of a great many contemporaries in antiquity it marked the dawn of an extraordinarily happy time, because the Mediterranean world, which had already been culturally interconnected by Hellenism, was now also growing together into a political unity. Ancient historians in particular have referred to this power of political integration in the 'Roman peace' as a positive factor. For organizational reasons alone it would have been impossible to sustain a giant empire of – at the beginning of the second century – more than five million square kilometres exclusively by an occupying force constantly exerting brutal pressure. Down to the second century almost half the Roman army stationed in the frontier provinces was recruited from indigenous auxiliary troops – and must therefore so to speak have consisted of potential rebels. In reality, as a rule the provinces of the empire were not ruled by the governors with their small personal staffs, i.e. without any fixed bureaucratic apparatus; rather, under their control there was communal self-government by the various indigenous upper classes. So in the world empire there was not only Roman society but also 'countless societies with different structures as ethnic and cultural units (urban communities, tribes, etc.), which often had barely comparable states of development. Moreover their languages, legal orders, political cults and therefore also norms of behaviour and orientations were different.'[34] The everyday brutality of an antiquity which nowadays is called 'classical' was mitigated rather than increased by the *pax Romana* – a fact which criticism of the more favourable picture of it tends to overlook. At the end of the fourth century, for example, a senior Roman soldier, Flavius Bonus, *comes et dux Arabiae*, is certified by 'his' population to have 'ruled over us in peace and to have preserved constant peace and security' for travellers and for the people.[35] These and other texts show that particularly on the unruly frontiers of the Roman empire and in the metropolises, which were forcibly extended, the population felt the *pax Romana* to be more a blessing than a curse. That the political, economic and social 'crisis of the empire' which began at the end of the second century in some respects quickly put an end to the previous 'golden age' does not overthrow this basic assessment. The emperor, rather than indigenous bodies or subordinates, was still looked to for hope in difficult situations, as is shown by a contemporary appeal from the provinces: 'Come and help us, and as we poor countrymen . . . eke out a living with the toil of their hands . . . have pity on us, that we need not pay more than we owe according to the basic statute of Hadrian and the letters of your procurators.'[36]

Regional differences

Of course the question keeps arising what characteristic differences there were between the various regional forms and expressions of Christianity in the Roman empire. However, a really deep political, cultural and ecclesiastical regionalization of the empire began only in late antiquity. For the previous decades it may be said that the wider the categories of comparison chosen in a quest for regionalisms, the more unyielding the question becomes. Thus for example there continues to be a vigorous dispute as to whether really characteristic distinctions between the Christianities in the two halves of the empire can be demonstrated before the fourth century, and if so how.

Language

That the two halves were separated is already evident from a look at the languages. At the latest after the early third century, we have an 'official' bilingualism in Christianity. However, in the Roman community the establishment of the Latin language (in place of the Greek which was previously dominant) took essentially longer; it came about in a process which lasted from the beginning of the third century to the middle of the fourth. Latin Christian texts (like the translation of the 'Shepherd of Hermas', a partly apocalyptic, partly admonitory work) from the second century seem correspondingly clumsy from a literary point of view. We can also note how the first theologian to write in Latin, Tertullian, struggles in places to discuss theology in Latin. Granted, it is disputed whether he himself formed individual characteristic terms like *trinitas* (Trinity), but at all events he provides the first evidence for a whole series of expressions of Christianity in Latin. From the beginning of the third century the evidence for Christians corresponds to the situation in the empire as a whole: west of a line which ran from the confluence of the Danube and the Sava southwards, people spoke Latin (e.g. in Pannonia, Dalmatia and Tripolitania); east of that Greek (from Moesia to Cyrenaica in North Africa). This dividing line between East and West, which initially was purely linguistic, took on deeper political significance when the administrative division of the empire into an Eastern and a Western half was consolidated dynastically in the fourth century. What Diocletian, emperor from 284, had wanted to avoid took place at the latest after the death of Theodosius on 17 January 395: one dynasty produced both emperors, but neither of Theodosius's descendants possessed sufficient authority to keep the empire functioning as a unity. So the two halves increasingly went their own ways – and within the church, too, tensions deepened between West and East; they were especially virulent after the fourth century. They resulted in a definitive schism, i.e. a split in the church and reciprocal excommunication between Rome and Byzantium, in 1054.

The Mediterranean and the 'interior'

As well as this split into an Eastern and a Western half of the empire, however, there was also a sharp division between the Mediterranean area proper and the 'interior', which extended in an eastward direction to the frontiers of the empire: regions of Egypt and Palestine, Syria and of course Mespotamia, Armenia or Georgia. It does not seem to be fortuitous that in the middle of the fifth century a theological split finally opened up between the core area of the Mediterranean and these outer regions. It is most unfortunate that these churches on the periphery of the empire, called 'Monophysite' after a detail in their christology, have been described as a 'third world of Christian experience'.[37] This conceals the rich theological and spiritual tradition of cities which for urban Roman eyes were in fact on the periphery, like Edessa (now the Turkish Urfa) or Seleucia-Ctesiphon (Tel Umar, just under sixty kilometres north of Babylon). Moreover, the opposition between the provinces shaped more by monasteries and country places, and the metropolises, shaped more by bishops, played a major role in this split in the church – this is therefore a differentiation within the major geographical regions.[38]

Town and country

Early Christian authors reflect these differences between town and country – the Antiochene preacher John Chrysostom (he was called Chrysostom, 'golden mouth', because of his extraordinarily popular sermons) was presumably only giving a positive twist to current prejudices when in a sermon to candidates for baptism in the 390s he declared of those living in the country around: 'So we should not just want to look at their outward appearance and their language and in so doing overlook their virtue; we should get to know their angelic life, their wise way of living. For they have cast off all excess and gluttony, and not only this, but also the other careless ways of living which prevail in the cities. They eat only as much as they need to sustain life, and devote all the rest of their time to singing hymns and constant prayer; here too they imitate the life of the angels . . . Just look at these simple people, who have no great knowledge, but some understanding only of cultivation and agriculture, and give nothing to earthly things but have their minds on the good things above. They know how to reflect on the good things that cannot be put into words, and have a precise grasp of what the philosophers, who pride themselves on their beards and their staves, can never imagine.'[39] But despite such testimonies, the contrast between city and country should not be exaggerated either. For example, the educational level of village Christianity must not be underestimated. Thus a papyrus found in the monastic town of Oxyrhynchus in Lower Egypt shows that Irenaeus of Lyons' *Refutation of the Gnostic Heresy*, an important theological work by the bishop in Gaul, written in Greek, was in circulation (in the twofold sense of the word) in the Egyptian province only a few years after its composition.

Translations

The considerable linguistic and theological problems of understanding between the different geographical regions, which were not just caused by differences in language, were resolved within the church, as they were also coped with in the private sphere, in business or by state institutions. Bilingual theologians – like Tertullian, mentioned above – were go-betweens: a large number of Greek texts were translated into the language of the Western half of the empire by gifted individual Latin theologians; there was simultaneous translation from the different languages used in the great episcopal gatherings of Eastern and Western theologians from the fourth century on, with up to five hundred participants. At the beginning of the second century, Bible translations were made into the different vernaculars of the empire (e.g. Syriac, Coptic, rather later also Georgian, Armenian, Ethiopian and Arabic), initially probably often as *ad hoc* renderings of texts in worship.

We can already see from these relatively external details how little a rigid division into two halves does justice to the reality of early Christianity. On the one hand there is the 'Mediterranean *koinē*'[40] in many manifestations of movements of Christianity transcending the parts, for example in monasticism. On the other, to speak of a split into two is not sufficient, as we can already see in the question of language. Alongside the two main languages in the two halves of the empire, of course in the conquered provinces vernaculars like Coptic in Egypt or Syriac were important, not least in theology. Greek and Latin were spoken in these provinces in the larger cities and by the authorities – the official bilingualism is documented by the inscriptions – but in country communities and monastic settlements the vernaculars were used. In the larger cities even the sermons were occasionally translated into the vernacular: thus in the main church in Antioch there was a simultaneous translation of the sermons into Syriac for the countryfolk who came to the metropolis from the land around. So when from the fourth century on theological language increasingly uses these vernaculars instead of Greek, and no longer just makes translations from original Greek texts, we have an expression of the increasing loss of grip by the central authority.

East and West

Whether the linguistic frontier is also appropriate for dividing an 'Eastern' from a 'Western' Christianity still remains very disputed. Whereas at the beginning of the twentieth century it was possible to describe the 'spirit of the Eastern church as distinct from the Western church',[41] the growth in knowledge of the historical material has made such descriptions very much more difficult today. The apparently striking differences between the

Christianities of the two halves of the empire are much more strongly dependent on individual theological personalities than on the 'mentalities' of wider strata, to which the relatively crude categories of 'West' and 'East' do not do justice. We cannot lump together communities of Christians in Cappadocian villages with a port like Ephesus and a great cultural metropolis like Alexandria, any more than we can the different North African churches. In truth, personal continuities govern what seems to be the profile of a district. For example in North Africa the question of the limits of the church's institution of penance (i.e. the question of which sins can no longer be forgiven by the church) plays a major role. A dispute broke out over this topic, but presumably not so much because the North African Christians were all such died-in-the-wool rigorists as because the first North African theologian whose writings we have, Tertullian, for a while argued to this effect, and later authors like Caecilius Cyprianus (died 258) revered him as an authority here. The same is true of other differences which scholars like producing in a comparison of the Eastern and Western churches: since the theology of the West from the end of the fourth century was very strongly stamped by the North African Bishop Augustine (died 430), the question of salvation from sin and the topic of sin generally played a very much greater role in it than in Greek theology – this topic had also very much shaped the life of the bishop of Hippo. And the fact that in the incarnation of the only Son of God stood more at the centre of Eastern piety, and his death on the cross and its atoning effect stood more at the centre of Western theology, must first of all be explained in terms of the history of theology: the Alexandrian patriarch Athanasius (died 373) composed a treatise *On the Incarnation of the Word* which was often copied or quoted in extracts from the fifth century on. The claim that Eastern Christianity was closer to Roman culture and society can easily by demolished by examples to the contrary in the West: L.Caecilius Firmianus Lactantius, author of a multi-volume *Apology* and an important source work on the persecutions of Christians, worked until 303 as a teacher of rhetoric under the emperor Diocletian at the residence in Nicomedia and from 317 at the court of Constantine in Trier, as tutor to Constantine's son Crispus. The important Latin theologian Ambrose held office as governor of the province of Liguria-Emilia in which the imperial residence of Milan was located before being elected Bishop of Milan in 374. At most some time-lag can be noted. Latin parallels to the first great clashes between Alexandrian Christian theology and pagan philosophy at a high scholarly level from the beginning of the third century on can be produced only at the end of the fourth century.

All in all, a stronger 'regionalization' would benefit this question and the historiography of early Christianity. Thus individual Western regions agree with Eastern regions over some disputed points against the 'official' line in their own half of the empire. For example, the communities of Africa and Asia Minor both regarded baptism performed by schismatics and heretics as null and void and rebaptized.[42] By contrast, the Roman church did not put the validity of the sacrament in question and contented itself with a subsequent laying on of hands.

However, it remains difficult to describe 'regionalisms' in a way which commands a consensus. For example, we can say that the theology and church order of North Africa put some emphasis on practical problems and were restrained in speculative discussions of the kind that were popular in Alexandria: questions of discipleship, of martyrdom, of penance and persistence in everyday life occupied this region in particular. It is easier to observe differences in the experience of worship in both halves of the empire. The impression that the earthly liturgy unites a community with the liturgy of the angels in heaven still stamps Eastern experience today: 'Mystically we represent the cherubim . . . all worldly care we lay aside, that we may receive the king of the universe.'[43] By contrast, at the forefront of the Western celebration stood the individual sacraments, penance with forgiveness and eucharist. Perhaps this difference is connected with the fact that high and popular theology in the East had been shaped to a much greater degree by Platonic philosophy than the West – at least earlier and more thoroughly.[44] If we transfer the Platonic notion of a constitutive relationship between original and copy, between idea and reality, to worship, we can say of worship that it is 'heaven on earth', the divine liturgy of the angels in the copy of earthly worship.

Time: the division and contours of eras

What we today call 'the period of the Roman empire' and occasionally still subdivide into early or high empire and late antiquity was regarded by the Christians of those times as a single epoch.

When at the beginning of the fifth century a close friend of the North African bishop Augustine, the Spanish priest Paulus Orosius, composed the first Christian universal history, he divided 'the Christian times because of the intensified present grace of Christ' from the 'times of error through unbelief', i.e. those years between the creation of the world and the appearance of Jesus. For him, these two periods were parts of a divine plan of time (in theological terms, a plan of salvation); this consists in the fact that 'from the beginning the human race has been created and destined to live in the fear of God and without labour and to merit eternity as the fruit of its obedience'.[45] Such a Christian perception of time understands time as a course directed towards a goal; here world history strives to restore the state of paradise which was there at the beginning but lost, and history becomes an event on a finite stretch which can be interpreted and calculated, in which the present position can be indicated accurately. Of course pagan historiography, too, knew such an entelechy of historical development. The Roman empire was largely regarded as the goal of history and the best form of state order so far. In the middle of the second century the orator Aelius Aristides propagated this commonly held view with his 'Speech on Rome'. In contrast to previous empires, he argued, under Roman supremacy all the people of the earth had been brought together under a just rule. By contrast, Alexander the Great had not succeeded in establishing such a rule permanently. Among other things as a result of citizenship, a greater equality among the inhabitants had been achieved than ever before. Whereas hitherto the empires had embraced only parts of the world, now, 'Your possession coincides with the course of the sun'.[46] Aelius Aristides ends with a fine notion which occurs in Virgil, that of the kingdom without end: 'We shall beseech all the gods and sons of the gods to grant their favour that this empire and this city flourish for ever': *Roma aeterna*, the eternal Rome.[47]

So pagans and Christians do not differ in their view that historical development has a goal; they differ in defining this goal and therefore also in diagnosing any particular present. However, it immediately has to be said by way of qualification that this Christian diagnosis of time altered considerably in the five centuries after the birth of Christ. Common to Christians of all times is a criticism of the ideology of history focussed only on the pagan *imperium Romanum*. The biblical apocalypse of John, by general agreement to be dated at the end of the reign of Domitian (AD 95/96), describes Rome as the 'great whore Babylon' (17.3–5). After the eternal city had fallen into the hands of the West Goths in AD 410, Augustine declared in Carthage: 'Heaven and earth will pass away. If what God himself has made will pass away, how much more quickly will pass away what Romulus has founded.'[48] On the other hand, in the course of five centuries of the history of early Christianity there was some adaptation to the pagan *Roma aeterna* ideology. Its hymnic view of Rome was transferred to Christianized Rome, with certain deletions and corrections like those of Augustine just quoted. A central presupposition for this was the retreat of the expectation of an imminent end (Greek *parousia*), i.e. the original notion that Christ will appear on earth during the lifetime of his first disciples and usher in the end-time. When this generation died without the events described taking place, people more or less resigned themselves to a long continuation of this earthly world. There were some attempts to cope with this 'delay of the parousia' theologically; in a New Testament letter the attribution of which to Paul is disputed, for the first

The delay of the *Parousia*

time there is a mention of 'the one who still restrains it (viz. the end)' (II Thess. 2.7). Already at the end of the second century, in the context of the letter, this still undefined restraint is identified with the Roman empire: 'In praying for a postponement we contribute to the ongoing existence of Rome,' writes Tertullian.[49] In the first decades of the third century the Roman historian Hippolytus identifies the fourth and last kingdom of which an Old Testament prophet speaks in metaphorical garb (Dan. 7.7: 'After that I saw in my night visions a fourth beast') with the Roman empire and asks: 'Who is it that is restraining up to now, if not the fourth beast?'[50] However, the author warns his readers against brooding on precisely how many years the Roman empire will still continue to 'restrain' the dawn of the final event. The fact of the end is certain; speculations about the date bring danger. Of course there were such speculations nevertheless: Hippolytus himself engaged in them and believed that with the help of various biblical passages he could calculate a period of still more than two and a half centuries to come.

At any rate, such considerations by Christian theologians closely connect with earthly Christianity a Roman empire the majority of which was still pagan and which was by no means always well disposed towards the church. Already in the second half of the second century Bishop Melito of Sardes in Asia Minor links the growth and flourishing of 'our philosophy' (i.e. Christianity) with the 'greatness and splendour' of the 'Roman power': 'For our philosophy at first flourished among barbarians; but after it had appeared among your peoples during the mighty principate of your ancestor Augustus, it became especially an auspicious benefit to your empire. For from that time the power of the Romans increased to something great and splendid.'[51] Even if here Melito is using terms and themes from contemporary panegyrics – a rhetorical training communicated the art of composing such a panegyric – a first step in the direction of a 'political theology' has already been taken. In his *Church History*, which appeared in a fourth and last edition in AD 325, Bishop Eusebius of Caesarea (in Palestine) also associates the appearance of Jesus Christ with the beginning of the

Roman empire. Moreover he quotes Melito's passage to this effect.[52] Finally, at the end of the fourth century, probably the most gifted poet of Christian antiquity, Aurelius Prudentius Clemens, hopes for the complete fusion of these two: 'Come then, Almighty, here is a world in harmony, enter it. An earth receives you now, O Christ, which peace and Rome hold in a bond of union.'[53]

Periodization

By figures in the biblical history

But how did Christians divide up the eras of the Roman empire which they often judged positively? Initially the normal points of division corresponded precisely to those of pagan historiography: simple numbers of years in the chronicles, those of the reigning emperor in more extended accounts. The usual form of reckoning time, by Olympiads, by an era, by consular fasts, indictions, years of a ruler's reign, etc. – were of course also used by Christians. We can see this from what is probably the most significant surviving Christian chronicle of antiquity, the 'Chronological Orders and Composition of the Different Histories of the Greeks and Barbarians' which the Palestinian church historian Eusebius wrote in AD 303. Eusebius gave three dates to events, which were described very briefly. First came the number of the year 'after Abraham', i.e. after the birth of Abraham, so his main date betrays a deliberate theological decision and a Jewish-Christian view of world history: he puts the 'beginning of salvation and truth' with Abraham, the ancestor of the Jews (and Christians). Then he adds the Olympiad and the regnal year of the particular ruler. Only in the sixth century did a Roman monk by the name of Dionysius Exiguus establish the way of counting the years from the birth of Christ (*ab incarnatione Domini nostri Iesu Christi* = 'from the incarnation of our Lord Jesus Christ') which is still customary today and put the 'turn of the ages' in the year 754 *ab urbe condita*, after the foundation of the city of Rome. Although by present reckoning Dionysius substantially miscalculated the dating of the birth of Christ, and put it around five years too late, his basic model for dating quickly became established – not least because he connected it with the fixing of the dates for Easter.

By persecutions

But in addition to these basic possibilities of 'Christianizing' the calculation of time, specific means of dividing it were also available: in his first Christian history of the world – one based on Eusebius and continuing the line taken by Jerome, Orosius counted ten persecutions of Christians, connected them with particular rulers, and moreover reported the divine punishment which had befallen the empire and the emperor concerned. Thus after the description of a 'first persecution of Christians' under Nero in connection with the burning of Rome in July AD 64 we read: 'Soon misfortunes which arose in great number everywhere caught the unfortunate citizens in a stranglehold.' Orosius counted Domitian as the second persecutor and reported that shortly after the measures concerned, the emperor was 'cruelly murdered by his people in the palace'. The third persecutor of Christians, Trajan, was punished by fires in Rome and earthquakes in the empire; the fourth, Marcus Aurelius, by plague in Italy. 'The notorious audacity of Septimius Severus towards the Christians and the church was followed by heavenly vengeance,' namely the civil war. Punishment hastened on the sixth and seventh persecutors of Christians by Orosius' count, the usurper Maximin Thrax and his successor Decius, in the form of speedy deaths. Orosius interpreted the end of the emperor Valerian, which shook even his contemporaries, as a divine punishment on the eighth persecutor of the Christians: 'Immediately Valerian, the author of the notorious law (viz. against the Christians in June 260), was taken prisoner by the Persian king Shapur I: the emperor of the Roman people grew old among the Persians in the most shameful servitude.' Orosius counted Aurelian as the 'ninth from Nero': 'When he . . . commanded that the Christians should be persecuted, lightning struck him . . . not much later, he was killed on a journey.' The last persecutors of Christians, Diocletian and Maximin, were punished by an earthquake which caused many thousands of deaths. That ends the series of persecutions of Christians: just as after the ten plagues the Pharaoh of Egypt felt the power of God and set the people of Israel free (Ex. 7–11), after the ten persecutions the Roman emperor had 'let Christianity stand'.

Constantine is presented relatively dispassionately by the author as the first Christian emperor.[54] Moreover Orosius quotes a pagan commentary on his interpretation of history: evidently he has been accused of 'associating to some degree artificially and slyly the chance changes of history with (divine) actions of vengeance for Christians'.[55] But Bishop Augustine of Hippo, his teacher, who also commissioned his universal history, was not content with this presentation either. Like the pagans he saw at work 'the conjecture' which 'sometimes may err, as well as not'.[56] Already before Nero there had been persecutions, and the church continued to be oppressed even after Constantine, for example by the last pagan emperor Julian. He pointed out that the various anti-Christian measures among the Goths and Persians had been completely omitted from Orosius' count.

Before and after Constantine

Fundamentally, modern scholarship also still divides the history of early Christianity by this scheme when it distinguishes between a 'pre-Constantinian' and a 'post-Constantinian' Christianity, the former being characterized as an 'era of persecutions' and the latter by the gradual introduction of 'state church' conditions, which initially are more free of persecutions. Among other things, this strict division is connected with the catchphrase 'the shift under Constantine', which divides the history of early Christianity radically into two parts: this is problematical and in nucleus goes back to mediaeval theologians. The correct insight in this view remains that under Constantine there were decisive changes in the legal status of the Christian religion. The process even began slightly earlier: in 311 the senior member of the imperial college, Galerius, issued an edict of tolerance and allowed Christians, too, to practise their religion. They might 'establish the places of their religious assemblies; yet so as they do not offend against good order'.[57] In 313, in Milan, Licinius and Constantine agreed unlimited freedom of religion for Christians also. Laws and ordinances which had imposed conditions were abolished and confiscated property was restored.[58] In 318, Constantine recognized an episcopal jurisdiction alongside state jurisdiction and allowed the church to appoint its bishops: in 321 he regulated by law

Sunday observance for judges, for townspeople and for craftsmen (but not farmworkers).[59] Finally, in 326 he banned meetings by some movements which the church had excluded as heretical, and confiscated the house that they used for these meetings.[60] His son Constantius II clearly deviated from this policy of tolerance, in 341 forbidding 'the madness of (pagan) sacrifices'; in 346 (or 354) he commanded that infringements should be punished with the sword: pagan temples were to be closed and entry into them forbidden.[61] Finally, at the end of February 380 the emperor Theodosius I declared Christianity in a particular trinitarian theological interpretation to be the state religion – expressly naming the bishops of Rome and Alexandria ('the faith . . . which the [Roman] Pontifex Damasus and also Bishop Peter of Alexandria . . . publicly confess'): those of other beliefs 'whom we hold to be crazy and insane, must suffer the disgrace of being heretical teachers. Nor may their gatherings be called churches. In the end, first divine retribution and then also our penal justice, transferred to us by the verdict of heaven, will befall them.'[62]

This short survey shows how much the legal position of Christians altered in the course of the fourth century. Given the revolutionary changes, the twofold division into a 'pre-' and 'post-Constantinian Christianity' is certainly justified and meaningful – even if often the pagan officials sabotaged the change to the new legal situation by passive resistance. In some circumstances this resistance was offered at the highest level: in the Life of Bishop Porphyry of Gaza it is reported with a nice touch of candour that the East Roman emperor Arcadius forbade him at the beginning of the fifth century to destroy the main temple in the city of Gaza in Palestine because the emperor was concerned about the honesty of his commune in paying taxes: 'I know that that city is devoted to idolatry, but it fulfils its tax obligations loyally and brings in a high revenue.'[63] In view of the importance of the port of Gaza, from which not only inland produce but also long-distance wares from Damascus and 'Aqaba were shipped, the emperor's concern does not seem completely unjustified.

Continuities

Of course the new legal status had an effect on the form of the church and the nature of its theology. But at the same time, so many continuities in church order, the form of the liturgy and hierarchy, theology and ethics, connect the 'pre'- and 'post-Constantinian church' that too strict a bisection of the history of early Christianity becomes problematical: the following sections in this account will present these continuities in detail. Therefore a rather more refined periodization of the era seems natural. In research a five-stage division is almost as established as the two-stage model; this works with the centuries but defines these by their content. The widespread terminology goes back in essence to works by Albrecht Ritschl (1822–1889), when he was a lecturer in Bonn, and the philosopher of religion Ernst Troeltsch (1865–1923). The account with the most consistent methodology is that by Carl Andresen, *Die Kirchen der Alten Christenheit* (1971). The Göttingen church historian distinguished between different 'types' of church in antiquity and used them to illustrate the interaction between ecclesiological self-understanding and the historical situation. Andresen distinguished an 'early catholic church' (up to the end of the second century) from an 'old catholic church' (up to the so-called 'Constantinian shift'), an 'imperial catholic church' and a 'Roman catholic church' in the West (until the period of the migrations in the fifth century), or a 'Byzantine Orthodox church' in the East. Here he is using a word '*catholikos*', 'universal' (catholic: the term entered our language through the Latin loan word *catholicus*[64]), which throughout Christian antiquity had a positive sense, but through its present use in a Christian particular church – namely the 'Roman Catholic' church – has taken on at least one additional connotation. This terminology involves the whole of Christian antiquity in the confessional polemic of Central European modernity. Does a straight line lead from an 'early catholic' to the 'Roman Catholic' church? Is the Protestant church then directly linked to the 'primitive church'? Hardly any schemes using these key terms have no underlying positive or negative qualification of the term 'catholic', in accordance with a model of progress or

Characterization by centuries

decadence. Nowadays, it is time to get rid of these terminological fetters which go back centuries and which necessitate the constant repetition of circumstantial justifications for concepts like 'early catholicism', which at the least are open to misunderstanding. Apart from this somewhat unhappy terminology, which unfortunately has been introduced nevertheless, the division by centuries makes sense, and the term 'imperial church' also remains appropriate as a designation for the new legal situation of Christianity in the fourth century.

A brief characterization of the centuries might look like this. The Christianity of the second century differs from that of the first simply by the various highly-educated theologians who were concerned to provide a scholarly understanding of the new religion. In the big cities, people from the widest range of classes were won over on the broadest of fronts, and the church acted as a kind of laboratory in which different forms of theology, hierarchies of ministry and ethics were tried out. Only very gradually does a 'majority church' become recognizable, which excludes divergent positions as 'heretical'. This process came to some sort of a conclusion in the third century: movements like Gnosticism and Montanism separated from a 'majority church'; this developed a hierarchical ministry and a consensus over a kind of 'minimal dogmatics', worship and the ethical demands of a Christian life. The different Christian metropolises begin with a mission into the land around and develop into self-confident dioceses with their own theological emphases. The North African theologian Tertullian described this great increase in numbers: 'The outcry is that the state is filled with Christians – that they are in the fields, in the citadels, in the islands: they make lamentation, as for some calamity, that both sexes, every age and condition, even high rank, are passing over to the profession of the Christian faith; and yet for all that their minds are not awakened to the thought of some good they have failed to notice in it.'[65] The changes in legal status after the end of the persecutions which have already been indicated show that from this point the fourth century has a stamp of its own and what its new character is. The fifth century can be marked off from the fourth simply because now the Roman empire clearly changes its appearance as a result of activities of the various Germanic tribes which, in the framework of the migrations, had been shaking the frontiers of the empire for almost two centuries. The fall of Rome in AD 410 to the hordes of the West Goth Alaric made a traumatic impact, as did the devastating military defeat of Rome at Adrianople in 378 (along with the emperor Valens, many more than 10,000 soldiers may have fallen). Moreover the empire finally broke into its two part-empires. It makes less sense to apply to the history of early Christianity the periodization of the Roman empire widespread in classical studies, into 'principate' (30 BC–AD 192), 'imperial crisis' (AD 192–284) and 'late antiquity': the 'imperial crisis' does not change either theology or the organization of the church to any significant degree.

Everyday life

Alongside the great breaks in eras, of course the rhythm of time experienced in everyday life often plays a disproportionately greater role in human life: the change from weekday to Sunday and the succession of the different church festivals and everyday life with no particular distinguishing mark.

Sunday

Sunday comes from the Jewish tradition. The community in exile in Babylon introduced such a day of rest, the sabbath, in the sixth century BC so as not to lose its own identity completely in the midst of alien peoples and religion. By contrast the pagan world knew no such day of rest, which in the Jewish tradition was immediately also given theological and social legitimation (Gen. 2.3; Deut. 5.12–15). Jesus of Nazareth usually visited the synagogue on the sabbath and there read aloud from scripture (Luke 4.16). Evidently he valued this day very highly as a sign of divine salvation: at any rate, he attempted to bring out its significance, rescuing it from the sometimes strict set of regulations with which this solemn day had been surrounded by Jewish scribes. With the words 'The sabbath is made for man and not man for the sabbath' (Mark 2.27), he commented on a symbolic action aimed at demonstrating this. The first communities of his followers were communities within Judaism, which means that they observed the sabbath by resting from work and visited the synagogue, or in Jerusalem also the temple and temple worship. For instance Paul was arrested on a visit to the temple (Acts 21.27–39; around AD 57). James the brother of Jesus, who led the Jerusalem community after the execution of Jesus until he himself was stoned in AD 64, was called 'the Just', among other reasons because of his particularly zealous temple piety.[66] But probably already in Paul's missionary communities the custom arose of holding a meeting of Christians on the day of the resurrection, i.e. on the day after the Jewish sabbath (I Cor. 16.1). The name which was predominantly given to Sunday in Christian antiquity, 'day of the Lord' (Rev.1.10) or *dies dominicus*, already appears at the end of the first century. Bishop Ignatius from Antioch in Syria writes in the second century of Christians 'who have come to a new hope, no longer living for the sabbath but for the Lord's Day, on which also our life sprang forth through him (viz. Christ) and his death'.[67] The equivalent of our name 'Sunday', *dies solis*, occurs only rarely in the pre-Constantinian period, above all in writings addressed to non-Christians. After Sunday had been established as a free day all over the empire under Constantine in AD 321, the traditional pagan designation after a planet was combined with the interpretation in terms of the resurrection: in the fourth century Eusebius of Caesarea spoke of 'the day of the Redeemer which is also named after the light (viz. of Easter morning) and the sun (i.e. Christ as the sun)'.[68] Of course in the pre-Constantinian period 'Sunday observance' did not yet imply a main morning service, but gatherings in the morning or the evening (for more detail see below, 159–64).

An address which was probably given in the fourth century by a bishop Eusebius (perhaps of Emesa, present-day Homs in Syria) on the topic of Sunday rest and work offers an interesting insight into the idea and reality of Sunday in early Christianity.[69] 'Why,' the bishop is asked by way of introduction, 'is it necessary to observe the holy day of the Lord and not to work? What gain do we have from it if we do not work?' Eusebius explains to the person asking the question that on Sunday the memory of the Lord, or more precisely the supper instituted in his memory (thus the so-called 'words of institution' e.g. in I Cor. 11.24f.), is celebrated. Moreover the church remembers the beginning of the creation of the world, the resurrection of Jesus and the beginning of the week: 'Combining three beginnings, this day points to a beginning of three good things.' Rest from work gives time for worship – Eusebius admonishes his hearers not to leave before the final blessing, but the community prefers to go elsewhere. 'When the herald gives the summons to church, everyone claims to be too tired. If there is flute and zither music, they rush as though they had wings.' Nor is the bishop silent about the social dimension of the day of rest: 'A day labourer comes into your house and takes your work on his shoulders; he toils in sweat and effort, and for six days of the week hardly ventures to raise his head and look at the position of the sun, but consumes himself in your service, and he is not even allowed to look up. And he awaits the day of the Lord with great longing, so that at least once he can shake the dust from his body and rest. And will you not allow him that? Please tell me, what is your excuse?'[70]

The date of Easter

One controversy in the early church was sometimes extremely vigorous; it could only be resolved at last in the fourth century by the intervention of the political authorities. It too provides interesting information about notions of time and concepts in early Christianity. This is the dispute over the date of Easter. In many Christian communities in Asia Minor and Syria the Christian festival of the crucifixion or resurrection of Jesus was celebrated on the eve of the Jewish feast of Passover, 14 Nisan. So Easter was celebrated as the Christian Passover according to the chronological tradition for which the evangelist John laid the basis: according to the information that he gives, the crucifixion of Jesus took place on the 'day of rest' of the Passover feast (John 19.31: 14 Nisan) on which according to Jewish custom and the Jewish calendar the Passover lamb had to be eaten (Ex. 12.6–11; the rest of the evangelists assert that Jesus celebrated the last supper on the evening of 14 Nisan and was executed the next day, 15 Nisan, the first day of the feast of unleavened bread). Already in early Christianity, groups which celebrated Easter in accordance with this custom on 14 Nisan, i.e. without taking note of the day of the week, on the day of the first spring full moon, were called 'Quartodecimans'. It is quite possible that relatively close contacts between the Jewish and later also the Christian communities of the Diaspora in Asia Minor and the Palestinian mother country are responsible for this Easter practice, which is very strongly orientated on the Jewish calendar.[71] The Jewish and Christian Passovers had in common the expectation of future redemption – of course understood among Christians as the return of Christ.[72] The Christian celebration in Asia Minor began with a fast on 14 Nisan which lasted until the morning of the next day. The worship in the evening (a so-called 'vigil') consisted of a reading and an exegesis of the Old Testament Passover narrative (Ex. 12), which was followed on the early morning of 15 Nisan (from 3 a.m. at the first cock crow) by an agape, i.e. the shared meal, and the eucharist. Possibly we still have a sermon intended for such a liturgy by a bishop of Sardes composed between AD 160 and 170.[73]

This practice in Asia Minor contrasted with the Roman custom of celebrating the Christian feast of Easter in principle on a Sunday (probably at the latest after AD 165). The date of Easter was largely calculated according to the Jewish calendar, but because of the theological significance of this day was shifted to the following Sunday, thus adapting the festival to the normal time of worship. Unfortunately we do not know precisely when, why and in what circumstances this practice arose; the only thing that is certain that it is secondary to the practice in Asia Minor, and that the Christian feast of Easter and the Jewish feast of Passover were uncoupled. So the Roman custom attests to the increasing separation between the two religions: whether for that reason we should already call this 'anti-Jewish' is another question. That the difference over the date of Easter was an important conflict in the church is evident from the fact that already in the middle of the second century there were negotiations about it between the bishops of Rome and Smyrna. Bishop Polycarp of Smyrna was sought by the communities of

Asia Minor as a mediator: he was highly respected there, if only because of his age (he was over eighty), but he had been in contact with important figures of the founder generation. On the question of the date of Easter, he appealed to 'John the disciple of our Lord, and . . . the other apostles with whom he had conversed'.[74] Somewhere in the years between 155 and 166 he travelled to Rome to discuss a variety of church problems, including the date of Easter, with Anicetus of Rome. Although they could not agree on the date of Easter, they preserved church communion, and Polycarp celebrated the eucharist in Rome. However, Bishop Victor of Rome (189–198) attempted to establish his practice in Asia Minor also, possibly because a presbyter from his community had begun to introduce the Quartodeciman practice from Asia Minor. When within the framework of these controversies he threatened to excommunicate the churches of Asia, a storm of indignation broke out over the arrogance of the Bishop of Rome.[75] Victor had to withdraw and be instructed by Western theologians that the difference in the dates of Easter 'did not first originate in our time, but much further back . . . Yet none the less . . . we live in peace. The difference concerning the fast enhances the unanimity of our faith.'[76]

The dispute was finally resolved when with the emperor Constantine in AD 325 a strong political power tackled this problem which endangered unity. The monarch wanted a unified church in what was now also a politically unified empire, and in his traditional office as chief priest (*pontifex maximus*) defined this unity in essentially cultic terms. The first synod of bishops from all over the empire, in his summer residence of Nicaea (in Bithynia, present-day Iznik), resolved under the presidency of the emperor against the Antiochene form of an independent Christian calculation of the date of Easter and against all models orientated on the Jewish calendar. Whether at the same time it sanctioned a uniform date for Easter according to the Roman or Alexandrian usage, i.e. on the first Sunday after the first spring full moon, was already disputed in antiquity.[77] The encyclical in which the emperor instructed the churches about this result contained malicious and sharp attacks against Judaism: 'It appeared an unworthy thing that in the celebration of this most holy feast we should follow the practice of the Jews, who have impiously defiled their hands with enormos sin and are therefore deservedly afflicted with blindness of soul . . . Let us then have nothing in common with the detestable Jewish crowd.'[78]

A clear 'Christianization' of the calculation of time and of people's sense of human time also certainly developed through the formation and extension of a 'church year', i.e. a cycle of church festivals orientated on the history of the life of Jesus Christ, into which commemorations of saints and martyrs were inserted. In the fourth century, to the movable feast of Easter and a subsequent fifty-day period of rejoicing until Pentecost (*he pentakoste hemera*, Greek for 'the fiftieth day') was added the fixed festival of the birth of Christ (for details see below, 62–4); this became the second climax of the church year with its own preceding period of fasting. The festal calendar with such feasts of Christ and a wealth of further commemorations of martyrs at the same time replaced the pagan calendar simply by its fullness, as a random example for the early summer shows: in Rome on 29 June the festival of the apostle Peter was celebrated, on 30 June that of the apostle Paul, on 2 July followed the holy martyrs Processus and Martinianus (according to later legend the gaoler of the chief of the apostles), and finally on 10 July among others came the festival of the martyr Felicitas and her seven sons.[79]

The Individual

Conversion to Christianity

Conversion in paganism

A Greek or a Roman who knew nothing of Judaism and Christianity could hardly have imagined in the early period of the empire that 'a person could give up the religion of his native *polis* and his ancestors in order to attach himself exclusively and whole-heartedly to a different religion'.[80] This of course was because of the lack of any claim to exclusiveness on the part of the gods of a polytheistic pantheon. None of the gods who were worshipped at this time in Rome or Athens said of themselves, 'I am the Lord your God . . . you shall have no other gods before my face' (Deut. 5.6f. in the version of the Greek Bible). No one turned the intrinsically clear truth that one cannot serve two masters (cf. Mark 6.24) into the question 'Zeus or Apollo?' On the contrary, through the integration above all of originally Greek or oriental deities, the history of the religion of the city of Rome now also offered other masters (and mistresses) to serve: as early as 205 BC the cultic sign of the 'Great Mother of Mount Ida' (*Mater deum Magna Idaea*) from Pessinus (present-day Balishar) in Galatia was brought to Rome. Such 'cumulative' piety, which could integrate cults of very different origin, survived well into late antiquity and indeed even increased, as a random example shows: according to an inscription, a high administrative official of the post-Constantinian era, Alfenius Ceionius Iulianus Camenius, the *Vicarius Africae* of 381, was 'Father of the sacrifices of the invincible Mithras, hierophant of Hecate, Archibucolus of the God Liber and Tauroboliatus'.[81] So he had undergone a ritual of sacrifice or initiation belonging to the cult of Cybele, in which the blood of a slaughtered bull flowed over the candidate. The Tauroboliatus 'holds forth his filthy head to meet every drop and getting his robe and his whole body covered with corruption. Laying his head back, he even puts his cheeks in the way, placing his ears under it, exposing lips and nostrils, bathing his very eyes in the stream, not even keeping his mouth from it but wetting his tongue, until the whole of him drinks in the dark gore' – thus at any rate the shocked report of another high state official of the same period, the Christian poet Aurelius Prudentius Clemens.[82] Even intellectual scepticism about the gods (as in the case of Cicero) did not lead to a departure from traditional cultic actions: antiquity did not know a 'conversion' in our present understanding of the world except for a 'conversion to philosophical life'. Of course in such an environment there were also practices like self-purification, improvement and special devotion to a divine power. The well-known romance *Metamorphoses or the Golden Ass,* which the north African Platonist Apuleius of Madaura composed in the second century and which describes such a 'conversion', is a singular example of that. After a restless life (symbolized by his being in the form of an ass), the first-person narrator, called Lucius, finds rest and peace: he is turned back into a human being and initiated into the mysteries of Isis.

Conversion in Judaism

'Conversion' in Judaism is different: there, after the end of the Babylonian exile and with the spread of Jews also outside the core territory of Palestine, in the Diaspora the possibility developed of converting to Judaism and joining it (and not just being born into it as the son of a Jewish mother). As a term for people who joined in this way, post-exilic Judaism coined the word 'proselyte'; by that it understood people 'who have given up their vain nature and taken refuge under God's wings'.[83] As the unity of national and religious community had been done away with in the Diaspora, the Judaism there redefined itself over against Hellenistic culture and opened itself up to non-Jews. However, an antisemitism which occasionally flared up vigorously in antiquity and the fear of circumcision stood in the way of the conversion of large numbers of people. Therefore there was a group of people far larger in quantity than the proselytes, people who, while affirming Jewish monotheism, visiting the synagogue and even observing parts of the ceremonial law, did not have themselves circumcised. Those who belonged to this group were called 'godfearers' (*sebomenoi* or *phoboumenoi ton theon);* they are well attested by inscriptions. Remarkably, women predominated. Even now in the city of Miletus in Asia Minor there is still a row of seats in the theatre from which in antiquity one had an attractive view over the water (today, unfortunately, the bay is now land), above which there is an inscription more than a metre long in somewhat clumsy letters: 'Place of the Jews, who are also called godfearers'. The information is not completely correct, since it blurs the distinction between circumcised Jews and uncircumcised 'godfearers'; but that may because of the social level or the payment of those who had had this inscription made. At all events, the inscription in the fifth row right reserves some places for the community and its sympathizers. Like the whole theatre, it probably comes from the imperial period, perhaps the second century.[84] Young Christianity also gained many new adherents from the circle of the 'godfearers'.

Conversion in earliest Christianity

A new model of 'conversion' which was distinct from conversion to Judaism came about through Jesus' call to discipleship. The Gospels paint the picture of people who at Jesus' call 'Follow me!' drop everything to follow the one who calls (Mark 1.16–20). Alongside that, already in the movement around the historical Jesus there were evidently also supporters who despite their conversion continued to live in their ancestral abode and maintained their established ties. At any rate, Luke mentions prominent women who, we may suppose, performed such a role (Luke 8.2f.). As with John the Baptist, who called people to conversion and repentance in the face of the imminent end, and made the forgiveness of sins possible with baptism, in the Christian community baptism sealed the process of conversion: the power to forgive sins was attributed to it (and because of that, it was sometimes postponed until death). The later apostle Paul associates his call with a personal experience of conversion on the way to Damascus, a vision of Christ (Acts 9.3–9; cf. I Cor. 14.8). The Acts of the Apostles knows conversions only as a result of preaching by missionaries (Acts 13.48f.) and by miraculous acts in the name of Christ, for example in Jerusalem itself: 'Now many signs and wonders were done among the people by the hands of the apostles . . . And more than ever believers were added to the Lord, multitudes both of men and women' (Acts 5.12–14). The 'initial experience', the origin of the Jesus community in Jerusalem on the Jewish Feast of Weeks, evidently consisted of a combination of an outbreak of miraculous enthusiasm and a comparatively matter-of-fact sermon by the Galilean fisherman Peter (Acts 2.1–36; of course the text of the speech was not noted down at the time but composed later, as was the custom of contemporary historians). The success of the mission sermon is described like this: 'Now when they heard this they were cut to the heart' (Acts 2.37) and had themselves baptized.

Christian conversion accounts

Unfortunately for subsequent centuries we have only heavily stereotyped 'conversion accounts' from the circle of theologians with a passable (or – more rarely – even very good) philosophical training. This stereotyped form and the lack of interest in any psychological details are of course connected with the degree to which, in differing forms of intensity, the accounts of conversions in the New Testament remained the model for similar narratives at a later time. Even the accounts of conversions from the very early period are very sparing in details. The apologist Justin, who taught in Rome around the middle of the second century, describes his own conversion from Platonic philosophy to Christianity in a correspondingly brief form in a dialogue with a Jew (i.e. in a text which is itself meant to lead to the conversion of others). However, according to this account conversion is a purely intellectual process, which moreover is brought about with literary allusions and topics: it remains unclear whether Justin, who was born in present-day Nablus (Flavia Neapolis in Samaria), really retreated to the sea in complete solitude, there met an 'older man with an attractive appearance and a gentle, earnest character', and discussed philosophy, happiness, God and the knowledge of God with him. His acceptance of Christianity is then described in a way which combines an emotional and an intellectual act: 'Straightway a flame was kindled in my soul; and a love of the prophets, and of those men who are friends of Christ, possessed me; and whilst revolving his word in my mind, I found this philosophy alone to be safe and profitable.'[85] However, even in this description, which seems to be so personal, Justin again uses a language shaped by conventional themes. As well as the references to the model of the New Testament (Acts 2.37, quoted above, 42) and philosophical terminology,[86] this is demonstrated by an example which originated almost a century later. Gregory the Miracle Worker, shortly after 238 bishop in his ancestral city of Neocaesarea (Pontus, present-day Niksar), describes his own final conversion from paganism to Christianity as a result of lectures by the theologian Origen like this: 'Like some spark kindled within my soul there was kindled and blazed forth my love both towards him, most desirable for all of his beauty unspeakable, the Word holy and altogther lovely, and towards this man his friend and prophet.'[87] The lectures of Origen, the important Christian scholar and preacher from Alexandria, thus awoke in this son of distinguished parents a 'love of the Logos', i.e. of Christ, the Word who rules over the world and also holy scripture – these formulations used by Gregory show how much in five years of teaching by Origen he had taken in the synthesis of biblical (John 1.1) and philosophical thought which his teacher attempted to communicate. His words reflect precisely the specific mixture of scholarly theology and intensive Jesus piety which marks out Origen's biblical commentaries and sermons. If we may take seriously Gregory's own brief remarks in his panegyric on his teacher, he was particularly convinced by the thesis, which Origen put forward energetically, that a rational method with a scholarly basis and knowledge of philosophy were necessary for knowledge of God.[88] Accordingly, in Caesarea in Palestine, after conversion one could go through a canon of education focussed on Christianity as the most scholarly form of knowledge of

God: exercises in logic and dialectic, the natural sciences, moral teaching and theology (initially in philosophers and poets, and finally in the Bible). Because of this 'canon', Origen's lectures have been described as a 'mission school' for educated pagans: the real instruction in the special features of Christian dogma (the doctrine of the Trinity, christology, sacramental theology) probably took place only in the context of instruction for baptism. However, the example of Gregory shows that there were also pupils who attended such mission instruction with prior knowledge: at the age of fourteen he turned 'for the first time to the truthful Logos which brings salvation'.[89] Unfortunately Gregory does not indicate how we are to imagine this first encounter by an adolescent. According to a somewhat dubious account, a North African teacher of rhetoric was moved to accept Christianity through dreams.[90]

We have virtually no accounts of the conversion of less educated people from this period – all we have are the very brief and stereotyped remarks of theologians from middle- or upper-class circles. Thascius Cyprianus, the later bishop of Carthage (who called himself Caecili[an]us after his godfather), described his conversion to Christianity in the work *To Donatus* with matter-of-fact words. It is striking that he emphasizes its suddenness: 'How is such a conversion possible, that there should be a sudden and rapid divestment of all which is either innate . . . or has become inveterate by long accustomed use?' Only after baptism did 'doubtful things at once begin to assure themselves to me, hidden things to be revealed, dark things to be enlightened'.[91] We do not get much concrete detail or even a psychological picture of this event (or would it be better to say process?), which can be dated to the 240s. It is hard to decide whether the disturbed circumstances of the empire, which was in a political and economic crisis – Cyprian describes this in moving detail – were a motive for the conversion or whether in retrospect this conversion did not allow a calm look at the chaos of the world with its highwaymen and pirates, bloody wars, abhorrent cruelties in the circus, moral corruption in theatres and homes, economic crime and the failing authority of the emperor.[92] But one would not want to rule out the possibility that sensitive people who were shaken by the collapse of morality felt attracted to Christianity as a movement obligated to comparatively rigorous ethical laws. However, just how overwhelming what is reported so briefly was is shown by the changes in the life of the convert: Cyprian abandoned his profession as an orator in order to be able to lead a continent life and gave up the majority of his possessions for the benefit of the community.

At any rate the circumstances of the conversion of more ordinary people to Christianity can be reconstructed from the mockery of opponents: Celsus, a second-century Middle Platonist philosopher, claims that 'in private houses also we see wool-workers, cobblers, laundry-workers, and the most illiterate and bucolic yokels, who would not dare to say anything at all in front of their elders and more intelligent masters. But whenever they get hold of children in private and some stupid women with them, they let out some astounding statements as, for example, that they must not pay any attention to their fathers and school-teachers, but must obey them; they say that these talk nonsense and have no understanding, and that in reality they neither know nor are able to do anything good, but are taken up with mere empty chatter. But they alone, they say, know the right way to live, and if the children would believe them, they would become happy and make their home happy as well.'[93] We know of this polemic from the retort of the theologian Origen, already mentioned above, who in the middle of the eighth century devoted eight books to the refutation of Celsus. If we leave aside the exaggerated polemical charge that only rebels, women, children and common people propagated the new religion, or that it achieved success only on a mission to such people – Celsus finds such propaganda for a cause highly disreputable anyway – it follows that in the great cities, at any rate, the conversion was often preceded by conversations with prominent teachers. This alienated the candidates from their own family background (or their current teachers). Of course the circle of those addressed by Christian preaching differed from that for popular or specialist philosophical lectures. 'You say that we gossip among women and boys, among girls and old women' are the charges made by the non-Christian environment which another apologist reports;[94] obviously no complete description of those converted to Christianity in the second century can be derived from this. As appears amazingly accurately through the mockery of Celsus, conversion is not just about intellectual knowledge but about the right way to live and about salvation. Since in the one case we have God's revelation and in the other God's commandment, conversion means adopting, believing and confessing the authoritative claim to truth and validity. According to Celsus, the Christian teachers declare 'that one is obliged . . . to obey'.[95]

Conversion of Augustine

Probably the most famous conversion scene in ancient Christian literature was written by the North African Augustine when shortly before being consecrated bishop at the end of the fourth century he described his 'conversion', to be dated to August 386 (really the last part of a three-part series of conversions or conversion processes). There have been long arguments over the historicity of this 'garden scene', narrated around ten years after the event, but the majority of studies at present argue with good reasons that this is an account of what really happened. Augustine had spent two years in the imperial residence of Milan as city orator, and had enjoyed – initially for purely rhetorical reasons – the sermons of Bishop Ambrose, who had been head of the local church since 374 and had previously been governor of the province. But Augustine had also made contact with a group of Christian Neoplatonists who provided him with 'Platonic books'.[96] So his intellectual 'conversion' to Christianity in part preceded the famous 'conversion scene', but could not put an end to the North African's uncertainty. A clergyman from Milan and a high official from his native Africa deepened his inner restlessness by giving him examples of other prominent converts from among philosophers and ascetics around him. The models caused a severe inner conflict in Augustine over his own career, which he increasingly felt to be unsatisfying and immoral. At the climax of such an inward struggle, Augustine was in the garden of a house in Milan and later gave this report: 'I flung myself down somehow under a certain fig tree and no longer tried to check my tears, wihch poured forth from my eyes in a flood . . . And suddenly I heard a voice from some nearby house, a boy's voice or a girl's voice, I do not know: but it was a sort of sing-song, repeated again and again, "*Tolle, lege; tolle, lege.*"' The famous Latin words first of all mean 'Take, read', but they are also interpreted in the context of a children's game. Augustine goes on: 'I ceased weeping and immediately began to search my mind most carefully as to whether children were accustomed to chant these words in any kind of game, and I could not remember that I had ever heard any such thing. Damming back the flood of my tears I arose, interpreting the incident as quite certainly a divine command to open my book of Scripture and read the passage at which I should open . . . So I was moved to return to the place where Alypius was sitting, for I had put down the apostle's (Paul's) book there when I arose.'[97] Augustine went on to narrate how through this special form of the 'book oracle' (he opened Rom. 13.13f.) 'peaceful certainty flowed like a stream of light into my grieving heart, and all the night of doubt disappeared'. The 'conversion' was first of all expressed in a changed attitude to marriage and sexuality (Augustine henceforth renounced them) and to his profession (he resigned the Milan post and became an ascetic). As a result of the events in the garden he gained certainty and the power to implement in his own life the truth that he had recognized. The ethical implications of Christian faith no longer seemed to him to be a burden; he took them for granted as part of a new existence. In keeping with the style of his *Confessions,* the Bishop of Hippo concludes the scene in the garden with a direct address to God in the form of a prayer: 'And so you converted me to yourself.'[98] This remark indicates that in the meantime the author had occupied himself not only with two verses of Paul but in detail with the apostle and his theology: both understood conversion not as a decision made by an individual himself but as the effect of the divine election of grace. Augustine also preached this theology by the example of his own life in his autobiography.

Until well into the fourth century the Christian church gained more members from outside than through growth 'from within', i.e. through the education of children by their Christian parents. With the official tolerance of this religion, and even more with its rise to become a state religion (see above, 29), of course the question becomes more pressing whether the change of faith did not often take place for political, military or socio-economic reasons. For in some circumstances it was an advantage to be a Christian: in Phrygia, a place named Orkistos asked the emperor Constantine between 324 and 326 for the restoration of its lost civic rights, giving as one of the reasons that everyone was a Christian.[99] However, as in the fourth century the military still largely consisted of 'pagans', one should not overestimate this 'attraction' to conversion. The topic of compulsory conversion was a controversial one, as again we can see from Augustine: 'He (viz. Christ) never used force, but always persuaded and admonished.' He wrote at the beginning of the nineties.[100] We can see that Augustine changed his position over the course of his life from his *Retractationes*, a work which he wrote in the seventy-third year of his life, in 427. In it he quoted the earlier passage about Christ and made the critical comment that at that time he had not thought of the expulsion of the money changers and merchants, which Jesus had indeed carried out by force. But that was nothing, he said, compared with the violence with which demons could torment people. Already in a letter of 407 he had argued against giving heretics free rein, and among other things backed this up with a verse from the New Testament: 'Compel all whom you find to come in.'[101] He said that his view was once different; he thought that 'no one should be forced to the unity of Christ; one must let the Word work . . . so that we do not get conscripted Catholics from those whom we knew as upright heretics'. His correspondent had written to Augustine completely along this old line, stating what today is the consensus: 'One must not compel anyone to righteousness', i.e. to enter the Catholic church. But Augustine had been convinced of the opposite by his fellow bishops and no longer accepted any compromises in matters of salvation or damnation: it was not important 'whether anyone is compelled or not, but what he is compelled to, be this good or evil'.[102]

Conversion in late antiquity

How did 'conversion' function under the conditions of the state church in the fourth century? One answer by way of example which at the same time gives an interesting insight into the process of conversion in this period is the account of the life of Bishop Porphyry of Gaza, which is said to have been written by his deacon Mark. Even if details have been changed or invented in a later redactional revision,[103] this work gives a lively impression of the atmosphere of conversion to Christianity at the end of the fourth century. The Greek ascetic Porphyry accepted consecration as bishop in 395 in this city which was especially stamped by the cult of the city god Marna(s) (i.e. 'our Lord'). However, the pagan population of the city, who were the majority, regarded his elevation as a serious misfortune. But when the 280 Christians of the place (about one per cent of the estimated population) performed a petitionary procession for rain in time of drought and it actually rained, 870 men, 530 women and 14 children were converted.[104] The motivation for conversions provided by miracles, already attested in the New Testament, thus lasted into late antiquity. Around the turn of the century the bishop helped a woman who could not bring her child into the world without complications because of its unfortunate position in her womb. When with the intercessions of Porphyry after just a week the baby finally came into the world alive, the 'woman's parents, her husband and all the relatives and members of the family' asked for baptism. The author sums it up: 'And the number of those who were baptized through this occasion was sixty-four.'[105] Ninety-three men and women were converted when a statue of Aphrodite fell apart – allegedly in full view of a procession. And when after long efforts the Marneion, the famous chief temple in the city, was set on fire 'with liquid pitch, sulphur and pork fat', and 'burned for many days', 'many adhered to the holy faith, some from fear and others condemning their former life'.[106] Significantly the text also hands on a discussion within the community about such forcible conversions (at any rate soldiers had searched the houses for pagan cultic images and images of gods and pagan literature): 'But some of the believers told the holy bishop that he should not have accepted those who had joined out of fear, but only those who came with good intentions.' However, as the bishop also accepted the others in the hope that here 'time would soften their hearts', the number of those seeking baptism increased yet again: 'Now in any year around three hundred names were added to Christ's flock.'[107] The bishop graphically told the remaining pagans: 'Now when the ashes of the burned main temple were removed, the holy bishop resolved to use the remaining pieces of the marble covering of the Marneion (which were said to be holy and were in a place which could not be entered, especially by women) for paving the square outside the temple, so that they might be trodden on not only by men but also by women, dogs, pigs and all kinds of cattle. This offended the idolaters more than the burning of the temple. So most of them, especially the women, have not trodden on the marble to this day.'[108] New excavations in Aphrodisias in Asia Minor and elsewhere have produced archaeological evidence for this practice, which was evidently widespread;[109] it satisfied both demands for economical building and the revenge of a minority which was finally triumphing. When in reaction in Gaza some members of the council started a small revolt against the bishop in which the mob killed seven people, the provincial governor had to intervene with troops. Thus – if we are really to believe the surprisingly precise figures given, since in the end they are what gives a 'historical romance' authenticity – through the activities of the bishop the community had almost doubled in five years; within a year of the destruction of the main temple, as many Christians again had been gained. Nevertheless, after five years in the building, the church had evidently become too big for the urban Christian community: 'This was also the reason why some of the faithful accused the holy Porphyry of having made the church so big, although the number of Christians in the city was only few.'[110] So there were no real mass conversions within the – at a cautious estimate – between fifteen and twenty thousand inhabitants of the city.[111]

Obstacles to conversion

Obviously, after 380, when Christianity had been declared a state religion, there were also adherents of pagan cults elsewhere who had not converted – above all in the city of Rome there were energetic and highly gifted adherents of the traditional religion who argued shrewdly and skilfully, but ultimately unsuccessfully, for the preservation of their ancestral rights. When in 382 the emperor Gratian for the second time had the altar of the Goddess of Victory removed from the Roman Senate (Julian had had it restored), these groups of educated pagan senators sent a highly-respected orator and official, Quintus Aurelius Symmachus, to the court in Milan to have the measure repealed. After the complete failure of this mission, which was probably caused by the energetic intervention of the bishops of Rome and Milan, Damasus and Ambrose, a second attempt was undertaken in 384. Symmachus had meanwhile risen to become *praefectus urbi*; in addition it could be expected that because of his youth (he was only twelve), Gratian's successor Valentinian II would be more dependent on advisors. That proved to be the case, but in quite the opposite way from what the Symmachus group had hoped for: Ambrose influenced the ruler by two letters against the restitution of the altar, which stood as a symbol for the victory or the defeat of the traditional religion. In its famous petition dated 384 to the emperor, the pagan group argued on the highest level: 'We therefore pray you to reintroduce the religion in the form in which it was useful to the state for so long.'[112] In a series of arguments a plea is made quite openly to restore the traditional decoration to the building, as the place where for centuries the oath had been taken. Then there was an argument for religious toleration: 'Everyone has his own custom, everyone has his own belief. The divine spirit has assigned different cults to the cities for their protection . . . This form of worship of the gods has subjected the earth to my (viz. Rome's) laws . . . Therefore we pray for peace for the gods of our fathers and for the gods of our homeland . . . We see the same stars, we share the heavens, the same universe embraces us. Why is the question of the teaching by which each seek the truth so important? One cannot attain to such an exalted mystery by a single way.'[113] By contrast, the level of Christian reaction in Rome declined (evidently in the community there after the death of Bishop Damasus in AD 384 there were few with any poetic or theological capacity). A little verse in bad Latin accuses the pagan circle in the city of Rome of being responsible for the death of one of its members: 'What is the use of having worshipped the Lares and the two-faced Janus? What (is the use of) the mighty earth, the fair mother of the gods?'[114] Of course the pagan resistance to the (at least partially) mass conversion did not just consist of a few highly-educated intellectuals: whole regions either did not change their religion or, if they did, did so very reluctantly – the proportion of Christians in the population in the 360s has been calculated at between thirty and forty per cent (but such figures remain extremely uncertain). Around 400 a Jerusalem synod wrote to the patriarch of Alexandria[115] that 'thanks to the grace of Christ, all Palestine' need not endure 'any discord through heretics'. But the Christianization does not seem to have been completely straightforward: 'Thanks to the intercession of the saints, we were not made anxious by the Jewish serpents, the incredible stupidity of the Samaritans, and the quite manifest godlessnesses of the pagans, whose extraordinarily numerous host shuts its ears to the preaching of the truth and, as it circles Christ's flock like lions, causes us no little attentiveness and labour.' The inhabitants of such pagan Palestinian villages strewed 'thorns and splinters in the way' of the new Bishop of Gaza, Porphyry, when he wanted to enter 'his' city from Caesarea in March 385, 'so that no one could go past and they poured out piss and made evil-smelling smoke, so that we almost choked from the stench and our eyes watered.'[116] Here is so to speak an *adventus* turned upside down.

'Semi-Christianity'

Finally, reference should be made to a phenomenon which has been called 'semi-Christianity': people 'who, although they are Christian, join in the celebration of pagan festive occasions

. . . those who want to investigate human life and its events from the course of the stars or study the flight of birds and the like that one can observe in the world'.[117] Cyprian, bishop of Carthage, wrote his polemic shortly after the middle of the third century against a Spanish colleague who 'has long frequented the disgraceful and filthy banquets of the pagans in their college, and placing his sons in the same college, after the manner of foreign nations, among profane sepulchres'.[118] Evidently the Bishop of Saragossa belonged to a pagan association or college which met for meals on specific days, and of course these meetings also involved religious activities. Moreover at some point at the beginning of the fourth century the Synod of Elvira in Spain attacks priests of the imperial cult (*flamines*) who had had themselves baptized yet nevertheless still performed pagan sacrifices. Such people were excluded from the eucharist (excommunicated) for life.[119] Certain forms of 'semi-Christianity' could hardly be avoided at the latest after the third century, if one did not want to leave public life. Even the Synod of Elvira deals with Christian imperial priests, i.e. members of the community who could exercise their office – a top civic office bestowed anew every year, with considerable obligatory representative functions; such *flamines* were by no means finally expelled from the Christian community, but might be readmitted after a break of two years, i.e. after the end of their activity. Evidently at that time many pagan festivities had also already largely lost their original cultic character. For the Spanish bishops, only a lapse into pagan cultic practices was tantamount to murder.[120] The synod also attempted to regulate such 'semi-Christians' on another point which would probably have been almost unimaginable in the first and second centuries, on the basis of the principles of Christian ethics: those holding such civic offices were usually expected to engage in sponsorship at a relatively high level – for example, the *flamines* were expected to give games and theatrical performances. But the synod forbade members of its communities to do this: neither the murder of fellow human beings in the gladiatorial games nor unseemly scenes at the theatre were to be supported by the money of

Christian office-holders.[121] However, a warning must be issued against the view that this 'semi-Christianity' was limited to the well-to-do or to common, uneducated or at least barely educated Christians who could not strip off the relics of pagan religion because of public prestige or spiritual naivety. The highly educated Christian military strategos, architect and polymath Julius Africanus reported a whole series of magical practices at the beginning of the third century in his twenty-four volume collection *Cesti,* which unfortunately has largely been lost. Thus for example he presents a technique for poisoning the air in war as being extremely successful: two precisely specified snakes are to be put in a watertight pot which is to be exposed to the scorching midday sun. When the snakes have been destroyed by attacks on each other, by heat and by time, the stench is to be driven in the direction of the enemy on a favourable wind. To quote him: 'Here are some examples of the effect: a horse galloping past will fall and so will a man standing by; and a bird will not fly over, but drop out of the air dead.'[122] In the *Geoponica*, a Byzantine collection of earlier ancient agricultural writings, it is reported that a verse from a psalm on a wine-jar protects the contents from going off (Ps. 34.8: 'The angel of the Lord protects all those who fear and honour him'), and a verse of Homer spoken over the first cup (*Iliad* VIII, 70: 'Three times the mighty Zeus thundered from Ida') will be a protection against drunkenness.[123]

So – contrary to all the assurances in Christian literature – conversion to Christianity does not always represent a radical break with all forms of pagan life and thought.

Birth, baptism and death

Birth

In the period before Constantine, Tertullian's remark 'We are yours – one becomes a Christian and is not born one'[124] applied to the great majority of people. In the first centuries, an overwhelming majority of those who joined the Christian community were still born in pagan surroundings, though we also keep hearing of famous children of Christian parents. For example,

Names

already in antiquity there was an argument as to whether the Alexandrian theologian Origen was born the son of a Christian father or a pagan father who became a Christian shortly after Origen's birth: the Greek pagan Neoplatonist Porphyry, whom Origen had known in his youth,[125] claimed that Origen had been the son of a pagan father; the Palestinian church historian Eusebius claimed the opposite. The meaning of his name 'Origen', 'offspring of the Or', i.e. 'child of Horus', was regularly cited for the 'pagan' variants. However, such pagan names for Christians keep occurring well into the fourth century, as is already clear from a look at a history of ancient Christian literature: Apollonius after Apollo (Apolinarius is not connected etymologically with the Greek god); Dionysius (a comparatively frequent name among Christians, which could at a pinch be explained from the Athenian Dionysius in Acts 17.34); Hippolytus after the eponymous hero worshipped as a god in Troizen, or Serapion after Serapis, the syncretistic god of Alexandria. So evidently there was no compulsion for Christian parents to give their child at birth a name which occurred in the Bible or that of a well-known martyr or saint. On the contrary, such names were not given very often. In the earliest acts of a North African synod dated AD 256, just two 'Christian' names, Peter and Paul, appear among eighty-seven bishops. Adolf von Harnack once commented, 'The martyrs died because they refused to sacrifice to the gods whose names they bore,'[126] and pointed out that after the year AD 212 it was legally possible for any free person to change his name. He explained the manifest indifference of Christianity towards pagan names by saying that 'the general custom of the world in which people lived was initially stronger than any reflection'. Only in the fourth century did it become customary in wider circles to drop pagan names at baptism and assume a 'Christian' name. Eusebius reports on five individuals who at the beginning of the fourth century dropped the 'names given to them by their parents, probably derived from idols', and assumed the names of Old Testament prophets: Elijah, Jeremiah, Isaiah, Samuel and Daniel:[127] this corresponded to a practice among proselytes who had gone over to Judaism.[128]

Theodoret, the bishop of Cyrrhus, a pilgrimage centre in northern Syria, says around a century later that those who make efforts to give their children the names of martyrs and saints will achieve security and protection for them,[129] and a little later even makes a few indirect suggestions: Peter, Paul, Thomas, Sergius, Marcellius, Leontius; names of apostles, martyrs and saints. The inscriptions also confirm that his views are generally correct: more than 400 publishable inscriptions, mainly from the early Byzantine period, were found in the excavation of a seven-aisle basilica outside ancient Carthage (near the residence of the President of Tunisia). Among them appear the names of Carthaginian martyrs (Cyprian, Felicitas, Perpetua – the excavators thought that the place was the *basilica Cypriani*, where the local bishop Cyprian had been buried after his execution in AD 258); New Testament names like John, Mary, Paul and Peter; names which refer to topics of Christian doctrine (Anastasia as a reference to belief in the resurrection; Redemptus, Reparatus, Renovatus, with reference to the renewal of people through baptism), and names alluding to religious festivals (Paschasius [Pascha = Easter], Sabbatius). Names which are abbreviations of theophoric and religious maxims (Dominicus, Cyriacus, Adeodatus, Deogratias, Deusdedit, Habetdeus, Quodvultdeus, Spesindeo) are as widespread as ordinary African, Germanic and Greek names.

Abortion

It was by no means taken for granted in the world of the empire that children who had been conceived would in fact be born. From the beginning, Christian preaching was opposed to abortion, which was practised comparatively frequently in antiquity among non-Christians, above all in extra-marital or semi-marital relationships like concubinage (cf. 136). The satirist Juvenal in the early empire mocked: 'But how often does a gilded bed contain a woman who is lying in? So great is the skill, so powerful the drugs, of the abortionist, paid to murder mankind within the womb.'[130] As most people did not regard the foetus as a living being with a soul, abortion was not felt to be murder; however, after the second century AD it was punishable by temporary banishment. By contrast, the very first

Christian church order to have been preserved, the so-called Teaching of the Twelve Apostles, lays down: 'You shall not procure abortion or commit infanticide.'[131] The punishment threatened was correspondingly strict: an apocalypse composed in Egypt in the second century and attributed to Peter depicts a division of hell like this: 'And near that place I saw another gorge in which the discharge and the excrement of the tortured ran down and became like a lake. And there sat women, and the discharge came up to their throats; and opposite them sat many children, who were born prematurely, weeping. And from them went forth rays of fire and smote the women on the eyes. And these were those who conceived children outside marriage and procured abortions.'[132] The episcopal Synod of Elvira (presumably at the beginning of the fourth century) decreed that an abortion after adultery should result in lifelong exclusion from communion – but only for the woman! However, this strict rule was soon relaxed: at the Synod of Ancyra (Ankara), already in the fourth century a penitential period of ten years was ordained, and at the Synod of Lerida in AD 546 a period of seven years.[133] The notion occurs in many passages of ancient Christian literature that a guardian angel takes up aborted children and keeps them until they testify against their parents in the last judgment. 'Lord, you did not grudge us a common light. But those people there put us to death because they despised your commandment' (thus a Christian teacher from Lycia by the name of Methodius, perhaps in the late third century, in his *Banquet)*.[134] This ethic is based on the view that the foetus is already 'God's creature' and as such has a soul – at any rate the Didache and the Apocalypse of Peter agree in saying this.[135] Clement of Alexandria therefore made efforts to support the Christian prohibition of abortion on this basis by a philosophical consideration, and in this connection cites an 'elder', i.e. a Platonizing Christian teacher of the second century, who said that 'the embryo in the womb is a living being'. This theory was also put forward by some Platonists on the basis of the movement of the foetus, whereas Stoics spoke of part of the womb and compared it with the fruit as part of the plant. The anonymous Christian teacher quoted by Clement writes that the soul is 'prepared for and introduced' 'by an angel set over the procreation who knows the time of conception in advance'.[136] Even Tertullian thought that 'the entire process of sowing . . . forming and completing the human embryo in the womb is no doubt regulated by some power . . . We on our part believe the angels to officiate in this for God.'[137]

The process of conception

Through this idea Christian theologians Christianized the pagan medical and philosophical theories so to speak 'at the roots' and could then simply take over many other elements: Clement wrote that the 'power' contained in the seed – a Stoic conception – mixed with 'the pure residue of the menses'. The blood coagulates through the power of the seed, 'as rennet curdles milk, and so effects the essential part of the formative process. The right mixture leads to happy growth.'[138] In a didactic work, Clement innocently packages his own very detailed advice on the topic 'what one must discuss about procreating children', 'the right time for sexual union' and birth control in the metaphor of a countryman who sows seed either in the field or on the rocks. The maxim, derived from the Bible and converging with Stoic ethics, is clear: 'God has commanded: Multiply! (Gen. 1.28). And he must be obeyed.' Stoicism also shapes Clement's ideas of what may go on between a married couple and what had better not. Again a metaphor is used – this time from the animal kingdom. The hyena is an animal which is 'greedy for copulation'. It is said 'that every other year it exchanges the male sex for the female sex' – one must not behave like this.[139] To see sex above all as there for procreating children was in accordance with the Stoic notion of it as useful activity.[140] Accordingly Clement warned: if what is 'useful' turns into what is 'enjoyable', if pleasure dominates, rational human beings become beasts. This reversion of God's creation cannot be intended. There is nothing intrinsically reprehensible about sexual intercourse – however, that does not apply to the time of menstruation, pregnancy, breast feeding[141] and extramarital relations. Clement even claims the authority of Plato for his views: 'And do not touch any woman but your own wife.'[142]

These comparatively direct and clear counsels of Clement are addressed more to an educated public; the concerns of wider groups were described at the beginning of the third century by Julius Africanus in his *Cesti* as follows: 'Should a man want to beget a child, before he comes together with the woman, if he smears his member with hare's blood he will beget a male child, but if he smears it with goose fat he will beget a female child.'[143] An amulet with the inscription 'Let the crooked become straight! Let (the young one) come to light! . . . It is I who say this, the Lord Jesus who gives healing'[144] should be put on the stomach of the mother giving birth, or the verse should be spoken over a drink for her, so that the birth goes smoothly. As protection from the evil eye children were smeared with dirt from the bath.[145] Individual Christian men and women were also fond of using the rich astrological methods and techniques in antiquity.

Arguments against motherhood

The increasingly critical attitude of Christian theologians to marriage and sexuality in the fourth century is also expressed in essentially harsher attitudes to birth. Ambrose, bishop of Milan, described at length the labours on the way to the blessing of children in order to promote the option of becoming a nun: a woman marries and weeps, she conceives and becomes pregnant, she gives birth and is sick. The first movement of the child spells danger, and so does its arrival; thus birth represents pain and inconvenience, and virginity is to be commended.[146] It has been remarked pointedly that since the wilderness of the Egyptian and Syrian ascetics was not available in fertile northern Italy, Ambrose had to make the bedroom the monastic wilderness;[147] there has been talk of a 'carefully maintained siege mentality'[148] which is directed against the body and its needs, indeed against the trend of the times generally. On the other hand, these texts could also be read as an attempt to put into practice a Paul interpreted against the background of the hostility to the body widespread in antiquity, under the conditions of an urban society in northern Italy.

Religions as midwives

From the fourth century onwards, monks and ascetics in part took over the role at birth which had previously been performed by astrologers, magicians and midwives. The *Lausiac History*, a collection of monastic biographies made by Bishop Palladius of Helenopolis (Hersek) in Bithynia in the early fifth century and dedicated to one Lausus, often relates such instances – for example about Poseidonius of Thebes who lived in the Shepherds' Fields by Bethlehem. There a 'certain woman approaching her confinement had an unclean spirit and, when she was about to be delivered, she had difficult labour, the spirit tormenting her. The husband therefore . . . came and he sought that holy man to come. So he stood up . . . and prayed, and after kneeling down the second time he drove out the spirit.'[149] Saint Melania the Younger, who came from a Roman senatorial family, had founded a convent on the Mount of Olives in Jerusalem, and lived there until AD 439, once healed a woman whose child had died in the womb – in accordance with the custom of ancient medicine this should have been destroyed with an appropriate instrument, but here it miraculously emerged from the body, after Melania had put a girdle on the mother's body and healed her. Moreover this magical girdle is mentioned among the pieces of clothing that Melania took with her to her grave.[150]

Birthdays

It is possible that in early Christianity there were no special celebrations for birthdays. But perhaps Christians also simply took over the pagan custom of celebrating them without giving them any 'Christian' basis – uncertainty remains here because we have virtually no clear information. As the pagan birthday began and ended with the invocation of the 'good daemon' (thus in Greece) or the Genius or Juno (thus in Rome), which accompanied the person through life, the more serious members of the Christian community will have had difficulties with this date. 'From beginning to end appropriate prayers are offered to the gods of birth and family, and before and after to the saviour and leader in life (viz. Asclepius)' – that is how the orator Aelius Aristides from Asia Minor begins his address in AD 147 on the birthday of the eminent Roman senator C.Iulius Apellas from the Quadratus family in Pergamon. And the conclusion of his speech is again about a god, Zeus, and the ruling family on which Zeus has bestowed the rule.[151] Thus as a rule 'the emperor's birthday' was celebrated in a markedly religious way, and appropriate speeches on this occasion have also been preserved. For Christians who nevertheless took part in such celebrations, this connection between the birthday and the individual guardian deities of life must have represented a considerable problem. However, no great polemics against birthday celebrations have been preserved, even in the early period; at most we can infer disapproval of them from the fact that Tertullian would like to see the dead commemorated on the day of their death and not on their birthdays.[152] It is not until the third century that a critical shift against the celebration of birthdays becomes perceptible in literature. In his multi-volume commentary on the Gospel of Matthew, Origen explains: 'One of our predecessors observed what is written in Genesis about Pharaoh's birthday (viz. Gen. 40.20) and says that only the bad person who loves something connected with procreation celebrates birthdays. We have been stimulated by that exegete and found that nowhere in scripture is there a mention of the celebration of the birthday of a just man.'[153] Christian theologians could even reverse the pagan evaluation of birthdays and days of death: as Bishop of Hippo, around 417 Augustine preached on the festival of the Maccabean martyrs, declaring that Cyprian of Carthage incurred original sin on his birthday, and conquered it on the day of his death.[154] That explains the custom, particularly in the fourth century, of describing the days of martyrs' deaths as 'birthdays' (*dies natalis*). But at the same time there is increasing evidence in this century that birthdays were celebrated in the communities. Accordingly theologians also begin to justify this practice, a move which may simply be connected with the increasing social integration of Christianity. An anonymous Bible commentator of the late fourth century discusses the problem of birthdays in a series of questions on biblical texts. In Jerusalem the festival of the consecration of the temple was once celebrated: the temple had been destroyed, but the body is the temple of God (I Cor. 3.17). Now as the body is destined for eternity, one should be grateful to God for birth and should celebrate one's birth: 'We would not be reborn, were birth not useful.'[155]

The celebration of the birth of Christ

Moreover – probably again from the fourth century on – the birthday of Jesus Christ was celebrated, but initially on two different dates. The earliest evidence for this is a report by Bishop Ambrose of Milan about a sermon by the Roman bishop Liberius on 'the Day of the Birth of the Redeemer',[156] on 25 December 353 or 354. And for a slightly later date, namely 6 January 361, there is a first piece of evidence for the 'feast of the Epiphany' in Paris, a festival on which some of the Christian communities in the East down to the fifth century celebrated both the baptism *and* the birth of Christ.[157] Above all at the beginning of the twentieth century, it was assumed that both festivals were simply meant to 'Christianize' two pagan festivals: 25 December as the *dies natalis solis invicti*, the day of the invincible sun, and 6 January as the birthday festival of an Alexandrian god Aion (Greek *aion* = time, eternity) or a Nile festival. However, there is also evidence that the two dates were simply arrived at by calculation. Such learned calculations were made at a very early stage (though with completely different results): North African work on calculating the date of Easter in 243 still gave as the date of Jesus' birth the day on which the sun was also once created, 28 March.[158] Thus the parallel between Christ and the sun had already been drawn long before the usurpation of the pagan feast of the sun on 25 December.[159] By contrast, at the beginning of the third century Clement of Alexandria established the birth of Jesus by an indirect dating ('from the birth of the Lord to the death of Commodus', i.e. 31 December 192, '194 years, 1 month and 13 days') on the 18 November in the year 2 BC – and at the same time distanced himself from such calculations by showing that the real birthday of Jesus was already no longer known at that time. 'Some want with exaggerated precision to indicate not only the year but also the day of the birth of our Saviour' (these people favour 20 May).[160] Finally, a treatise the date and location of which is disputed calculated the date as 25 December and concluded: 'They also call (this day) the "birthday of the invincible sun". Truly, who is so unconquered as our Lord, who overthrew and conquered death? And if they call this day the birthday of the sun, he is the sun of righteousness!'[161] To begin with, East and West still differed over the date of Christmas, but then most regions of the East changed over to the Roman practice of celebrating it on 25 December – Cappadocia already in the fourth century, Jerusalem only in the sixth. Only the Armenian church has still maintained to the present day the old custom of celebrating the birth of Christ on 6 January. Correspondingly the West introduced a separate 'feast of the Epiphany'; in Milan, already under the episcopacy of Ambrose in the last third of the fourth century the birth of Christ was celebrated on 25 December and the visit of the three magi from the East, the baptism of Jesus and the wedding at Cana (John 2.1–11) were celebrated on 6 January. An interesting piece of evidence for the differing practice of the two halves of the empire is contained in a Christmas sermon which the Western theologian, biblical translator and ascetic Jerome delivered in Jerusalem at the beginning of the fifth century against the practice there of celebrating the birth of Jesus on 6 January. He opted for 25 December: 'Some think that his birth falls on Epiphany. We do not condemn the views of others, but insist on our view.' To substantiate his remark, in a brief historical excursus he told his hearers that there were unbroken apostolic traditions only in Rome, and not in Jerusalem. In the events following the Jewish rebellions, 'all who were Jews and Christians were, without exception', driven out. Jerome also confirmed the date both with the solstice and with chronographical considerations: 'If you compare the birthday of John with the present day, you will see that there are only six months.'[162]

Through the practice of the communities in the fourth century of connecting the birthday of Jesus so emphatically with solar and cosmological mythology, already at that time this church festival was presumably very reminiscent of the emperors' birthdays. We know from a famous inscription of the year 9 BC which was attached to two pillars in the northern hall of the market place of the town of Priene in Asia Minor (the so-called

'Calendar Inscription') that in the province of Asia people thought that the 'birthday of the divine emperor (viz. Augustus . . . might rightly be identified with the beginning of all things'. He had 'restored everything that had been destroyed and left in an unpropitious state'; his birthday was regarded by the people of the province 'as the beginning of their own life and existence'.[163]

Baptism

As well as physical birth, for Christians in antiquity there was also a 'second birth' or even 'rebirth', *baptism,* as the real beginning of life, in which divine salvation was conveyed, sins were washed away and the overcoming of death was promised. These two functions of baptism as protection and transference to a new Lord were briefly summed up by the widespread description of it as 'seal'. Had one asked a Christian in the third century about the central liturgical action of the church he would have referred to baptism, not to worship and the eucharist. It was because of the insights of the apostle Paul that baptism could be understood as rebirth (*anagennesis/ regeneratio).* Granted, Paul himself did not use this word-field (it occurs for the first time in I Peter 1.3: 'God . . . who has born us again . . . to a living hope'), but he linked baptism with the death of Jesus and as a result first made the later terminology theologically possible: 'Do you not know that all of us who have been baptized into Christ Jesus were baptized into his death? We were buried therefore with him by baptism into death, so that as Christ was raised from the dead by the glory of the Father, we too might walk in newness of life' (Rom. 6.3f.). These notions can hardly be compared with ancient mystery cults: with these remarks the apostle did not want to suggest to the Roman community that baptism was a mystical prelude (or postlude) to their own individual deaths. Rather, baptism gives those baptized a part in the death of Christ, which for Paul was significant for world history, and marked a turn in the ages. Merely to convey the apostle's argument here in a concentrated form, focussed on its goal, Christ's death opens up the way to God (Rom. 5.2). However, in Paul there is an even more interesting linguistic reservation in the form of a future: 'If we have died with Christ, we believe that we shall also live

Theology of baptism

with him' (Rom. 6.8). The 'rising with', i.e. the share in Jesus' resurrection, is reserved for the future, but the life of believers has taken on a new direction as a result of baptism, from sin and death 'in the constant direction of God'.[164] The considerably later New Testament letter attributed to Peter now combined these Pauline theologoumena – like the Fourth Gospel (John 3.3–5; also I John 3.9. etc.) – with the 'rebirth terminology' which occurs with varying content and focus in very different contexts of the religious landscape of antiquity. The Johannine statement that no one who is not 'born of water and the spirit' (or 'born from above') can enter the kingdom of God is quoted by the apologist Justin in the middle of the second century and at the same time made more precise: 'Unless you are reborn, you will not enter the kingdom of heaven.'[165] Towards the end of the second century, Irenaeus, a Bishop of Lyons who came from Asia Minor, described Jesus' activity in his work against the heresies like this: 'He has . . . come, to save all through himself; all means those who are reborn through him to God, infants, little children, boys, young men and mature men.'[166] Moreover this and other passages played an important role in a vigorous discussion among scholars over the question whether[167] or not[168] the early church baptized children before the middle of the second century. In principle the sources allow both answers, although it is at least possible that infant baptism was practised from the beginning in the framework of baptisms of whole families. By contrast, the interpretation of baptism as a rebirth or second birth had clearly already established itself in Christian theology in the second century. Presumably this was possible because this connection also corresponded to Jewish conversion theology: 'One who has become a proselyte is like a child newly born.'[169]

Infant baptism

Origins

Presumably Christian baptism also comes from Judaism: from the New Testament period on (along with circumcision and sacrifice), proselytes had to submit to an obligatory bath of immersion, having previously made their intentions clear, undergoing an examination and receiving detailed instruction. The baptismal washing sealed the conversion and obliterated the sins committed previously. Christianity took over from Judaism both the admission procedure and the baptismal instruction (= catechesis) along with the theological interpretation. However, primitive Christian baptism derives directly from a baptismal movement within Judaism centred on John, a penitential preacher who was active by the Jordan (half-way between Jerusalem and Amman) in the early first century. Jesus and at least some of his disciples came from the circle of those baptized by John. However, they themselves did not baptize, but merely took up John the Baptist's penitential preaching. Only after the execution of Jesus did the community begin baptisms 'in the name of Jesus' (Acts 2.38); so here it organized itself on the model of the group around John and other baptist groups in the world of Jesus' day. The fact that baptism took place 'in the name of Jesus' indicates that – in contrast to the other groups – baptism was not seen only as a purification ritual or a rite of initiation and acceptance; the reference to the person of Jesus was thought to be decisive. Paul also says words to this effect in his reflections on baptism quoted above.

Practical details

From a similarly early period, namely at the latest from the second century, we have a first explicit testimony to the practical administration of Christian baptism. The so-called Didache refers to the trinitarian baptismal formula already mentioned by the evangelist Matthew (28.19) when it stipulates: 'Baptize in the name of the Father, and of the Son, and of the Holy Spirit, in living (i.e. running) water. If you have no living water, baptize in other water. If you cannot baptize in cold water, baptize in warm water. And if you have neither, pour water three times on the head in the name of the Father, Son and Holy Spirit. Before baptism let the baptizer and those who are to be baptized fast, and any others who are able. And command those who are to be baptized to fast one or two days before.'[170] Thus the Didache for the first time attests so-called 'baptism by infusion' and baptismal fasts; however, there are no reports of laying on of hands after baptism, the gift of the Spirit associated with it and the anointing which was sometimes customary – nor are there any remarks about the person who administers baptism.

But to want to conclude from this silence the lack of church ministers or a 'priesthood of all believers' would be to over-interpret a passage which is concentrated on the baptismal liturgy.[171]

Baptism and confession of faith

Already at an early stage the accounts show how closely baptism and some form of confession of faith belong together: baptism seals the act of conversion, and the person being baptized is questioned on his or her new confession. In a brief work shortly before the end of the second century, Irenaeus of Lyons spoke of 'three points of our seal (of baptism)': by these he understood God the Father, above all as Creator; the Son, especially the 'saving ordinance of his incarnation'; and the Spirit, especially as the originator of the prophetic gift, 'by receiving which human beings bring forth life in God'.[172] All this still seems comparatively free and individual; it alludes to short formulae of faith, the language of which is very variable but the content of which roughly follows a norm which one can call *regula fidei* ('rule of faith') or *kanon tes aletheias* ('guideline of the truth'). Here – as also elsewhere in liturgical contexts – the development is 'from freedom to formula',[173] i.e. to more markedly stereotyped texts. For the act of baptism, specifically this meant that the candidate had to answer stereotyped questions. However, our first certain evidence of the candidate being asked questions directly within the framework of the act of baptism comes only from the third century. The North African bishop Cyprian around the middle of the third century mentions such a question: 'Do you believe in eternal life and the forgiveness of sins by the holy church?' At another point it becomes clear that the questions are called *symbolum*, that like the so-called 'baptismal command' (Matt. 28.19) they have a trinitarian structure, and that they are answered with 'I believe'.[174] For want of earlier and clear sources certainty can be gained only in the fourth century. For this is the date of the revised text of a church order which probably originates in Egypt: this is called the *Apostolic Tradition* (*Traditio Apostolica*), and the writing underlying it is attributed – but probably wrongly – to the Roman theologian Hippolytus.[175] This order ordained that 'at the time of cockcrow' first there is prayer over the running (spring) water, then the candidates, who have undressed, go into the water, first children, then men and finally women, 'who shall all have loosed their hair and laid aside their gold ornaments'.[176] This is probably meant to prevent demons from hiding under them. At any rate women were normally required to bind up their hair in church (in accordance with what was for the longest time the general fashion).[177] The bishop prepared two kinds of oil and the priest called on the candidate to renounce the devil. After an anointing, the baptizer, a deacon and the candidate went down under the water (there was usually a font provided with steps). The baptizer than asked the questions already mentioned while laying on his hands: 'Do you believe in God, the Father Almighty?' – 'Do you believe in Christ Jesus, the Son of God [etc.]?' – 'Do you believe in the Holy Spirit in the holy church and in the resurrection of the flesh?' After each answer the deacon poured water over the candidate, and then followed another anointing (in some circumstances even two anointings), the sign of the cross and a kiss from the bishop. Finally those baptized took part in the eucharist.

Baptismal instruction

But before this ceremony was performed on Easter Eve, those seeking baptism had to complete baptismal instruction; therefore a special 'class' of people also developed within the Christian communities, the catechumens (from the Greek *katechoumenos* = someone who is trained or instructed). Before admission there was an entrance examination, the form of which allows us to make interesting inferences about the social circumstances of the communities. According to the *Apostolic Tradition* the 'teachers' were enjoined to inquire into the way of life of those seeking baptism, 'whether one has a wife or is a slave'.[178] Those seeking baptism had to bring sponsors along: slaves were admitted to baptismal instruction only if their master allowed it or gave them a good testimonial. The unmarried were instructed either to remain continent in this state or to 'take a wife after the (Roman, profane) law'. An examination of their professions was also to be carried out: we shall be returning to this question (see below, 120–3). Acceptance was 'sealed' by the sign of the cross, and after the sixth century other actions also followed, including the giving of salt as a sign of the new fellowship. The instruction lasted for three years, 'but if someone is earnest and perseveres well in the matter, let him be received, because it is not the time that is judged but the conduct'.[179] The instruction consisted of two halves, the period of the catechumenate proper and the period of preparation immediately before baptism during the time of fasting, which was usually carried out by the bishop himself. Admission to the second half depended on whether the catechumens 'lived piously, whether they honoured the widows, whether they visited the sick, whether they fulfilled every good work'.[180] Therefore it was noted whether the candidates had succeeded in putting what they had learned into practice in a 'Christian life'. Later a terminological distinction was also made between the catechumens and the photizomens (*photizomenoi* = the enlightened ones) or between the hearers and the *competentes* or *electi*. In her report on a pilgrimage in 381–384, a nun from Aquitaine also mentions the topics of the second part of the instruction: an exposition of scripture which begins with Genesis and explains both the literal and the spiritual meaning of the texts, along with remarks about the resurrection and faith: 'That is called catechesis.'[181] During the preceding period of their three-year instruction, the catechumens joined in part of the community worship but were not yet admitted to the eucharist.

Blood baptism

If a catechumen was persecuted for the Christian confession before he could receive baptism, it was ordained: 'For if he suffers violence and in put to death before baptism, he shall be justified, having been baptized in his own blood.'[182] As well as this 'blood baptism' there was also 'clinical baptism', an emergency baptism in the case of serious illness with in some circumstances a considerably reduced rite. Here if possible members of the family had to attest the sick person's decision for baptism, if he or she was not in a position to express their own will on the sickbed (Greek *kline*) because of unconsciousness or other

Clinical baptism

problems. The 'possibility' of clinical baptism became increasingly attractive as Christianity advanced into public life and embraced official circles.[183] Such people did not need to make deep changes to their professional and social status and postponed baptism, which would require this of them, until shortly before death. Two emperors of the fourth century, Constantine and Theodosius, are probably the most prominent witnesses to the practice of such a postponement of baptism: they received their baptisms only on the occasion of a life-threatening illness, although they had become Christians long before and attempted to act accordingly. Nevertheless Constantine still bore the title *pontifex maximus* during his lifetime, and thus held office formally as the supreme pagan priest of Rome.

This 'Christianity without baptism', which was evidently widespread in imperial church Christianity in the fourth century, does not seem remarkable only to a modern observer; many prominent theologians of this time delivered sermons against the misuse of a postponement of baptism. Thus while still a presbyter of his community in the 360s, Basil of Caesarea, later metropolitan of the church province of Cappadocia, gave the following admonition on baptism: 'Having been instructed in the faith from childhood, do you still not assent to the truth? Are you still learning and have you not yet come to knowledge? You are making trial all your life, seeking until your old age. When will you become a Christian? When may we greet you as ours?'[184] In the course of his sermon his tone gets increasingly irritated: 'If I were to distribute gold in the church, you would not say "I will come tomorrow, give it me tomorrow." You would take it immediately, you would press for distribution and be reluctant at any kind of delay. But as the great-hearted giver is not offering you shining metal but cleansing of the soul, you look for excuses.' And the tirade comes to a climax: 'We have already lived long enough for the world; let us now live for ourselves.' 'So come here – to me! Give your heart completely to the Lord! Give in your name! Have yourself enrolled in the church.'[185] Basil and others also criticized the postponement of baptism because they were afraid that here people would be concerned about the social and economic consequences of joining the Christian community.[186]

Catechetical addresses

Above all from the fourth century on, a whole series of bishops in East and West gave catechetical addresses. These show that the preachers were particularly concerned with putting Christian life into practice, and so the sermons are like a course in etiquette, occasionally motivated by biblical texts. John Chrysostom, a priest in Antioch in Syria, declared in AD 387: 'The goal of my discourse has not yet been reached when you hear it; rather, you are to keep what has been said in mind and prove it to me through your actions.'[187] The community is to repay Christ the benefactor – here the Greek term used is *euergetes*, the usual designation in antiquity for the sponsor on whose gifts any commune was dependent – 'by an unobjectionable form of life'. And such sermons became quite concrete: 'Has a member of your household insulted you and irritated you? Then overcome your anger!' (1.10). 'Are you an artisan? Then sing songs while you are sitting at work. If you do not want to sing with your mouth, then sing in your heart!'[188] The constant presence of biblical texts prevents Christians from having 'worldly, unreasonable and fruitless conversations' and not watching their tongues: the mouth should be used 'only for singing hymns and praise, for reading scripture and for spiritual conversations'. 'If we go to the market place, our gait should be so peaceful and controlled that it attracts the gaze of all those who meet us. Nor should the eye look round everywhere; the feet should not move in an undisciplined fashion and the mouth should produce its words restfully and respectfully. In short, the whole exterior should announce the good inner disposition of the soul.' Life after baptism is a battle, the time of the catechumenate 'a training ground, a battle school'.[189]

Baptisteries

A word about the buildings in which baptism was performed, above all after the fourth century. Previously, running water was enough; from the fourth century on, the very mass of those seeking baptism who now had to be instructed made separate rooms necessary. However, the ground-plan and situation of the building varied considerably: a font is always the safest way

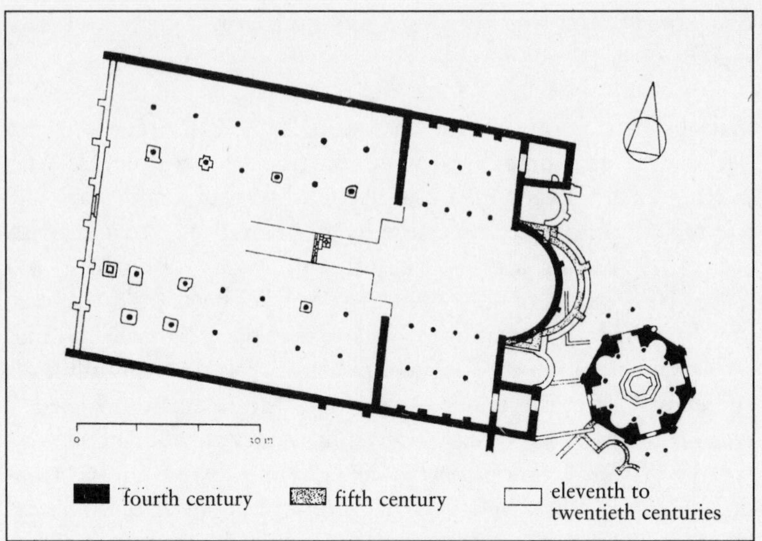

A. *Milan, St Thecla with Ambrose's baptistery*

of identifying rooms for baptism in excavations. Although the buildings were based on existing types, efforts were made to have meaningful relations between the building and the cultic action taking place there. Thus Bishop Ambrose of Milan had an octagonal baptistery erected south-east of his cathedral, the buttresses of which on the external corners and the inner niches recall Diocletian's mausoleum in Spalato (Split) and the usual form of the hot room in Roman baths (*caldarium*) (see above). Thus it followed the model of other baptisteries; here the functional form of a bathroom with its water container in the centre was combined with the significance of rooms with this shape, above all in the imperial mausolea, which represented the immortality of the divinized ruler. [190] Ambrose composed an inscription for the octagonal structure in Milan which connected the octagon with the event of baptism.

'With eight niches the temple rises for holy use.
Octagonal is the form of the well, worthy the (holy) gift.
In the number eight the house of holy baptism had to arise,

in which in truth salvation returned to the peoples
in the light of the rising Christ, who loosens the reins
of death and raises the dead from the graves
and frees the penitent sinners from the stain of sin,
as he purifies them in the water of the baptismal spring
flowing clear as crystal.'[191]

Death

Not least, baptism with its redefinition of birth and life may be responsible for earthly death playing a different role in pagan Christianity from that in the pagan environment – or at any rate people were concerned to give this impression. Of course it is even less possible to generalize here than elsewhere. A certain indifference, a certain resigned pessimism towards death can nevertheless be demonstrated in the early empire: 'Predominantly . . . people thought that death was nothing, an eternal sleep. The vague notion of shadows which lived on in an indeterminate way after death was merely a fable, as was constantly emphasized. Certainly there were numerous speculations which spoke in detail about the ongoing life of the soul after death and about its fate in the beyond, but they were known only to a few small groups. No generally recognized teaching claimed anything other than that after death a body without a soul was left behind.'[192] Thus the Roman historian Tacitus wrote in an obituary of his father-in-law in AD 93: 'If there be any habitation for the spirits of the just; if, as wise men would have it, the soul that is great perish not with the body, may you rest in peace.'[193] Around thirty years earlier, Seneca wrote to his friend Lucilius on the occasion of the death of a friend: 'Now is the time for you to reflect not only that all things are mortal, but also that their mortality is subject to no fixed laws. Whatever can happen at any time can happen today. And perhaps, if only the tale told by wise men is true and there is a bourne to welcome us, then he whom we think we have lost has only been sent on ahead.'[194] A pagan letter of sympathy from the second century says: 'However, one cannot do anything about it. So comfort one another.'[195] The Christian writers were fond of polemically focussing these uncertainties: 'There is nothing after death, according to the school of Epicurus. After death all things come to an end, even death itself, says Seneca to like effect.'[196] But their texts, like other reports, show that the idea of a universal immortality increasingly seized ever wider circles in the society of late antiquity. Among other reasons that was because other cults as well as Christianity propagated the idea of a raised (or revitalized) hero, for example the cult of Adonis in Syria; in the second century the satirist and sophist Lucian reported such festivals in Byblos.[197]

Resurrection

However, in the early empire the Christian message of the universal resurrection of the dead was not all that attractive; even in the founding of the first communities there were people who rejected it. Therefore the apostle Paul attempted to consolidate the hope of a general resurrection of the dead (which was also widespread in certain circles in ancient Judaism) in his communities. 'If there is no resurrection of the dead, then Christ has not been raised; if Christ has not been raised, then our preaching is in vain and your faith is in vain. If for this life only we have hoped in Christ, we are of all men most to be pitied' (I Cor. 15.13f.). In the continuation he showed – here too in clear contrast to the world around him – that according to the notion of the first Christians the resurrection affected the whole person, soul and body. As the whole person is mortal, Paul could not imagine resurrection as the redemption of an imperishable part of a perishable body, but only as the redemption and transformation of a whole bodily person. Thus around 150 years after Paul, Tertullian formulated the Christian hope: 'The resurrection of the dead is the Christians' trust. By it we are believers.'[198] At the same time he raged in vigorous polemic against those who 'only half recognize the resurrection, namely merely that of the soul'; and that, although he had to concede : 'There is greater difficulty in believing in the resurrection of the flesh than in the oneness of the deity.'[199] Above all philosophical and popular philosophical circles argued against the notion of a resurrection of the flesh: 'This is simply the hope of worms! For what sort of soul could have any desire for a body that has rotted?' (a question asked by the Platonic philosopher Celsus).[200]

In less sophisticated circles belief in the resurrection of the flesh may have been more widespread, as is evident from a nice narrative from a romance about Paul which was extraordinarily popular in Christian antiquity – a priest from Asia Minor wrote it towards the end of the second century. When Paul was brought before Nero and threatened with decapitation, according to this legend the apostle warned: 'I will arise and appear to you (as a proof) that I am not dead, but alive to my Lord Christ Jesus, who is coming to judge the world.' His actions were as good as his words. After the execution, 'Paul came about the ninth hour, when many philosophers and the centurion were standing with Caesar, and he stood before then all, and said, "Caesar, here I am, Paul, God's soldier; I am not dead, but alive in my God."'[201]

Confidence in bodily resurrection evidently stamped the attitude to death among many early Christians to death and distinguished them from those who denied life and were weary of it: 'My desire is to depart and be with Christ, for that is far better,' wrote Paul to the Philippians (1.23). One could certainly also read similar statements on the walls of houses in Alexandria ('I pray that I shall soon be with you'[202]), but of course the motivation is different. Christian confidence bore up the martyrs through trial, torture and execution. Thus one of the martyrs from the small African village of Scilli (see above 10) said to the Roman consul after the death sentence: 'Today we are martyrs in heaven. Thank God!'[203] However, we should have no illusions about the general steadfastness of communities when faced with the danger of death. After a serious persecution in the middle of the third century, Cyprian, bishop of Carthage, wrote a kind of 'pastoral letter' against members of the community who had failed, under the title 'On Mortality', and warned against the fear of death: 'We should consider, dear brothers, and constantly reflect that we have renounced the world and live here only as guests and strangers (Eph. 2.19/I Peter 2.11). Let us greet the day which assigns each of us to his own home, which snatches us hence, and sets us free from the snares of the world, and restores us to paradise and the kingdom. Who would not hasten to return home if he lived abroad . . .? We regard paradise as our home . . . A great many loved ones await us there, a noble, dense crowd of parents, brothers and sisters, and children is longing for us . . . There is the glorious company of the apostles, there the host of jubilant prophets, there the innumerable multitude of martyrs, crowned for the victory of their struggle and passion, there the triumphant virgins who sudued the lust of the flesh and of the body by the strength of their continency, there are merciful men rewarded, who by feeding and helping the poor have done the works of righteousness.' [204]

Burial

In their burial customs the Christians largely followed the pagan environment: the mouth and eyes of the dead were closed; restrained weeping and prayer for the dead were to replace the loud lament for the dead, tearing out the hair and similar drastic gestures. When Augustine's mother Monica died in November 387 in the Roman port of Ostia, her son closed her eyes; and when her grandson Adeodatus broke out in loud weeping he was reprimanded by all. A bystander took the Psalter and prayed Psalm 101 alternately with those present. The body was carried away and the son went to bathe – in the expectation that 'it will drive anxiety from the mind'.[205] There was a eucharist for the dead at the tomb: as a Syrian church order from the third century ordains, 'In accordance with the gospel and in the power of the Holy Spirit you shall also gather in the cemeteries and read in the holy scriptures, and perform your service and your prayer before God without murmuring, and offer acceptable eucharist.'[206] The obligation to provide burial lay with the family; first of all the death had to be notified as quickly as possible to the authorities, so that there was no obligation to pay tax and other duties. As a rule, for Christians the community took over the function of the burial clubs and funeral funds; Tertullian already attests that the burials of the poor were financed from general church funds. The bodies were washed, anointed with myrrh and clothed. The simplest clothing consists of cloths or linen towels, but finer linen garments and the usual upper garment were usual. After a time of lying in state, the bier was carried from the house of mourning with candles and torches, in later times first into church for the vigil of the dead, and finally the body was buried. Christians apparently hardly ever, if at all, practised the burning of corpses which was usual up to the beginning of the time of the empire. The traditional dark clothing which the survivors already wore in antiquity was criticized by the clergy. 'No occasion should be given to the pagans for them deservedly and rightly to reprehend us because we mourn as dead and lost those whom we claim to live with God.'[207]

From the late third century on, the dead of Christian communities were buried separately from non-Christian dead. Cyprian already forbade burial among those of other faiths;[208] it was worth making efforts to lie beside the tomb of a martyr or a saint (a burial 'by the saints', *ad sanctos*). This was thought to promise special help on the day of resurrection. In the fourth century it was quite customary in more well-to-do circles to get relics of such a 'special' dead person, put them in an oratory of one's own, and bury the family there. In 421, in his writing *The Care of the Dead*, Augustine of Hippo did not criticize this practice, but he did warn against its misuse: 'I do not see how the dead are helped by this; though it serves for the survivors, mindful of the place where their loved ones rest, to commend them in their prayers to those saints as their chosen helpers and guardian patrons before God.'[209] In Rome it is still possible today to see how Christian cemeteries developed in the third century. They came into being on the great roads out of the city, where the pagan necropolises also lay. In individual sites it can be seen how prominent Christian families gave a last resting place on their land outside the city not only to their own relatives, but also to poorer members of the community. Best known are the 'catacombs' – occasionally the whole of Christianity before Constantine is described as the 'church of the catacombs'. Catacombs are subterranean cemeteries made mainly in Rome, but also in Sicily and North Africa; the designation derives from such a cemetery which lies under the Roman church of San Sebastiano on the *Via Appia Antica*, which is still in use today. The neighbourhood bore the designation '*in/ad catacumbas*' (the clear meaning of this expression is disputed; either 'in the valley' or 'by the ship[monument])'. However, these corridors and chambers deep in the earth were not made as a hiding place for the community because of persecution by the state; they simply represented a normal form of burial which saved space – very important in a city with a population of millions. The great Christian catacombs in Rome were made by the urban community. A church order which has already been mentioned many times, the *Apostolic Tradition,* lays down: 'Let there be no heavy charge for bringing people into the cemetery, for it is for all the poor; except they shall pay the hire of a workman to him who digs and the price of the tiles. And the bishop shall provide for the watchman there who takes care of it from what they offer at the assemblies, so that there is no charge to those who come to the place (viz. through begging).'[210] Wall paintings in the catacombs give us a very clear idea of the cemetery workers (*fossores,* presumably also at the same time the 'watchman' mentioned in the *Apostolic Tradition*): they wore the short tunic of the ordinary man, and carried a pick, a lamp, and probably also a basket or a bag for picking up loose bits of rock. Of course they could reserve the best places for themselves – and in some circumstances other people then had to buy these from them; from the fourth century at any rate the distribution and sale of place lay in their hands: 'Tomb of Filominus, which he bought from the *fossor* Florentinus for his family,' we read on an inscription in the Roman catacomb of Callixtus.[211] Niches were hewed out by the workers in the subterranean passages in which bodies were laid; these *loculi* were closed up with polished tiles or a marble plate with an inscription, depending on the financial resources of those concerned. The earliest epitaphs content themselves with the names of the dead persons without any addition; later the wish was added that the dead person might rest 'in peace' or 'in God'. Only from the third century – contrary to pagan practice – did the burial date also appear on the inscriptions. There was also often a symbol – a fish, an anchor or a dove – in place of the acclamation. As well as the simple form of the *loculus* there was also a niche tomb covered with a round or a flat arch (*arcus*), the *arcosolium*; prominent families and communities also had their own rooms hewn out as a kind of mausoleum (*cubiculum*). Of course graves were also dug on the surface in the open air (*sub divo*), possibly with tiles in the form of a saddleback roof laid on them (*alla cappuccina*); from the fourth century onwards there were sometimes also more artistic mausolea of different kinds (plate 3).

Confident dying

The calls from theologians to be confident in death are reflected in the many reports of Christian martyrs and saints dying comforted. When the famous Bishop of Ambrose of Milan lay in bed, terminally ill, in AD 397 and was urged to pray for the lengthening of his life, he refused, saying: 'I have not lived among you in such a way that I am afraid of death, for we have a gracious Lord' – at any rate, that is what is reported in the Life, written around twenty years after the death of the saint by his former secretary Paulinus, at the request of a great pupil of Ambrose, the North African Bishop Augustine of Hippo.[212] Gregory of Nyssa, the brother of the metropolitan Basil of Caesarea, described the last moments of their sister Macrina in 379 in a remarkably skilful literary form: 'Rather did it seem as if some angel had taken human form with a sort of incarnation, to whom it was nothing strange that the mind should remain undisturbed, since he had no kinship or likeness with this life of flesh, and so the flesh did not draw the mind to think on its afflictions.'[213] Macrina passed away with prayer and the sign of the cross, and her brothers clothed her in a fine upper garment, as there was no appropriate garment among the extremely limited possessions that the ascetic left behind. When those around her thought that this decoration was excessive, her mother's dark cloak was laid on her, 'that this holy beauty be not decked out with the unnecessary splendour of clothing'.[214] At her own wish, Macrina was then buried beside her parents.

In the Mediterranean room at the Louvre there is the epitaph from the beginning of the fourth century of a little Sicilian girl called Julia Florentina; she died at the age of eighteen months.

And the text ends: 'While her parents were mourning her death at that hour, the voice of (God's) majesty rang out in the night and forbade them to lament the dead child.'[215]

Christian life and its piety

Christian piety includes not only the attitudes in which early Christian attempted to shape their individual everyday life by their faith, but also the forms which led to these attitudes: the way in which they used the Bible, prayer, the veneration of angels and saints and further forms of expressing piety like almsgiving or fasting. An examination of Christian life and its piety in antiquity is apparently a relatively new interest of scholars. However, in reality everyday piety is a phenomenon which was already perceived as such and made a specific topic of interest long before the time of the Roman empire. The Greek expression *eusebeia* (Latin *pietas*) was used to denote respectful behaviour towards the gods. Ritualism and conservatism were a special characteristic of pagan *eusebeia*. Almost in analogy to this, Christian theologians define *eusebeia* as subordination to God's will, devotion to God and discipleship, and then also as deeper knowledge. The Christian piety of the second and following centuries has been described as a 'piety of observances'[216] and has been distinguished quite clearly from that of the primitive community: Jesus of Nazareth, and the apostle Paul in his footsteps, energetically oppose a particular form of piety of observances, namely a piety orientated on the observance of external precepts or even on public effect (Mark 3.23–28; Matt. 6.1–9). In the Gospels this tends to be called 'Pharisaic' (contrary, moreover, to historical reality). But the relevant Christian texts of the first century show that this term is a rather unhappy one because – in keeping with the widespread prejudice about the Pharisaic movement – it sees to imply a peevish and thus forced observance of concrete norms. In a Christian letter from the beginning of the second century, later called the 'Letter of Barnabas', we read: 'Consort with those who fear the Lord, with those who meditate in their heart on the meaning of the word which they have received, with those who speak of and observe the ordinance of the Lord, with those who know that meditation is a work of gladness and who ruminate on the word of the Lord.'[217] Certainly 'precepts' are mentioned here, but in connection with an 'act of cheerfulness' (however this is to be translated). Equally problematical is the widespread characterization of Christian piety as a 'piety with a conformist stamp, the basic conservative – because conserving – feature of which is unmistakable'.[218] This assessment, too, must be supplemented with a reference to the criticism of earthly circumstances which was always more or less intensively presupposed in piety. For the basis of all such criticism was the Christian experience of alienation and homelessness in this world, which stamped many texts, particularly in the early period. Carl Andresen calls that a 'Diaspora mentality'. The letter of the Roman community to the Corinthian community (at the end of the first century, so-called I Clement) begins with words to this effect: 'The church of God which dwells in Rome as a stranger, to the church of God which dwells in Corinth as a stranger.' Already in the New Testament it is said that although Christians are subject to all state authority (Rom. 13.1),they have their commonwealth, their state (*politeuma*), in heaven (Phil.3.20). Another New Testament letter describes them as 'elect strangers' 'who live dispersed in Pontus, Galatia, Cappadocia, the province of Asia and Bithynia' (I Peter 1.1). The most extensive and at the same time the best known description of the situation appears in an apologetic writing *To Diognetus*, which is very difficult to date; it probably comes from the second century. The unknown author writes to these non-Christians: 'But you cannot expect to learn the mystery of the Christians' own religion from a human source. For Christians cannot be distinguished from the rest of the human race by country or language or customs. They do not live in cities of their own; they do not use a peculiar form of speech; they do not follow an eccentric manner of life . . . Rather, they live in Greek and barbarian cities alike, as each man's lot has been cast, and follow the customs of the country in clothing and eating and in other practices . . . They live in their own countries, but only as aliens. They have a share in every foreign land as their fatherland, and yet for them every fatherland is a foreign land. They marry, like everyone else, and they have children, but they do not expose their offspring (viz. which was the right of a Roman father within the framework of his paternal authority C.M.). They share their table with one another, but not a (common) bed. They obey the established laws, but in their own lives they go far beyond what the laws require. They love all men, and by all men are persecuted. They are unknown, and still they are condemned.'[219] Anyone who felt himself to be not only a citizen of the Roman empire but also the subject of a heavenly king would have a touch of unworldliness and criticism of the world in his piety. It is popular to describe these features today with the modern term 'contrast society'. Nevertheless, this society consists of many members who are concerned to 'immigrate' into the everyday life of ancient society. The popular notion that this process of wandering came to a standstill in the fourth century and that the Christian attitude of following times was 'essentially a piety of discontinuous moments of contrition'[220] ignores a tension between two worlds which already existed beforehand, and was not dissolved by the measures of the emperors Constantine and Theodosius.

For of course 'Christian piety in antiquity' is in truth an extremely variegated phenomenon to which one cannot do justice by means of crude differentiations (e.g. 'upper-class' versus 'popular religion'). However, one differentiation seems to have been significant at all times: that between Sunday piety and everyday piety. At any rate John Chrysostom begins one of his Antioch sermons in the 380s like this: 'I hear many say, "While we are here, and enjoy the privilege of hearing, we are awed, but when we go out, we become changed, and the flame of zeal is quenched." What may be done to prevent this?'[221]

Using the Bible

The New Testament already shows that Christians used the texts which had been canonized, i.e. brought together as normative holy scripture, since the second century, and how they did so. Whereas Paul argues only at two points using words of the historical Jesus (I Cor. 7.10f.; 9.14), another New Testament letter provides evidence that people substantiated their own positions with Pauline texts – but also had difficulties with the apostle's letters, which circulated in collections and were read aloud in worship. In support of his own views, the author of a New Testament letter attributed to Peter refers to what 'our dear brother Paul . . . says in all his letters, which in some things are difficult to understand, because the ignorant and the frivolous twist them . . . to their own damnation' (II Peter 3.15f.). But it is already evident in the letter which the Roman community writes to the Corinthian community at the end of the first century (I Clement) that greater authority is attributed to the words of Jesus than to 'the Bible' – in other words, in the circumstances of the time, what from the middle or end of the second century was called 'the writings of the Old Testament'. Jesus is introduced as 'Lord', i.e. with the designation used for God in the Greek Bible (and also an established title for the emperor). There follows a free paraphrase of words of the Sermon on the Mount (I Clement 13.2). So the use of the Bible here means primarily the use of words of the Old Testament and of Jesus for theological argument, but also the presentation of an outline of Christian existence in the light of the texts, establishing its criteria and limits.

The formation of the canon of the NT

A clear reflection of such use of biblical texts becomes evident in the process of the 'canonization' of the New Testament, i.e. the establishment of the second part of an authoritative word of God alongside the Greek Jewish Bible – however, the history of the canon is 'one of the most complicated parts of critical church history'.[222] Here the term 'canon' (really 'reed', but also 'measure') was only applied to the subject-matter much later, namely at a synod in Asia Minor in the middle of the fourth century. One of its regulations reads: 'No psalms composed by authors shall be used in the church, nor any extra-canonical books, but only the canonical books of the Old and New Testament.'[223] The following definition by the synod (which moreover in Greek is also called 'canon') gives a list of the books concerned: this is in keeping with the procedure in such legal texts. However, what is designated with the words 'canonical writings of the Old and New Testament' can already be found at an earlier stage, namely the demarcation of particular writings as an authoritative word of God from other less authoritative texts, and their use as such in liturgical readings and theological argument. Contrary to the views of some scholars, the impulse towards canonization was not simply the increasing need in the middle of the second century for the majority community to set itself apart from heretics.[224] The ultimate motive for establishing a canon may have been the unprecedented freedom with which Jesus used his Bible, the present-day 'Old Testament'. The carpenter's son simply abrogated biblical laws (like that on divorce, Mark 10.2–12), quoted commandments formulated in the Bible with divine authority, and introduced his correction with the words 'But I say to you'. It has proved possible to demonstrate formal parallels to this phrase, but not its use in the sense described. The historical Jesus himself authoritatively stood over against the old word of God with a quite extraordinary self-awareness of being the revealer of a new word; it was natural also to attribute this authority to his words, and to this degree to set them alongside the Hebrew (or Greek) Bible as the word of God of the new covenant *(kaine diatheke*, Jer.31.33). The use of the title 'Old' or 'New Testament' for a book appears clearly for the first time in Clement of Alexandria at the beginning of the third century; all the evidence from the second century remains uncertain. At the same time, however, the early church could not give up Jesus' Bible, nor did it want to; had it done so, it would have rejected the framework of interpretation within which Jesus' activity became comprehensible to it and in which indeed it saw that activity. The present-day 'New Testament' rests so to speak on three pillars, two of which were already linked during the course of the first century: first, an early collection of authoritative sayings of the Lord; secondly, an oral tradition of community confessions on the authority of the one who uttered them (these two were brought together in the various narratives of the life of Jesus, the Gospels); and, thirdly and finally, on the letters. But evidently the four Gospels were rapidly thought of as an inter-related unity, at an early stage, since their earliest manuscripts already bear the titles 'Gospel according to Matthew', '. . . according to Mark', '. . . according to Luke' '. . . according to John'. This title makes sense only if one understands the writings as four parts of a single Gospel: the one Gospel *according to* author X.[225] The last of the 'three pillars' to be mentioned is a collection of apostolic letters from the early period: they were understood by the communities in Italy and Asia Minor which formed the canon as the 'beginning of the gospel', i.e. as those sacred texts which stood at the beginning of the proclamation of the gospel and thus the history of the particular communities (thus e.g. in the Roman letter to the Corinthians, I Clement 47.1). Moreover, at least in the second century they were in part understood as the 'main speculative and dogmatic book'.[226]

The exact historical course of the canonization can only be reconstructed in each case only after the event: thus we find the first evidence of the canonicity of the Four-Gospel canon in Irenaeus of Lyons at the end of the second century. In his work against the Gnostics he superelevates the canon of four[227] Gospels theologically by referring to the four points of the compass and the four beasts from the apocalyptic tradition: the lion, the bull, the human being and the eagle. Why this canon in particular came into being in the course of the second century is currently explained in different ways, either as a protective measure against the heretics[228] or as the 'survival of the fittest': the gradual establishment of the writings which were theologically 'strongest'.[229] The view at present being put forward that earlier and theologically more interesting Gospels than the canonical Gospels were wrongly excluded by the church as heretical dates writings which can more or less clearly be assigned to the second century back to the first century on ideological grounds.

An account of using the Bible limited to a description of the highly complicated 'process of canonization', which differed in part depending on the region, would register only what happened in church governments and synods. In any case the laity got to hear a large number of biblical texts in church teaching and in worship. Such pericopes were additionally fixed in the memory by the various expositions, explanations and sermons. Alongside this, the 'private use of the holy scriptures'[230] should be noted. Evidently – at least after the middle of the second century – it was not difficult to buy biblical texts in bookshops, depending of course on one's interests and resources. Only a century later, in his polemic against the Platonic philosopher Celsus, Origen attests that in the second century this declared opponent of Christianity evidently had no difficulty in buying biblical books, though he was not a Christian. In his commentary on Matthew, Origen complains about the malicious falsifications of this text in the pagan scriptoria.[231] Moreover one could also buy other Christian literature, even in pagan bookshops. As his extant writings show, Origen himself must have had a quite excellent library which contained philosophical and historical texts and some lexica, in addition to the Christian literature and the most important pagan literature. Even the sheer mass of books must have assumed considerable proportions; the sale of the pagan texts alone led to the scholar being paid a daily fee by the buyer at the level of a day labourer's wage.[232] At the beginning of the fourth century, the Christian library in Palestinian Caesarea, which among other things took over Origen's works after his death and with which Eusebius later worked, had around 30,000 scrolls (by contrast, probably the largest library in antiquity, the collection of books in the Museion of Alexandria, comprised around 700,000 scrolls). This is the extreme case of a scholar with an enthusiasm for literature, which is repeated a few more times in the history of the early church; the question what was the norm

The possession of biblical books

1. *Sarcophagus of Prosenes – Rome, park of the Villa Borghese*

2. *Simeon on the pillar – pilgrim badge from Qal'at Sem'an*

3. *Rome, necropolis under S. Sebastiano in Catacumbas*

4. *Christian amulet – Papyrus Vindobonensis G 16685*

5. *Gold medal on a girdle from Dumbarton Oaks*

6. *Madaba, Jordan, Church of the Apostles, detail of the mosaic in the nave*

is much harder to answer. It already arises in the big cities: how many people capable of reading actually read? From what point in time were there Christian books in public libraries? (According to the regional catalogue of Constantinople in the middle of the fourth century the capital had more than twenty-eight public libraries.) How were things in the smaller country communities? Did these have the interest and the money to get hold of biblical books as private copies or copies from booksellers? Did they have contact with Christian scribes or pagan booksellers?

We find a first interesting piece of evidence of the possession of biblical books by simple Christians in the acts of the trial of the Scillitan martyrs in Carthage (AD 180): when the case proper had been heard, the Roman proconsul asked the group what they had in their book chest. One replied: 'Books and letters of Paul, a just man.'[233] This sign of literary education among people who in his eyes had lost their minds made the official relent and offer the Christians the relatively long period of one month to think things over. Moreover the passage (and also the manuscript tradition) shows that the New Testament was initially handed down not as a whole, but in parts.

Reading the Bible

In the middle of the third century Origen expected his community to spend more than an hour a day reading the Bible. Here he was holding up to his community an ideal which could really 'be fulfilled only in the monastery'.[234] Later, particularly the Christian preachers in the fourth century made efforts to equip their communities, which had grown larger, to read scripture on their own. Thus for example John Chrysostom asked his community in Antioch: 'But in order that the word may be more easy to learn, we pray and entreat you . . . to take up beforehand that portion of the scripture which we are beginning to explain, that your reading may prepare the way for your understanding . . . There are many enigmas.' And some sermons later: 'For we ought not, as soon as we leave worship, to plunge into business unsuited to that worship, but as soon as we get home, we should take our Bible into our hands, and call our wife and children to join us in putting together what we have heard, and then, not before, engage in worldly business.'[235]

The hearer who does not memorize the sermon and the text of scripture on which it is based is like Sisyphus, and 'spends the whole day drawing water in a vessel with a hole in it.'[236] The exhortations presuppose that every household has bought a Bible – the preacher has asked his community to do this. But at the same time Chrysostom gave gloomy prognoses about the success of such admonitions: 'Tell me which of you who stand here, if he were required, could repeat one psalm or any other portion of the divine scriptures? There is not one . . . But what is the answer to these charges? "I am not," you would say, "one of the monks, but I have a wife and children, and the care of a husband." Why, this is what ruined all, your supposing that the reading scriptures pertains to those only. When you need it so much more than they . . . So that it is far worse than not reading to account the thing even superfluous, for these are the words of diabolical intervention.'[237] In the later sermons on Romans, Chrysostom has thus also given up the hope of educating his community to zealous Bible reading: he repeats the argument about being preoccupied with 'bringing up children, wife and household affairs' and adds in resignation: 'Therefore at least be prepared to accept the thoughts gathered by others.'[238]

An extraordinarily interesting and at the same time important form of using biblical books was reading at meals – not only in monastic communities but also at weddings of lay people and other solemn occasions. Poems consisting of biblical verses and scenes (*cento*) were prepared as 'seasoning' (*cena*). Zeno, bishop of Verona in northern Italy at the end of the fourth century, quoted such a piece in one of his sermons:

'The father of the house is giving you precious bread and precious wine . . . from his own table. First the three young men (Dan. 3.1–97) harmoniously bear the vegetables, and to make the taste finer, they sprinkle them with the salt of wisdom. Christ pours oil on them. With due haste Moses provides a one-year-old lamb, the first to be born from the ewe (Ex. 12.5), Abraham in his faith a fat and well-prepared calf (Gen. 18.7) . . . If anyone is lacking anything, Noah, the inhabitant of the ark, who has kept everything safe, will not refuse him. Peter the fisherman offers a sufficiency of fresh fish from the sea (Matt. 4.18), with marvellous aspic. Tobias, the wanderer, gets the roe of the fish from the river and bakes it with great care (Tobit 6.1–5). John, the humble forerunner of the Lord (viz. John the Baptist), in his camel-hair coat, brings honey and locusts from the forest (Matt. 3.4). Paul conveys the fare and admonishes people that none shall rebuke another at table (Rom. 14.3). David, the royal shepherd, provides silvery milk and cheese for all (I Sam. 17.18).'[239]

The veneration of the biblical books

Many reports point to an intensive veneration of the biblical books – and they did not necessarily have to be read for that. Even Augustine did not object to the books being used in a quasi-magical way: 'If you have headaches, we commend putting the Gospel on your head and not taking refuge in an amulet.'[240] And John Chrysostom mentioned that many women wore the Gospel (probably parts in miniature) round their necks. We get a very interesting impression of the sheer holiness of the biblical books – at least in the African church – from reports about the organized destruction of books during Diocletian's persecution of Christians; at the same time the measure represented a brutal break for most Christian libraries. After a first edict on the unity of the empire dated 24 February AD 303, the action started: in addition to the confiscation of movable church property and the destruction of church buildings, this included the surrender of the holy scriptures used in worship and the burning of them 'in public places'.[241] The official record of the confiscation of church property in Cirta in Numidia (present-day Constantine, in Algeria) on 19 May 303 has been preserved. The majority of Christians had fled to a hilly wilderness south of the city when the state commission entered the building 'in which the Christians were accustomed to gather'. First of all the investigating Roman official (the city curator) commanded Bishop Paulus to bring 'the books of the Law and anything else that you have here'. The bishop declared that the lectors had the scriptures, but that they would hand over the rest. The subdeacons also indicated that they had only one codex in their possession;[242] only with the six lectors were five large and two small codices then found, and in addition twenty-five unspecified large and items and four volumes. So the authorities confiscated thirty-six library 'units'; unfortunately it remains unclear how high the proportion of the Christian community was among the roughly 10,000 inhabitants of the place.[243] We can only make rough inferences from the number of clergy present in the church, the number of pieces of clothing confiscated there and the number of lectors sought out by the state commission (around one hundred in all). At any rate the handing over by the church of the holy scriptures to pagan magistrates for destruction was attacked with angry words (after all, simply to alter the letters was regarded as sacrilege); years later the clergy involved in the confiscation were accused of being 'handers over' (*traditores*); among other things the process of the 'handing over' led to a severe schism in North Africa. When after the end of the persecution (probably in 307) some bishops met in Cirta, it proved that of ten bishops, six had handed over the scriptures. Their laborious excuses did not convince the critics: one decided to hand over medical writings instead of the Bible, another had thrown the four Gospels into the fire with his own hands, but had used copies which were by then virtually illegible. The other side emphasized the special holiness of the biblical text, identified the material biblical text with the Word of God, and quoted biblical sayings to this effect.[244]

Lectionaries and anthologies

Though the Bible was regarded as an especially holy book, we must not deceive ourselves about the extent of knowledge of the text. Quite frequently people had only an indirect knowledge of the Bible, the selection offered by liturgical lectionaries or biblical anthologies. Almost two-thirds of the New Testament manuscripts from the Byzantine period came from lectionaries – the selected liturgical texts which came into being after the great liturgical reforms of the fifth and seventh centuries. A handful of inventories of community libraries from the fourth to the sixth centuries have been handed down on papyri; these show that people only rarely possessed complete books. The 'main books' of the community were the various liturgical collections of texts of the Bible. For a community, as for a monastery, it was less important to have complete manuscripts of the New Testament books, since these were not used in public worship. At most they could be of interest to the clergy or scholars. In addition we must remember that a complete Bible produced in the usual uncial script would have had the considerable extent of up to 400 pages, and the cost of procuring one would have presumably have placed excessive demands on the budget of a small community. When in the fourth century the emperor Constantine had fifty splendid parchment Bibles made, they were so expensive that the head of the financial administration of one of the twelve administrative regions of the church had to be involved, and two wagons of the state post were used for their transport.[245] As well as the lectionaries, anthologies, i.e. selections of individual passages of scripture, offered convenient access to biblical texts. For example Cyprian, Bishop of Carthage, had three books of such a 'collection of material' made for a certain Quirinius, which consisted of theses and biblical quotations to substantiate them. Here the statement that 'Christ was God' was substantiated with eighteen biblical passages;[246] Cyprian's literary work was limited to a few introductory remarks on where they were to be found. Simple as the work seems today, it had a great effect: we can mention at least four Christian theologians of late antiquity who used it as a quarry for their own theological arguments. We also have such anthologies by a few prominent authors; a papyrus combines biblical verses and their allegorical interpretation: '"On the third day there was a wedding in Cana, Galilee". "The day" is Christ. "Third" is faith. The "wedding" is the call of the Gentiles. "Cana" is the church.'[247] What is catalogued here in a brief and somewhat obtuse way was normally developed by a learned Alexandrian scholar like Origen into multi-volume commentaries on the Bible, in order to bring past texts up to date for community worship in the present. However, Origen is an exception in the midst of such 'atomizing' appropriation of biblical texts. His father Leonides had given him an exceptional knowledge of holy scripture: 'He made him learn a passage of scripture by heart every day and repeat it.'[248] However, such skills are related of monks from the fourth century on in a stereotyped way: once during a walk of forty miles the ascetic Hero of Alexandria recited 'fifteen Psalms by memory, then the letter to the Hebrews, Isaiah, a passage from Jeremiah, then the Gospel of Luke and after that the Proverbs'. And the narrator sums it up: 'Nevertheless we could hardly keep pace with him.'[249]

Apart from such exceptions among the theologians, it was probably possible to persuade only a few learned and yet fewer ordinary contemporaries to read the Bible for themselves – unless these were converts from the Jewish sphere, who were familiar with what in a number of respects was the somewhat remote world of the text. Basil dissuaded the youth from reading the Bible: 'As long as we are not in a position to discover the depth of its meaning because of our (youthful) age, first of all we practise with our spiritual eye on other writings which are not completely alien to the holy scriptures, but by comparison with them are as it were a shadow and a reflection.'[250] In missionary or community sermons it was easy – though also easily superficial – to speak of the venerable age of the Mosaic law, to rationalize its regulations and so to make them comprehensible (cf. the observations on the prohibition against consuming blood, 118 below). Everything looked rather different to readers reading the Bible by themselves. The outlines of a very strange world were opened up to the reader – or were not. The Roman theologian Justin reports at the beginning of his dialogue with the Jew Trypho a reference of the Christian teacher to the holy Scriptures: 'He who has read them is very much helped in his knowledge of the beginning and end of things, and of those matters which the philosopher ought know.'[251] However, only a very few passages of these texts can be used directly and without explanation for the topics of 'God, the world and the soul' and the question of the 'happy life'. Augustine is a significant example of the effect that the Bible, read without an introduction, must have had on educated people. In his religious autobiography, the later Bishop of Hippo reports on his attempt to read the Bible (probably at the beginning of the 370s): 'When I first read those scriptures, I did not feel in the least what I have just said; they seemed to me unworthy to be compared with the majesty of Cicero. My conceit was repelled by their simplicity, and I had not the mind to penetrate into their depths.'[252] On the other hand his contemporary Jerome managed to get women from Roman aristocratic circles to put aside the pagan classics with which they were familiar, read the Bible, enter into the scholarly exegesis of this text and learn Hebrew.[253]

Prayer and liturgical piety

Without doubt, the centre of personal piety in Christian antiquity was individual prayer – a tradition which the new religion had taken over from contemporary Judaism. But Jesus of Nazareth had already not only prayed the psalms of the Hebrew Bible in this tradition – even on the cross he prayed to the Father in this form (Mark 15.34 = Ps. 22.2) – but created the text of his own prayer, the Our Father (Matt. 6.9–13; Luke 11.2–4), with clear reference to Jewish prayers in both form and content. At the beginning it contains one of the key points of Jesus' message, Jesus' familiar way of addressing God as 'Father'.[254] Of course other psalms were used as well as this: thus for example a disciple of Paul called on the Christians in Colossae, a metropolis in Asia Minor, to 'Sing psalms, hymns of praise and songs to God with grateful hearts' (Col. 3.16). Individual prayer, too, is to keep the whole community in mind; at any rate Cyprian writes from Carthage around the middle of the third century: 'The teacher of peace (viz. Christ) . . ., did not want prayer to be individual and self-centred, so that if a person prays, he prays only for himself . . . Our prayer is public and communal, and when we pray, we do not pray for one but for the whole people, because we, the whole people, are one.'[255]

Prayer to Christ

Prayers were addressed both to God the Father and to his Son Jesus Christ, although individual theologians (Origen, for example) wanted to limit liturgical prayer strictly to an address to the Father. But from the beginning there is a strong tendency to turn to Christ, at least in personal prayer, presumably simply because through the reports of the New Testament authors Christ could come directly very close to people in antiquity. Thus for example Ignatius, the bishop in Antioch in Syria, asks the Roman community (probably at the beginning of the second century) to 'Pray to Christ for me.'[256] The piety of so-called 'simple people', i.e. those who had not had a theological training, of course also included a knowledge of quite different prayer texts – and this is true, although warnings not simply to make a schematic distinction between the piety of a poor and uneducated 'broad mass' and that of an educated class which thought rationally need to be taken very seriously.[257] From the fifth century an invocation of the blood of Christ has been preserved on papyrus: 'Blood of Jesus Christ, who for our sake became flesh of the holy virgin; blood of Jesus Christ who was baptized in the Jordan by his forerunner John, Amen.'[258] At around the same time a Christian in the monastic town of Oxyrhynchus in lower Egypt asked God in the style of questions to pagan oracles: 'Is it your will that I travel to Chiut?'[259] But even such texts as are strongly influenced by a pagan tradition of piety still betray the fact that the Christian prayers very much lived by biblical formulations and the liturgical formulae which can already be read there, for example the Old Testament 'Hallelujah'.

Times of prayer

Prayer accompanied the course of the Christian's day. The custom of praying three times a day was taken over from Judaism. Whereas Judaism offered a rhythm of three hours in the morning, at noon and in the evening, at a very early stage a further model became established: of prayer in the evening, at midnight and in the morning. The church order called the 'Apostolic Tradition' combines both series, and prescribes seven hours of prayer; these were later observed in the monastic hours, as they are still, in part, to the present day. 'And let the faithful man and woman when they rise from sleep at dawn, before they undertake any work, wash their hands and pray to

God, and so let them go to work . . . If you are at home, pray at the third hour and praise God, but if you are elsewhere and that time comes, pray in your heart to God . . . Pray also likewise at the sixth hour . . . And at the ninth hour also let . . . prayer be protracted and praise be sung . . . Pray also before your body rests upon your bed. And at midnight arise and wash your hands with water and pray. And if you have a wife, pray both together. But if she is not a believer, go apart into another room and pray and return again to your bed. Do not be idle in prayer.'[260]

Postures in prayer

Praying was usually done lying or kneeling on the floor; standing was the custom only on Sunday – this detail too was regulated by precepts of synods, here for example in a canon of the episcopal gathering in Nicaea (AD 325): 'Forasmuch as there are certain persons who kneel (when praying) on the Lord's Day and in the days of Pentecost, therefore, to the intent that all things may be uniformly observed everywhere, it seems good to the Holy Synod that prayer be made to God standing.'[261]

The cross and prayer

Acts of a Syrian martyr from the fourth century report that a certain Hipparchus had painted a cross on the east wall of his bedroom and prayed before this to Christ seven times a day.[262] Similarly, the apses of many Christian basilicas in antiquity which were orientated on the east displayed a cross. On journeys it was evidently also customary to set up a wooden cross in an easterly direction and pray kneeling in front of it. The cross generally plays a major role in individual piety: in his work 'The Soldier's Garland', Tertullian says that 'at every formal step and movement, at every going in and out; when we put on our clothes and shoes, when we bathe, when we sit at table, when we light the lamps, in couch or seat, in all the ordinary actions of daily life, we trace upon the forehead the sign of the cross'.[263]

The ascetic Nilus, head of a monastery in Ancyra (Ankara), probably at the beginning of the fifth century, advised his monks always to perform a kind of little liturgy before they left the monastery. First of all they were to repeat the renunciation of the devil from the baptismal liturgy and say with their hand stretched out in front of them: 'I renounce you, Satan, and all your works and all your splendour and all your services.' Then they were to recite the trinitarian formula from the baptismal service ('In the name of the Father and of the Son and of the Holy Spirit', cf. Matt. 28.19) and make the sign of the cross – and only then leave the protective walls of the monastery.[264] Finally a Syrian monk of the seventh century enjoined that after saying the Our Father on one's knees one should stand before the crucifix in the cell, embrace it, and kiss it with a feeling of penitence and love.[265] Here a gesture long familiar in antiquity was now also present in Christianity: it was in keeping with Roman religion to kiss sacred trees, images of gods, temple thresholds and altars, but also amulets and the domestic table. Kissing the table (for example after eating) was understood as a gesture of prayer, like kissing the altar. It was hoped in this way to make special contact with the divine, 'perhaps also because a power of life dwells in them (viz. the altars)'.[266] Everyday pre-Christian religion expected much of the religious kiss: the 'Great Paris Magical Papyrus', instructions in magic which one could probably buy from an appropriate source, says: 'Kiss the amulet and say . . . '"Protect me!" After these words you will see the doors open and seven virgins in robes of Byssos with serpentine faces coming from the depths.'[267] Such magical piety lived on even after the various legal measures taken by the Christian emperors against pagans in the fourth century. The pagan Neoplatonist Proclus (AD 412–485) was healed by a kiss from the arthritis which had affected his foot. A traveller who had come to Proclus in Athens from Epidaurus, the ancient cultic centre and centre of healing, kissed his knee – 'and from that day on he spent his whole life without any pain from arthritis. He reached a particularly great age without ever feeling any pain.'[268] At first the whole pagan practice of kissing was criticized by the Christian theologians; thus we read in a Christian Syrian apology of the third century: 'But rise above those who lie on the earth and kiss stones.'[269] But then the church too adopted pagan gestures of kissing. In his sermons on the Second

The kiss

Letter to the Corinthians, John Chrysostom, the preacher of Antioch, reports that people kissed the thresholds of churches and martyrs' chapels, or at least touched them with their hands and then brought these to their mouths.[270] Generally speaking, the gesture of kissing the hand also seems to have been used in prayer: 'Those who pray are accustomed to kiss the hand and bow the head,' writes the ascetic and writer Jerome, who lived in Bethlehem, in a polemic at the beginning of the fifth century.[271] The tombs of martyrs and the altars were kissed: 'the altar becomes warm from the mouth and the stone from the breast'.[272] The kiss was also important for healing: Martin of Tours (died 397) once went to Paris – at any rate this is what his biographer Sulpicius Severus reports shortly after the death of the saint. There 'to the dismay of all he kissed a leper who gazed at him in a quite pitiful way. Immediately all the sickness left the man. The next day he came to church with a shining white skin to give thanks for the health that he had regained.'[273]

It has already become clear that prayer binds the individual to the community. Liturgical piety is a further characteristic of early Christian religion. However, almost from the beginning there were complaints about its lack of intensity. Probably in the fourth century, a Bishop Eusebius, perhaps the Bishop of Emesa (present-day Homs in Syria), complained about the failure of Christians to observe Sunday: 'When Sunday comes, anyone engaged in a lawsuit spends the whole night cherishing hostile thoughts against his neighbour, and hardly has morning dawned than he girds himself for battle and goes to church. That is the custom, especially in the villages. They go to church and sit outside, and before the service the priest does the same thing; and they present their negotiations and legal disputes (and it comes) to taunts and fisticuffs. After that they go into church and look round grimly like wild beasts, gnashing their teeth at one another. And woe to the priest who does not above all offer prayers to God by the appointed hour. For if the appointed hour by which the prayer should have been completed has elapsed, and some leave the church to go home to eat, their sin falls on the priest.' And the bishop concludes: 'Do not keep away from the church and prayer! To the degree that you keep away from visiting the church, God too will keep away from you.'[274]

Eucharistic piety

A eucharistic piety also develops in the third century. Such piety was already prepared for in the case of the individual member of the community by an explanation of the sacrament in baptismal instruction; first participation in it was connected with the administration of baptism. Thus alongside baptism, the liturgical celebration of a ritualized meal, also described as a mystery (*mysterion*), was a high point of Christian life. Since most explanations agree that the elements of bread and wine represent the body and blood of Jesus Christ – in accordance with the words of institution, e.g. I Cor. 11.23–25 (explicit reflections on the mode of this representation are rare in antiquity) – this mediated presence of the divine in the material world naturally called for corresponding veneration of the eucharist by believers. In his writing 'On the Lapsed', Cyprian tells of a small girl who had been left behind by her parents fleeing from the Roman authorities in the persecution under Decius (AD 250). The authorities gave the child a morsel left over from a pagan sacrifice to eat, but the girl was still too young to tell her mother about the event when the mother again took her into her protection. When the mother again went with her child to Christian worship, the child wept and threw herself to and fro. She vomited up the contents of the cup which a deacon presented to her. This veneration of the eucharistic elements, which to modern sensibilities is quasi-magical, also found its way into church orders, as in the *Apostolic Tradition*: 'Let all take care that no unbeliever taste of the eucharist, nor a mouse or other creature, and that none of it fall or be lost. For it is the body of Christ, to be eaten by those who believe and not be thought lightly of.'[275] The designation of the eucharist as 'sacrifice', which already appears in the second century, itself provided a certain assimilation to pagan cultic practices – though of course any analogy to Jewish and pagan sacrificial practice was rejected. In the tradition of Hellenistic Judaism, on the one hand a bloodless sacrifice was offered to God through bread and wine;

on the other hand, the simultaneous collection of gifts for needy members of the community was a sacrifice as an act of mercy. It was possible to appeal to New Testament theology for these notions, as a passage from Cyprian shows: 'For if Jesus Christ, our Lord and God, is himself the high priest of God the Father (Heb.10.1–18), and has first offered himself a sacrifice to the Father and has commanded this should be done in memory of himself (I Cor. 11.24f.), certainly that priest truly discharges the office of Christ, who imitates what Christ did; and he then offers a true and full sacrifice in the church to God the Father, when he proceeds to offer it according to what he sees Christ himself to have offered.'[276] To this degree the emphasis on 'fear and trembling' with which one has to approach the Christ present in the meal is certainly one of the specific features of Syrian theology in the fourth century, but it fits in organically with pre-Constantinian eucharistic piety. Theodore, a friend of John Chrysostom, like him first a priest in Antioch and later (AD 392/393) bishop in Mopsuestia in Cilicia, spoke of this in a catechesis for those seeking baptism in Antioch: 'Every time this awesome sacrificial service is performed, we must at the same time imagine that we are like the one who is in heaven (viz. Christ), and through faith imprint the vision of the heavenly things on our minds. It (viz. the sacrificial worship) is manifestly the likeness of the heavenly realities . . . As our Lord Christ offers himself for us as a sacrifice, and thus has in fact become the high priest for us, there is the image of that priest which he who now stands at the altar represents, by which we have to imagine ourselves.'[277] It was in accordance with ancient practice to venerate persons alongside such institutions: angels, saints and martyrs, To a quite extraordinary degree, pilgrimages were made to the cultic centres of the last two groups, at the latest from the fourth century on.

Veneration of angels, saints and martyrs; pilgrimage

Veneration of angels

Not only in early Christianity but already in Hellenistic Judaism it was customary to personalize both good and evil powers alongside God and set a heavenly court with hierarchies of angels alongside the heavenly ruler. At the head of the hierarchy stood the archangels; according to the Greek version of Enoch they were called Uriel, Raphael, Raguel, Michael, Sariel, Gabriel and Ramiel (Greek Enoch 20). Different functions were assigned to the different classes of angels (which are partly of biblical origin: cherubim, seraphim, ophanim, with Isa. 6; Ezek.1; 10), from praise of God and service at the heavenly altar to the control of the stars, the bringing of news and the protection of individuals. In his account from the end of the fourth century the pagan historiographer Ammianus Marcellinus reports the view that 'there are associated with all men at their birth . . . certain divinities of that sort, as directors of their conduct. But they are visible to very few.'[278] Although here individual scholars have thought of Christian theologians and the notion of guardian angels, in fact the reference is to astrologers and their interpretation of the pagan notion of the genius of each individual. But these different interpretations only show how closely in the fourth century many notions originally deriving from different cultural circles had come together. In early Christianity there were both vocal criticisms of the veneration of angels and developed doctrines of the place and function of these beings. However, the vast majority was against cultic veneration: in the second century Bishop Ignatius of Antioch wrote to the Christian community in Tralles in Asia Minor that while he knew 'the hierarchies of angels, and the gathering of the ("angelic") principalities',[279] he avoided further information and played down his knowledge because of the danger of misunderstanding ('therefore I am no disciple').

It was not just many theologians and church leaders who were unhappy about forms of angel piety. Pagan critics also asked whether it was not merely a difference of name that differentiated God and angels: 'When you say that angels stand before God who are impassible and immortal and incorruptible by nature, whom we call gods because they are near to the deity, why do we dispute over the designation? Are we not obliged to regard it merely as a difference in terminology . . .? It does not make much difference whether someone calls them gods or angels, for their divine nature bears witness.'[280]

The veneration of angels can be demonstrated above all by archaeology; a few examples are enough to show that this was an important side of early Christian piety. In Umm El-Jimal, in present-day Jordan, which in antiquity was one of the frontier fortresses of the Roman empire against the barbarians and at the same time secured the frontier between the arable land and the wilderness, a tower from early-Byzantine times rises above the military camp. Its four sides visibly bear the names of the four archangels, 'Gabriel', 'Raphael', 'Michael' and 'Uriel', so to speak as a permanent written prayer invoking protection, as a reminder for the inhabitants, and an effective warning to Bedouin tribes who might possibly attack.[281] And anyone who climbs the steps of the cathedral church of the city of Jerash (ancient Gerasa), not far from Umm El-Jimal, will still find there a niche in which Mary is framed by two archangels: Michael, Holy Mary, Gabriel.' There were individual churches or sites with angels as patrons, like the Michaelion built in the fifth century in Huarte in northern Syria, around fifteen kilometres north of Apamea on the Orontes. Here two basilicas, each with three aisles, stand side by side at different levels and are linked by a baptistery (see p. 102). The building on the north side was given a fine figurative mosaic by four members of the gerousia (a village administrative body) and the five most important members of the council: at the east end of the north side-aisle the founders perpetuated their fame: 'A mosaic was laid in the Michaelion by the gerontes Eleutherius, Sergius, Thomas, Dorotheus, John, Thomas, George and the other Thomas.'[282] Evidently the people here had not observed the regulations of the synod in Laodicea in Phrygia which established in the middle of the fourth century that 'Christians . . . shall not worship any angels and hold liturgical gatherings (in their honour)'.[283] The letter to the community of the city of Colossae, a few kilometres from Laodicea, which comes from the school of Paul, already criticized angel worship (Col. 2.18), and the bishop in the Syrian pilgrimage centre of Cyrrhus recalled the

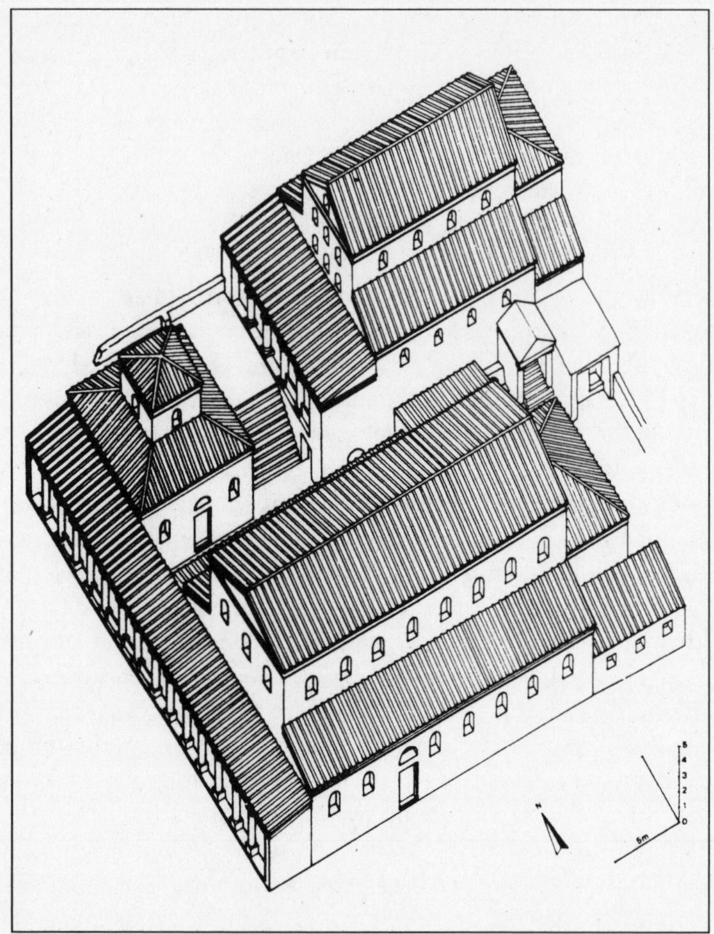

B. *Huarte (Syria), basilica of Photius (below), baptistery (above left), and Michaelion (above right)*

decision of Laodicea (barely a generation before the erection of the Michaelion in Huarte, which was not too far away). According to Theodoret of Cyrrhus in his commentary on Colossians, there were nevertheless oratories of the archangel Michael in Phrygia in his day; it was pointed out to those who visited them that angels were not as great as God in all things, but that it made sense for people to make sure of the divine good will by the intercession of the angels. On the other hand, at the same time Sozomen, the attorney from Constantinople, assured readers of his *Church History* that he had received great benefits at the site of the Michaelion in Constantinople. It was said that the archangel himself had appeared here; Sozomen could confirm that and likewise 'people who found themselves in desperate entanglements or unavoidable dangers or who had incurred sicknesses or unknown suffering', and after a prayer at the place had obtained sudden relief from their suffering.[284]

Saints and martyrs

The pagan world was irritated at the way in which the Christian communities worshipped saints and martyrs. The Platonizing orator Eunapius of Sardes from Asia Minor described the veneration at the end of the fourth century from his perspective like this: 'They gathered the bones and skulls of people who had been led out to execution for manifold crimes, people whom the state courts had punished, declared them to be gods, hung around the bones and thought that they would get better because they had defiled themselves with the tombs. They were now called "martyrs" and "deacons" and "messengers" of prayers to the gods.'[285] What happened in the Christian community in the framework of the cult of saints and martyrs is reported here quite precisely: the term 'messenger' (perhaps better 'bearer' or 'intermediary') occurs in a very similar way in Basil: he calls saints and especially martyrs 'powerful intercessors'.[286] This important theologian shows that the veneration of the saints was not a phenomenon of uneducated popular religion. Basil and his family particularly honoured the 'holy forty martyrs of Sebaste' from the *legio XII fulminata* (the 'lightning legion') who had been executed under Licinius around 320. The family also kept relics of those soldiers, whose cult had spread as far as Constantinople.[287] In his sermon on them given in 372, Basil showed with all the rhetorical means of a traditional panegyric (while at the same time distancing himself from this: 'The panegyrics on the saints are not subject to the laws of profane eloquence') that these saints had long taken over the function of state and community agencies: 'It is these forty who occupy our land and who like densely packed towers give sure protection against the attack of the enemy.'[288] Basil at the same time saw people with the most varied private concerns praying to the soldier martyrs. One sought 'deliverance from his suffering', another prayed 'that his good fortune might last. Here we find the pious woman who prays for her children, who begs for the return of her absent spouse, and for health in sickness.' Basil's sermon shows how the martyrs and their veneration made it possible for the Christians in the period after Constantine to distance themselves from the world and the state and reconstitute social ordinances by Christian standards: 'The ancestral city of the martyrs is the city of God, whose architect and creator is God himself, the heavenly Jerusalem . . . By natural descent they were of different origin, but together all formed a single spiritual family. Their common father was God, and all were brothers, not the offspring of the same two parents, but bound together in mutual love and harmony by being children in the Spirit.' The degree to which the forty martyrs constitute new ordinances – both political and social – is evident from a detail from the account which Basil gave of their martyrdom: they gave their personal names, but not that of their particular families: 'They no longer bore different names, but all called themselves Christians.'[289]

Faith and martyrdom in Hellenistic Judaism

The martyrs were felt to be 'holy' because their public confession of Christ as the Lord was regarded as the sign and working of the Holy Spirit (I Cor. 12.3), and through their execution they had become like Christ in a special way. A first very clear differentiation between the 'normal' Christian community, which bears the predicate 'holy' like its members (I Cor. 1.2), and particular 'saints' is evident in the account of the martyrdom of Bishop Polycarp from Smyrna in Asia Minor, presumably written by his community in AD 155/156. This important church leader was executed at the age of eighty-six and his bones were burned. Thereupon the Christians of Smyrna wrote to the community of Philomelium: 'We afterwards took up his bones, as being more precious than the most exquisite jewels, and more purified than gold, and deposited them in a fitting place, whither being gathered together, as opportunity is allowed us, with joy and rejoicing the Lord shall grant us to celebrate the anniversary of his martyrdom both in memory of those who have already finished their course, and for the exercising and preparation of those yet to walk in his steps.'[290] The beginnings of such a veneration of martyrs go back to Hellenistic Judaism; thus in Antioch people venerated the so-called 'Maccabaean martyrs', a scribe named Eleazar, seven young Jewish men and their mother, who had been killed, some in a very cruel way, in the religious persecution under Antiochus IV Epiphanes (around 168–166 BC: II Macc. 6.18–7.42). The bones of these nine persons, somewhat unfortunately called 'Maccabaean martyrs' (they have nothing to do with the priestly family of the Maccabees, though the designation comes from antiquity), were venerated in a separate Jewish tomb in Antioch over the ruins of which a church was built towards the end of the fourth century.[291] Soon after its consecration John Chrysostom gave committed sermons about these martyrs, and an anonymous pilgrim to Palestine from Piacenza, who visited the spot around 570, saw nine tombs, 'and over each tomb hang the instruments of their maryrdom'.[292] At the latest from the middle of the third century it became customary to hold a memorial eucharist on the day of martyrs' deaths (so-called *anniversaria*). Cyprian told the clergy of Carthage: 'Mark down also the days on which they left life, so that we may solemnly celebrate their memory!'[293] When the Synod of Elvira at the beginning of the fourth century forbade women to keep vigil at the tombs (of martyrs) and also elsewhere issued polemic against nocturnal excesses at such resting places, it was acting in keeping with a polemic against women current in antiquity, but probably also against what was actually an occasional degeneration of the anniversaries.[294] However, not only the mortal relics of martyrs, but also those of the *confessores*, i.e. men who did not pay with their lives for their confession of Christianity before the Roman authorities, enjoyed great veneration. The *Apostolic Tradition* stipulated: 'But if a confessor has been in chains in prison for the name, hands are not laid on him for the diaconate or the presbyter's office. For he has the office of the presbyterate by his confession. But if he be appointed bishop, hands shall be laid upon him.' However, the large number of such people caused problems: therefore ordination by the laying on of hands had to be given 'if he be a confessor who was not brought before a public authority nor punished with chains nor condemned to any penalty, but was only by chance derided for the name'.[295] After the great persecutions of the third century, however, the practice fell into disuse; the mass of persons involved might simply have been too great. At the latest in the middle of the third century, prayers were also addressed to martyrs themselves, as for example in Rome: 'Paul and Peter, pray for Nativus for ever!'[296] Moreover around this time we find the origin of a veneration of holy women and men who had not made a confession before the state authorities either as martyrs or as confessors. Peter Brown has repeatedly drawn attention to the social function of such saints in order to explain their 'rise' above all in the fourth century, when at least in the empire there were no longer any martyrs.[297]

Sainthood and patronage

The saints took their place in the ancient system of patronage, thus assuming the functions of protection and guarantee both for the individual and for communities. The intercession of the martyr brought about in heaven what the earthly patron secured for his client in the best cases: legal security and the occasion for modest prosperity. But at the same time it can be demonstrated that the ascetics also took over functions of earthly patronage: for example, they settled disputes over ownership of land (see below, 111). The saint or saints had power in the society around them – and the miracles that are reported of them are merely part of their influence on their environment, which was comparable to that of a patron. Moreover saints also put a stop to the strong centrifugal tendencies of Roman country life; they reinforced the identity of village communities and their capacity to function. Simeon Stylites, who died in AD 459 and whose pillar less than one hundred kilometres east of Antioch developed into *the* pilgrimage centre in the fifth century, evidently gave a Syrian village quite practical advice about weights and measures, about the level of interest (namely half a hundredth) and about dealing with notes for debt.[298] 'With a humble demeanour' he answered 'anyone, be he a craftsman or a beggar or a countryman', asking about everyday problems, for example in the case of childlessness.[299] The world-famous ascetic also gave advice not only to the inhabitants of the surrounding Syrian limestone massif, but also to 'Persians and Medes and Ethiopians . . . and even . . . Scythians and nomads', and indeed 'Ishmaelites, Persians and the Armenians subject to them, Iberians . . . Spaniards, Britons and Gauls'.[300] Even three emperors sought him out (Theodosius II [408–450], Marcian [450–457] and Leo I (457–474]), as did Arab Bedouin rulers. It need hardly be mentioned that Simeon also provided religious certainty as a professional in a world of religious amateurs: he gave advice about the right way to behave, made decisions and relieved anxiety – these are insights into the phenomenology of religion which apply to very different cultural circles. The saints of early Christianity combined functions which previously had been exercised by society as a whole, its patrons and authorities, the pagan priests and individuals. Why this remarkable concentration came about will probably never be completely explained; however, the uncertainties caused by the sometimes chaotic political developments (Syria, for example, had to live under a grave threat from Persia), must not be underestimated.

Such forms of 'piety towards saints and martyrs' as have just been described could develop only because the piety of the martyrs was itself felt to be a model. Bishop Cyprian of North Africa was executed in August 258, in the context of the persecutions of Christians by the emperor Valerian, on the estate of the proconsul of Africa near Carthage – and the sources take trouble to emphasize the combination of Stoic tranquillity and Christian joy shown by the martyr, and the quasi-imperial dignity with which he came down from the podium. A second edict of the emperor, a rescript to the senate, had ordered immediate execution for those clergy who refused to sacrifice. Cyprian commented on the governor's death sentence with a liturgical formula of prayer: *deo gratias* ('Thank God').[301] When led out to execution, first he took off his fine hooded cloak and then spent a long time praying, prostrate on the earth. Before he was beheaded he also took off his *dalmatica*, an upper garment with long sleeves and two stripes, and so stood there in his linen undergarment. Finally he even rewarded the executioner with twenty-five gold pieces – Roman emperors used to give soldiers precisely this sum on festal occasions.[302] We have good reason to assume that under all the literary themes here we have a firm individual piety.

Pilgrimages

Pilgrimages were made to the cult centres of saints and martyrs: by such a pilgrimage people in antiquity broke out of their normal life, shaped by status and role, into a 'total process'.[303] Their social structure was radically simplified, and they came to take part in a community which had a routine, but by comparison with the rest of their environment it was unstructured and undifferentiated. At their destinations, pilgrims could hope for 'an immediate experience of the holy, invisible and supernatural order, whether in the material form of miraculous healing or in the spiritual form of inner transformations of spirit or personality'.[304] Pilgrimage is one of the rites of passage; it transforms people from a normal order into a sacred order. Other people could be drawn into this process: 'Three miles further on we reached Cana, where the Lord was at the wedding (John 2.1–11), and sat down to table on seats; there I, the unworthy one' – writes the anonymous pilgrim from Piacenza towards the end of the sixth century – 'wrote down the names of my parents.'[305] Moreover pilgrimage shifted the balance between the metropolises of antiquity, the centres and the periphery. As we saw, Jerusalem and the Holy Land, central goals of pilgrimages, lay on the periphery of the empire. Sanctuaries were partly founded in the depths of the province as 'cities outside the city'.[306]

Pilgrimage centres

The giant pilgrimage centre which became established round 'the greatest wonder of the inhabited world' may serve as one example of the many pilgrimage centres – outside Jerusalem, and Rome, Tebessa, the City of Menas/Abu Mina, Simeon's sanctuary in Qal'at Sem'an, Thecla's sanctuary in Seleucia/

Meriamlik or Helenopolis/Hersek might be mentioned.[307] This arose round the pillar of St Simeon, who was born at the end of the fourth century a son of that prosperous class of farmers who made their mark on the limestone massif of northern Syria at that time. The Life composed in his lifetime by a friend, Bishop Theodoret of Cyrrhus, describes with the usual exaggerations of the genre how Simeon developed into the wonder 'that all subjects of the Roman empire know'.[308] After being thrown out of his monastery for an excess of ascetic zeal, he finally went up a mountain. He climbed up on to a pillar because the great stream of pilgrims grew constantly ('around his place one could see what looked like a burning sea of people) 'and all tried to touch him and get a blessing from his fur garment'. Even when raising the pillar three times served to detach him from the earthly tumult ('He wanted to fly to heaven and detach himself from earthly affairs'), as described above, Simeon remained caught up in the simplest earthly matters like the level of interest: a wanderer between the worlds.[309]

A profitable trade in devotional items was connected with pilgrimages; as well as small pilgrim badges made of clay (Plate 2, about the size of a one penny piece or a dime) which people could buy on the spot, small statuettes of Simeon were sold even as far away as Italy. 'For the man is said to have become so famous in great Rome that people set up little images of him in all the vestibules of workshops. These are meant to provide protection and security.'[310] A truly ecumenical saint, who could even hold together the two halves of the empire which had been driven apart! Though a great stream of pilgrims travelled to this 'wonder of the world' already during his lifetime, this throng further increased after his death – a whole pilgrim city was built in the last decades of the fifth century. The sanctuary stood on the top of the hill, at its centre, about 450 by 250 metres in surface area: in the south there were a baptistery and pilgrim hotels, in the north one of the largest Christian monuments in antiquity.[311] An octagon arose round the pillar, and there were four triumphal arches, each of which led into a three-aisle basilica; a tremendous substructure had proved necessary for the construction of the western basilica. The male pilgrims (women were not allowed to enter during the festivals) danced round the pillar with music and songs, sometimes also with wagons and carts. The noise was evidently so great that partitions were built between the octagon and the basilicas, to make sure that the places in which worship was carried on were quiet. At the foot of the hill was a small settlement with further pilgrim hotels and monasteries (Deir Sem'an); from here a pilgrim way led up the hill as a *via triumphalis*, finally bringing the pilgrims in through a triumphal arch in the southern basilica. It has been calculated that more than a thousand workers must have worked on this giant building at the same time;[312] they implemented an architectural programme developed in the imperial court.

Other expressions of piety

Amulets

Evidence of magical or semi-magical Christian piety is particularly widely attested, especially through archaeological remains. The desert sand has preserved amulets particularly well; thus a fifth-century Christian wore the following text: '† Christ be my witness! Above all it is a bad moment for the punishment of Theodorus. The moment is really bad' (Plate 4[313]). Thus evidently the person wearing it was attempting to preserve himself from punishment and relied on his centimetre-size piece of paper. Many mentions, above all polemical, show that a number of Christians, which should probably not be underestimated, wore such 'tangible' assurance of numinous support round their necks, round their heads, on their arms or on their thighs, carried them in their hands or put them on their pillows – in the same way as their non-Christian fellow citizens. Here too we must not see this form of piety limited to the area of 'popular religion': after the death of his sister Macrina (AD 379), the highly-educated Cappadocian theologian Gregory of Nyssa was given her amulet, in the form of a cross in a ring, which she had worn round her neck. A nun who had been close to Macrina explained to her mourning brother: 'You have made no mistake in choosing this treasure; for the ring is hollow in the hoop, and in it has been hidden a particle of the Cross of life.'[314] Here the boundaries between the cult of relics and the use of amulets becomes blurred – and this family certainly did not consist of simple people who had not understood the difference between paganism and Christianity. On the other side were critics of such customs: John Chrysostom, from 398 bishop in the capital, Constantinople, held up to his big-city congregation the picture of a mother whose child had fallen sick: 'The child fell sick and she did not hang an amulet around him. For her that amounts to martyrdom, since she sacrificed her son out of loyalty to her conviction. If those amulets are also no use, but rather empty deceit and foolery, what place have they here? Nevertheless, there were people who attempted to persuade her that they would really help; and she preferred to see her child dead than to tolerate pagan idolatry.'[315] Again it is the synod in Phrygian Laodicea which explicitly forbids the wearing of 'so-called amulets, which are fetters for the soul': 'Those who wear them are to be expelled from the church.'[316] However, this same legal definition by the synod indicates that there were evidently even clergy, senior and junior, who produced such pieces, had magical knowledge of other kinds, and engaged in magical practices.

Cursing

Of course other magical practices of antiquity were also adopted by individual members of the community; saints, ascetics and monks in particular made use of these techniques, which at the same time so vividly demonstrated their power in the society of late antiquity. In a collection of monastic biographies from the beginning of the fifth century, a story is told of an ascetic named Apollonius, who became a witness to a dispute between a pagan and a Christian village in Egypt over the boundaries of their respective arable land. After the dispute had already led to a several armed clashes, the ascetic sought to make peace. Monks and ascetics often assumed this function of an ombudsman or arbiter in Christian antiquity. But when the head of the pagan village resisted him and announced that he would continue the war 'to the death', Apollonius cursed the combatants: 'Be it now as you have wished. But no one but you is to be killed. And when you die, the earth shall not be your tomb, but you shall fill the bellies of animals and vultures. And while he was still talking, it came to pass.'[317] This cursing, to which a number of parallels could be added, above all from Syria,[318] is of course in contradiction to the vigorous polemic of the church fathers against such conduct: the historical Jesus already counsels his followers to bless those who curse them (Matt. 5.44/Luke 6.28) – but he might have found approval in that Christian village in Egypt. A prohibition of cursing in principle was a comparative new view in antiquity, so it was not surprising that the everyday Christian life of the apostles could not live up to this demanding commandment: according to the account in the Acts of the Apostles, Paul cursed a Jewish magician (13.6–12) and at the same time upheld Jesus' commandment (Rom. 12.14; I Cor. 4.12). But on this point the behaviour of Jesus of Nazareth was also evidently not very clear. If the narrative may be taken seriously, he cursed a fig tree (Mark 11.13)

Exorcism

Exorcism, the ritual expulsion of evil spirits and powers, played a rather different role – intrinsically it was similarly a magical technique, but stood on a different level from amulets and magical curses by virtue of the simple fact that Jesus of Nazareth and the apostles had practised it. Origen attempted to explain this striking fact in the middle of the third century by bringing similar artifices among magicians and sorcerers into discredit: 'But in fact no sorcerer uses his trick to call the spectators to moral reformation; nor does he educate by the fear of God people who were astounded by what they saw, nor does he attempt to persuade the onlookers to live as men who will be judged by God.'[319] But of course attempts were made to cope with the problems of life, greater and smaller, through exorcisms. In Heracleopolis Magna in Egypt, a prayer of conjuration has been found in the tradition of the ancient magical texts: 'Lord, almighty God, Father of our Lord and Saviour, Jesus Christ . . . I, Silvanus, address my prayer to you and bow my head before you with the petition and request that you will drive from me, your servant, the demon of witchcraft and headache and dispute, and remove any sickness and any weakness from me.'[320] Every member of the community took part in an exorcism at least once in his or her life, namely the exorcism contained – though in a strongly ritualized form – in the framework of the baptismal liturgy (see above, 67). The magical papyri, texts with magical instructions which could presumably be purchased, take us into a remarkable grey area between pagan and Christian religion.[321] They provided abundant material for exorcism formulae using the names of the Jewish and Christian God, Jesus and various angels. The canons of the Christian synods of the fourth century know a regular office of exorcist within the ministry, thus for example the Synod of Laodicea: 'No one of the priesthood, from presbyters to deacons, and so on in the ecclesiastical order to subdeacons, readers, singers, exorcists, doorkeepers, or any of the class of the ascetics, ought to enter a tavern.'[322] However, no one is to lay claim to this office for himself who has not been appointed to it by the bishop: of course one could not simply 'become' an exorcist, but first had to have shown one's charisma previously in some way, for example as a 'Christian physician and exorcist'.[323] Regular prayers for exorcisms have been attributed to the great theologians of the fourth century, thus for example John Chrysostom: 'Let us call on the Lord: Eternal God, who has freed the human race from the captivity of the devil, snatch this your servant from every influence of unclean spirits, command the evil and unclean spirits and demons to depart from the soul and body of this your servant, not to remain in him or to continue to be concealed in him. May they be made to flee from the creature of your hands in your holy name and in the name of your only-begotten Son and lifegiving Spirit.'[324]

Almsgiving

Almsgiving and fasting should be mentioned as other practical features of Christian piety – in Christianity, as in Judaism, almsgiving, fasting and prayer formed a triad of good works which were constantly emphasized. The earliest church order that we have, the Teaching of the Twelve Apostles from Syria in the late first century, understands alms as a 'ransom for sins', emphasizes the effect of such works of mercy in blotting out sins, and quotes a biblical saying as a witty warning against over-hasty giving to inappropriate recipients: 'Let your alms sweat within your hands until you know to whom you are giving.'[325] The instructions are clear: 'You shall not hesitate to give, and when you give, you shall not grumble. For you shall know who is the good paymaster of the reward. You shall not turn from the needy; rather, you shall share everything with your brother, and you shall not say that it is your own.'[326] Tertullian calls the contributions to the support fund for the poor 'as it were piety's deposit fund'. The North African theologian also attests the existence of a fixed fund for the poor for the end of the second century. 'On the monthly day, if he likes, each puts in a small donation, built only if he has pleasure and only if he be able; for there is no compulsion, all is voluntary. Their gifts are as it were piety's deposit fund. For they are not taken thence and spent on feasts, and drinking bouts, and eating houses, but to support and bury poor people, to supply the wants of boys and girls destitute of parents and of old persons now confined to the house, such, too as have suffered shipwrecked; and if there happen to be any in the mines, or banished to the islands, or shut up in the prisons, for nothing but their fidelity to the cause of God's church, they become the nurslings of their confession.'[327] It is already clear from this how important the gift of alms was for Christian piety. An apocryphal saying of the Lord, 'It is better to give than to receive' (Acts 20.35), is widely attested. The last pagan on the imperial throne, Julian, to whom the Christians gave the nickname 'the Apostate', also saw very clearly how relevant these Christian acts of love were for the spreading of the communities. As he wrote from Antioch in AD 362: 'It is a disgrace that not a single Jew needs to seek support, while the godless Galileans (i.e. the Christians, see above, 2f.) feed our people, who evidently lack any help from our side, as well as their own.'[328] 'We should see how godlessness (Christianity) has been able to gain ground only because it is lovingly concerned with strangers or has provided cemeteries for burial, not to mention its strict way of life, regardless of whether this was merely external or not!'[329] And at another point: 'As often as the poor have the impression that the priests take no notice of them, the godless Galileans immediately see this and use the occasion for beneficence.'[330]

John Chrysostom, who met Julian as a fifteen-year-old youth and was possibly taught by a close friend of the emperor, sheds more light on this practice in his sermons on the Gospel of Matthew: 'When the church is possessed of a revenue of one of the lowest among the wealthy, and not of the very rich, consider how many widows it supports every day and how many virgins; for indeed the list of them has already reached the number of three thousand. Together with these it supports those who are in prison, the sick in the hospitals, the healthy, those too who are away from their homes, those who are maimed in their bodies, those who wait upon the altar steps for food and clothing, and the beggars who come every day; and its substance is in no way diminished.'[331] And it emerges from his sermons on Corinthians that three thousand widows and virgins were listed in a similar catalogue of those in need of support.[332] Thus at the beginning of the fifth century, Bishop Porphyry paid beggars, 'strangers and citizens, six obols a day',[333] and during the time of fasting the sum was even increased to ten obols. He gave board and lodging for one day to any stranger who stopped in the city. In these texts, the regulations of the church orders, and Julian's remarks, we can see clear features of what has been called a 'contrast society': ordinances for a society which represented some contrast to that of the pagan environment, a diakonia which moreover did not stop at the church doors but had an effect on society as a whole. However, a picture that used to be a popular one, namely that pagan antiquity knew no almsgiving, is a caricature;[334] on the contrary, in the time of the empire many cultural and social institutions functioned on the basis of a developed and often strict system of sponsorship. But only in the Christian community was this system turned into a continuing institution and organized strictly. By increasingly putting care of the urban poor in church hands, in the fourth century Christian bishops also introduced new customs, to the degree that now the contributions no longer benefitted just their own fellow citizens, but all those in need, regardless. In the cities, the 'rules of the game' were so to speak abolished; at the same time, such a social policy of course allowed more effective care (and control) of the urban masses. Perhaps this, too, was a reason for the interest of state officials in Christian bishops from the second half of the third century on.

It is not surprising that the morality of giving did not always live up to these noble statements: in the middle of the third century Cyprian wrote a whole treatise of twenty-six chapters to emphasize the joy of giving. In it the Bishop of Carthage produced a whole arsenal of arguments against it put up by the community: 'But when you begin abundantly to practise good deeds, you become anxious and fear that this could make you poor as soon as your possessions are exhausted by generous giving.' – 'You fear that perhaps your patrimony might disappear . . .' – 'Moreover you have many children at home, and the size of your family prevents you from abundantly devoting yourself to good works.'[335] And he attacked his audience directly like this: 'You are wealthy and rich, and do you think that you celebrate the Lord's Supper, not at all considering the offering, who come to the Lord's Supper without a sacrifice, and yet take part in the sacrifice which the poor man has offered?'[336] In the fourth century John Chrysostom criticized the misuse of alms as an act that blotted out sin: 'There are now also those who take by violence countless things belonging to others, and think that an excuse is made for all if they cast in ten or a hundred gold pieces . . . It is better to give nothing than to give the things of one sort of person to others. For tell me, if you saw any two persons, one naked, one having a garment, and then having stripped the one that had the garment you were to clothe the naked, would you not have committed an injustice? It is surely plain to everyone!'[337]

Fasting

Like the Jewish community, the Christian community also fasted twice in the week – however on other days, so as to dissociate itself from its own origin. The Teaching of the Twelve

Apostles stipulated: 'But let not your fast days be with the hypocrites: they fast on the second and fifth days of the week, but you fast on the fourth day and on the day of rest.'[338] Alongside the Jewish roots, one could also point to the tradition of fasting in the cults of Demeter or Ceres, and in individual mystery religions, and to the instruction for all laity to be sober before performing religious actions. It remains uncertain whether Jesus himself fasted: to his contemporaries he appeared to be a 'glutton and drunkard' (Matt. 11.19). Over the course of the first centuries, however, numerous regulations for fasting developed: in preparation for baptism, before ordinations and consecrations, before receiving the eucharist ('every believer should make an effort to receive the eucharist before he has consumed anything else'[339]), and for the purposes of penitence or intercession. But at this point, too, the community discipline is evidently threatened time and again with erosion: 'In respect of fasting,' thus John Chrysostom, 'I hear many say that to go hungry is a strain on them and that they find it difficult; they plead bodily weakness, and made many other complaints, and said that the neglect of bodily care and drinking water incapacitated them.'[340] Accordingly the preacher tried to promote the religious custom by referring to the beneficial effects on health of moderate eating and drinking.

Everyday life

Differences between Christians and Pagans

How did Christians in towns and villages who were not monks live their everyday life? How, for example, did the commercial, social and political life of a metropolis shape community life? And conversely, did Christianity perhaps also shape the face of a city? What in the end were the differences between Christian life in the city and life in the country? Such fascinating questions about the interaction of Christianity with its natural or artificial environment are still difficult to answer on a broad basis. Moreover it is very difficult to estimate how far norms which were preached or set down in writing were observed in everyday reality. John Chrysostom once said in a sermon in Antioch in AD 387, after vigorously censuring his community for superstitious forms of behaviour, 'Do you hide your faces, put your hands to your brows and look at the ground? Do not do that when I say it now, but when you do what I am talking about!'[341] But how widespread really were the modes of behaviour which he was criticizing?

House doors

Christian life already differed from that of the pagan environment in quite small external details. In some circumstances, verses from the Bible were put on house doors (as Deut. 6.4f., 'Hear O Israel . . .', is still attached to the doorposts of pious Jewish homes today). A papyrus text which has survived, originally attached to a door, introduces all kinds of verse from the Psalms with the words: 'The power of our Lord has become mighty, and the Lord has gone to the door, and he has not allowed the exterminator (i.e. the devil) to come in. For Abraham dwells here. May the blood of Christ remove evil.'[342]

Eating

Differences between Christians and non-Christians also became evident in other features of everyday life like eating. Perhaps a somewhat crude example can illustrate these connections: since the Old Testament had already forbidden the consumption of blood (Gen. 9.4: 'But you may not eat meat in which there is still blood'), Christians had to give up eating black pudding *(botuli cruore distenti)*, which was extraordinarily popular in antiquity. As Tertullian wrote to the non-Christian authorities: 'You tempt Christians with sausages of blood, just because you are perfectly aware that the thing by which you thus try to get them to transgress they hold unlawful.'[343] A report on the martyrdom of Bishop 'Akebsema/Acepsimas and his companions under the sharply anti-Christian Persian king Sapur II in AD 379 shows that this was not an unsubstantiated rumour. Time and again the Sassanid state authority required Christians to drink blood: 'Drink blood and I shall let you go free and you shall not die.' And time and again those who had been arrested refused to do so; they even rejected the substitute of grape juice, which was meant to look like blood: 'Far be it from us . . . to conceal our faith and our truth for the sake of hostile and perverse men.'[344] At the same time, the Old Testament prohibition against consuming blood was supported or rationalized with quasi-scientific arguments, which suggests that the communities in fact had problems with the norm. Clement of Alexandria declared in his *Instructor* at the beginning of the third century: 'People should not touch blood at all, since their own body is none other than flesh, the growth of which depends on blood.' And John Chrysostom similarly preached about the commandment in this rationalizing way when he expounded the book of Genesis in the community in Constantinople at the end of the fourth century: 'How slight and easy are the commandments! The Lord does not require of our nature anything that is heavy, or any burden at all! Some even say that the blood of beasts without reason is difficult to eat, earthy, and therefore causes illness. However, we should not commend the observance of the commandment for such philosophical reasons, but simply because of the ruler's legislation.'[345]

Public life

Alongside private everyday life there was public life. But even the New Testament gives us relatively little information about what today we would call public, political and social life.[346] Reports of everyday Christian life concern questions of religious life, relations between Christians and non-Christians – but they are sparse. We have only a few remarks of Jesus of Nazareth on this subject; at all events he calls neither for a boycott of the Roman occupying forces and their exaction of taxes nor for armed resistance against them, but at best refers to the limits which are imposed by religion: 'Render to Caesar that which is Caesar's, and to God that which is God's' (Mark 12.17). First the writings of the New Testament are concerned for an integration of Christians into society, despite all the efforts to preserve the ethical legacy of Jesus and the 'heavenly citizenship' (Phil.3.20): 'Aspire to live quietly, to mind your own affairs and to work with your hands, as we charged you', writes Paul around AD 50 to the community in Thessaloniki (I Thess. 4.11). Committed work instead of begging and abstinence from political activity ensure that the community will be inconspicuous in cities and towns: 'If a man will not work, let him starve' (II Thess. 3.10 – a verse of the Bible which moreover appeared without attribution in two constitutions of the Soviet Union).

Tertullian attests how little everyday Christian life in the North African port of Carthage, which was above all stamped by trade, differed from that of the other inhabitants. He says that Christians are people who live alongside non-Christians, 'have the same food, clothing and education and the same needs in life'. He told the pagan audience of his *Apology:* 'We live with you in the world, abjuring neither forum nor shambles nor bath nor stall nor workshop, nor inn nor weekly market nor any other places of commerce. We sail with you, and fight with you and till the ground with you, and in like manner we unite with you in your trading – even in the various arts we make public property of our works for your benefit.'[347] Nowhere in antiquity do we hear the accusation that Christians boycotted non-Christian businesses and bought only from their own. Evidently in Carthage it was not even taken for granted or customary that Christians in financial difficulties would be able to get money from fellow believers – the community fund was limited to the support of the really poor, the orphans and widows. It was Bishop Cyprian, around fifty years later, who first used community money to make it easier for Christians who wanted to start a trade.[348] Thus the Christian community in Carthage was largely integrated into the everyday economic life of the city. The theologians' criticism of unfair business methods and dishonest maximization of profit probably also derived from Jesus' ethic of love of neighbour and the traditional criteria of Jewish legislation, but in content perfectly matched corresponding pagan demands.

Banned professions

However, this integration into professional life and society was true only in broad terms: specific professions were banned for Christians. The so-called *Apostolic Tradition* – like the precepts of later synodical law – prohibits a whole series of professions: people who worked as pagan priests, pimps, female or male prostitutes, actors, carters, gladiators, magicians, soothsayers or interpreters of dreams had to renounce their professions before they could be baptized. The craftsmen who worked for the pagan cult, sculptors, painters and makers of amulets were also not accepted unless they gave up producing work for the religion which was now alien to them.[349] However, by way of qualification it must be said that there were many professions in this list which even a contemporary non-Christian Roman would have regarded as dishonourable: prostitutes of both sexes, and also actors and gladiators, were infamous and had no civic rights. Finally, the church would not have been taking its own traditional principles seriously had it welcomed members of the twilight world and the underworld into its ranks and at the same time left them in their old milieu. On the other hand, time and again there are individual instances of people who continued to practise this kind of profession and were then accepted into the community again. That is true not only of those who made idols,[350] but also and above all of soldiers. We cannot discuss the topic in detail here, but a look at the settlement of Dura Europos, on the eastern frontier of the empire, which has already been mentioned, is enough (see 14 above). The Christian community of perhaps seventy members consisted predominantly of soldiers. The old claim that there was no evidence of Christian soldiers in the inscriptions for the period before Constantine (thus still Harnack[351]) has now been refuted. However, Christianity got a foothold in the army only after the emperors Marcus Aurelius (AD 161–180), Commodus (180–192) and then especially the Severi; at that time on the one hand the military extended its influence on the state administration, and on the other from then on non-Romans, freemen and even slaves could make a career in the military (and thus also in civil offices). These changes can be connected with the contemporaneous reports on Christians in the army.[352] To begin with, Christianity was represented only in the lower ranks, since at least in the second century the sacrifices which senior officers were required to make would have caused Christians an unavoidable conflict. But at a very early stage the mission was also successful among higher ranks, even in the Roman praetorian guard: for example, a 'Licineus, praetorian soldier', is buried in the Roman catacombs of Sant'Agnese,[353] and the *Apostolic Tradition* makes a kind of minimal demand: 'A soldier under orders shall not kill anyone. If he should be ordered to do so, he shall not do it.'[354] In relatively peaceful times, in which the military in part carried out police duties, it may indeed have been possible to observe this regulation. In time of war it seemed like a vain rearguard action, since the compatibility of being a Christian and being a soldier had been accepted in principle. Leaving aside the martyrdom of soldiers, the development continued in this direction: in 314 desertion from the army in times of peace was punished by exclusion from the community.[355]

In the third-century *Apostolic Tradition,* which has already been mentioned, it is interesting that if there is 'a military governor or a magistrate who wears the purple, let him desist'.[356] The decisive factor in this repudiation is the obligation on such officials not only to take part in the sacrifices and other actions of the pagan cults, but to supervise or organize their performance. It was a specific feature of the Roman administrative system of the imperial period that finance was also tied up with the performance of such actions; this form of compulsory sponsorship was a marked brake on interest in such offices throughout antiquity, despite all the honours that were bound up with them. Thus the tasks of a normal city magistrate posed considerable problems to relatively strict Christians and their communities. Tertullian gives evidence of discussions on such problems within the community. He had made the same decision as the anonymous church order: Christians might not take on such offices.[357] But the result of this attitude was quite clearly to isolate the Christian community in the communes. The community of Carthage therefore does not seem to have followed Tertullian in his strict attitude, and the Synod of Elvira, which was mainly attended by Spanish bishops, formulated a compromise solution which evidently gained a wide consensus. At the beginning of the fourth century it stipulated that *duumviri* – i.e. magistrates in the Roman civil colonies who held two positions – should voluntarily keep away from church and worship during their year in office because of their entanglement in pagan ceremonies.[358] Thus it became possible for Christians to accept such offices. Otherwise the inhabitants of communities in provincial cities like Carthage only rarely came into contact with the Roman state and its organs: with the military in times of war, in police service with the army (there was no police in our sense), and in criminal and civil legal proceedings.

Life in the metropolis

It is more difficult to reconstruct the everyday life of Christians in the period before Constantine in the three great metropolises of Alexandria, Antioch and of course Rome. At any rate Clement of Alexandria with his precise rules of conduct in the *Instructor* makes it possible for us to get a glimpse of the living rooms or *triclinia* of the more prominent Christian circles in the city at the beginning of the third century. Unfortunately, however, the first sources to depict the everyday life of the Christian community in Antioch with any degree of colour come only from the fourth century, and of course one cannot compare the conditions of this time, when almost half the inhabitants were Christians, with the beginnings. Only individual names of theologians have been preserved from this early period. How representative these usually well-educated writers were of the bulk of the community remains speculation. Only for the fourth century, i.e. about three hundred years after the founding of the community, is it possible to produce a rather more colourful picture of urban Christian life, and this is far from being really precise. In the homilies which he delivered in the city on the Orontes from AD 386 on, John Chrysostom mentioned at least a number of things which he did not like about his congregation, and over around ten years at some point touched on virtually all the problems of the everyday life of Christians. All these admonitions show how firmly rooted the everyday life of by far the majority of men and women in the community was in the social, political, economic and cultural life of their city.

Thus the delight of Antiochenes in festivities was notorious throughout antiquity; there were usually gladiatorial battles, circus games or theatre performances every other day. Now one might think that Christians would have stopped taking part in these events, which were always also associated with pagan religious occasions or ceremonies. But evidently the Christian confession did not lead to restraint over the Antiochene delight in festivities. Chrysostom criticized the interest of his community in such festivities and once appealed to them in a sermon in connection with a current event – a popular festival in the famous hedge of Daphne, a few kilometres outside the city: 'All of you who are present, go out to the city gate tomorrow and restrain them with good words.'[359] Did his community really follow such admonitions and go to the Daphne gate? One would hardly think so; at another point he soberly remarks on what is left when the festival has come to an end: 'Rubbish, ashes and dust.'[360]

However, the preacher from the 'mainstream church' does not see such festivals as a remnant of bourgeois paganism which his community is unable to shake off. He criticizes the way in which prominent Christian families as a matter of course use pagan slaves for educational purposes and also the wearing of amulets and coins with images of Alexander the Great as a talisman on head and feet: 'That is satanic frippery.'[361] Here the acculturation of the inhabitants of the city evidently sets very clear limits to the Christianization of a whole metropolis: certainly at a very early stage Christianity moved into the cities, but there in antiquity it threatened at least partially to lose its identity.

Chrysostom tries hard to resist such an adaptation of Christianity to 'the form of this world', faithful to the Pauline admonition 'Be not like this world' (Rom. 12.1). The point at which this critical attitude becomes particularly concrete is the question of property and private possessions.[362] In a sermon he analyses the comparative resources in his city like this: 'Around a tenth part is rich and a tenth poor; the rest are of the middle sort.'[363] From this he concludes: 'Although there are so many that are able to feed the hungry, many go to sleep in their hunger, not because those that have are not able with ease to help them, but because of their great barbarity and inhumanity. For if both the wealthy, and those next to them, were to distribute amongst themselves those in need of bread or clothing, scarcely would one poor person fall to the share of fifty men or even one hundred.' The preacher went on to propose that the richer ones could make at least a tenth of their possessions available for the care of the poor and concluded: 'By God's grace it would be possible for our city to nourish the poor of ten cities.'[364]

Such reports from Antioch show how far the Christian community at the end of the fourth century was removed from any form of conventicle piety. Its church services had become public events in the life of a great city, which of course also offered a breeding ground for all kinds of dishonest ways of making money: Chrysostom advised his hearers who had become the victims of pickpockets in church during the sermon to leave their purses at home in future.[365] There was simultaneous translation of the sermon into Syriac in the side asles for the landowners who had come to the city from their estates in the countryside around; at the foot of the mountain on which Simeon's pillar stood there was a dual monastery for Syriac- and Greek-speaking monks.

Life in the country

It is even more difficult to reconstruct the everyday life of Christian communities in the country. This is still easiest for Egyptian Christianity – above all because of the rich papyrus finds which the sand has preserved better here. This was of course not just stamped by the life of a great city in the imperial province (that also applied to the situation in Asia Minor). But despite the better tradition of everyday texts like letters, even now only very fragmentary statements are possible. One can hardly develop an overall picture of country Christianity in the around 30,000 small towns and villages of this area.[366] What is striking from the start is the intensive cohesion which stamps the communities, far beyond the limits of place and family. In a place in the so-called Great Oasis in the Libyan desert (El-Chârga, ancient Kysis) a letter was found in which a priest reported to a colleague how a Christian woman named Politike who had been banished by the state into the wilderness 500 kilometres south of Cairo was being given food and lodging. At the beginning of the fourth century the woman was taken under the protection of the 'excellent and believers among the grave-diggers', i.e. the Christian members of those responsible for burying the dead. Moreover, the letter has been preserved with the relics of the archive of the grave-diggers. The formula quoted, 'the excellent and believers' which is easily deciphered, shows that not all members of this class were Christians. But Politike's fellow believers gave their fellow Christian protection and lodging – just as their Lord in his speech about the last judgment (Matt. 25.31–46) calls for a welcome for the stranger and the homeless and food for the hungry and thirsty.[367] Another letter from the third century shows that this special fellowship was also practised in everyday business, for example in trade and money-changing. The sender organized his business in the region of Arsione, in the oasis of Fayyum, from Rome, and the bishop of Alexandria was to keep the surplus for buying linen cloths, barley, bread and fish until the sender had returned from Rome. So the Egyptian Christians turned to the chief clergyman of the province for quite everyday trade and financial matters; he assumed the function of a trading bank for the community.[368]

Forms of Life

Forms of life

'Between two worlds' – this title can also be used as a heading for an account of Christian forms of life. With marriage and a monastic-ascetic form of existence which was critical of marriage, from the beginning two fundamentally different models of Christian life were available – fundamentally different, but nevertheless related to each other and bound closer together than might appear at first sight by models of sexual continence.

Such a remarkable tension in the evaluation of marriage can, however, be discerned throughout the history of antiquity and late antiquity, right from the beginning. Positive and negative standpoints alternate. Like the collector John Stobaeus at the beginning of the fifth century, one could collect the attitudes under the very contrasting headings: 'marriage is very good', 'it is not good to marry', and 'for some marriage proves useful, for others intolerable'.[369] So the difference between Christian and pagan verdicts on marriage does not lie in differing evaluations of the phenomenon – it unites Christians and non-Christians, however strongly the assessments of marriage differ between different internal groups. For all their commitment to marriage, Christians are characterized by an awareness of its provisional nature, of a kind that the pagan environment did not know.

Probably this remarkable tension between an affirmation of marriage and references to its transitoriness go right back to the historical Jesus, who himself – like Paul – was unmarried. However, his message was in most cases addressed to people who were married, like Peter. The first people to bear responsibility in the communities and to carry the message from the narrow confines of northern Galilee and Jerusalem into the different regions of the Roman empire were also of course married. The advice for the selection of these people which has been preserved in the New Testament requires both the 'episkopos' and also the 'deacon' to be 'the husband of one wife', one who 'manages his household well, keeping his children submissive and respectful' (I Tim. 3.2/4, 12). Only on isolated occasions are there those in the first generation who renounce marriage 'for the sake of the kingdom of heaven'. They thought that the return of Christ and thus the end of this old world was imminent. For example the apostle Paul advised the members of the Christian community in the port of Corinth that in view of such prospects it was better to remain single, and he himself behaved accordingly. But he immediately added his own advice: 'But if you do marry, you are not sinning, and if a young girl marries, she is not sinning' (I Cor. 7.28). He regarded a 'mixed marriage' between a Christian and a non-Christian as a missionary opportunity (I Cor. 7.16). Here of course the apostle was putting forward a very optimistic, indeed calculatedly optimistic, view of a marriage between a Christian and a non-Christian.

Paul was completely in line with Jesus of Nazareth in his remarks, which are apparently so ambivalent, emphasizing the significance of marriage as an unbreakable divine order while at the same time referring to its transitoriness. Jesus on the one hand radicalized the contemporary Jewish practice of marriage by forbidding divorce and defining adultery not just in terms of sexual actions (e.g. Matt. 5.27). On the other hand he clearly put the kingdom of God and discipleship above the ties of marriage and family (Matt. 10.37). As Jesus made clear in a parable, in any case there will no longer be any marriage ties after the resurrection of the dead (Matt. 22.23–29). This evidence has been brought together as indicating that Jesus understood marriage as an 'interim ordinance' for the old world appointed by God and therefore to be preserved carefully; its validity was put in question by the dawn of God's new world. In a very similar way Paul advised his communities in Asia Minor and Greece, in view of the imminent end of the old world and the consummation of the new world, that those who were married should live as if they were not married (I Cor. 7.29–31). But of course the repudiation of any marriage can be legitimated by such statements – and this also happened.

Marriage and family

Marriage

In the NT

Circles of primitive Christian theologians who saw themselves as disciples of Paul then introduced this interpretation of marriage as an 'interim ordinance' into traditional views about this theme, above all in the sexual hierarchy of the Jewish and pagan environment, and legitimated it with the rule of Christ over his church. That is evident, for example, from the letter of a disciple of Paul to the community of Christians in Ephesus, the chief city of the Roman province of Asia: 'Wives, be subject to your husbands as to the Lord (Christ). For the man is the head of the woman, as Christ too is the head of the community . . . As the church is subject to Christ, so let wives also be subject in everything to their husbands' (Eph. 5.21–24). Such texts usually occur in the New Testament in the context of lists of rules which also regulate the behaviour of children, parents, slaves and other classes. All these catalogues of ethics propagate structures of rule, but define this rule more closely as loving care and the subordination more closely as adaptation in solidarity: no slavish subjection was ever intended. One of the central statements of Jesus about love of neighbour at least still shimmers through when husbands are required to love wives 'as themselves' (Eph. 5.33). The Christian definition of the relationship between wife and husband cannot, however, be emancipated from the patriarchal ethic of the sexes and classes which was dominant in the environment: timid attempts at a new ethic of freedom in primitive Christianity were suppressed by it. They are to be found, for example, in the unusually open and direct dealings of Jesus of Nazareth with women, but also in Paul's statement: 'There is neither Jew nor Greek, there is neither slave nor free, there is neither man nor woman' (Gal. 3.28). But it did not prove possible to transfer this devaluation of differences in earthly status and power relationships (for Paul grounded in the one baptism) into a concrete social reality. When a later New Testament letter calls on its male readers to deal respectfully with women, 'for they too are the inheritors of the grace of life' (I Peter 3.7), we simply seem to have a faded recollection of such radical statements.

Pagan and Christian marriage: identities and differences

So can we say that there were hardly any differences between a pagan and a Christian marriage in antiquity, and that only the ideological frame of reference of the religious contexts has changed? There is some evidence in support of this view – but here again it is the case that in antiquity, in the Roman empire, Christian marriage was moving in a very individualistic way between the two worlds of the religious ideal and everyday reality. Identities and differences can be demonstrated even from such an everyday piece of clothing as a marriage girdle: 'From God harmony, happiness and health', *ex theou homonoia charis hygi(ei)a*: these words are inscribed on the two central gold medallions of one such valuable girdle from Dumbarton Oaks (plate 5), which was probably worn by a well-to-do lady from Syria (perhaps in the sixth or seventh century AD). The two identical central medallions of the piece of jewellery show spouses, each of whom is extending the right hand to the other. For both guests and onlookers this gesture of binding the two right hands, Latin *dextrarum iunctio*, represented perhaps the most impressive action of any wedding in antiquity. Here pagan and Christian weddings did not differ at all. As the right hand was dedicated to *fides*, the goddess of faithfulness, at least for the pagan guest this gesture had a far deeper symbolic meaning than the modern handshake has for us. The joining of right hands signalized to a wedding assembly the will of the two partners to be faithful and live in harmony; it perhaps sealed the signing of the marriage contract or preceded it. Be this as it may, it belonged in the context of any marriage celebration, smaller or larger, depending on the social stratum. It was here that all the important things took place: in antiquity there was neither a church ceremony nor a civil ceremony for marriage. If we look simply at the couple and their joining of hands, apart from differences in style there is hardly any difference between the Byzantine silver medallions and the many depictions of weddings in Roman art from the early empire on: they all sought to depict 'harmony, happiness and health'. However, in the medallion on the Syrian chain, between the couple being married, blessing the alliance of their hands with his own slightly raised hands, is Christ with the nimbus of the cross. He is the 'God' from whom 'harmony, happiness and health come', and the two crosses over the couple indicate that they are both Christians, members of his church. Christ occupies the place which was first occupied in pagan depictions by a kind of bride's escort, the *pronuba*. As we read in one of the last important pagan poets of the fifth century AD, 'Then she took the right hand of the bridegroom, put it with the right hand of the maiden, and confirmed the alliance, saying: "Live in harmony."'[370] Similarly, on many pagan and also on some Christian depictions we find a woman between the couple who embraces the husband and wife and so protects and blesses their alliance. Juno, the spouse of Jupiter, was once distinguished with the epithet *connuba*, bride's escort; in the high empire she was regarded as the symbol of the goddess of harmony, Latin *concordia*. Thus the differences between the late Byzantine depiction of a wedding and its pagan models are reduced: in both, 'harmony, happiness and health' are made the theme through the gesture of joining hands; only the gods invoked as protection and as guarantor are different.

A sermon given by Asterius, the bishop of Amasea in Pontus (present-day Amasya, one hundred kilometres south of the Turkish Black Sea coast) in the first years of the fifth century, is an illustration of the scene on the Syrian wedding girdle: 'The very first escort of the bride is the creator of the world, who joined together the first human beings to be created by the marriage bond and imposed on those who were to be born unbroken life together, which cannot be dissolved and which one must honour as a law of God.'[371] Since Asterius here understood God to mean Christ, his description corresponds to the scene on the piece of jewellery from Dumbarton Oaks – Christ as the bride's escort between the couple, blessing their alliance. He has joined them together, as can also be read in the Gospel: 'So they are no longer two but one flesh. What God has joined together, let no man put asunder' (Matt. 19.6). The bishop advised the men of his community to accept God's gift of a 'wife' for what she is: a collaborator in coping with life, in having children, a help in sicknesses, a comforter in mourning, a guardian of the hearth, in short a treasure among possessions. 'She mourns and rejoices over one and the same thing (as her husband). In common with you she possesses the riches, if there are any; she copes with the most wretched poverty as a steward and resists the pains of poverty in a shrewd and powerful way. With perseverance she submits to the laborious nurture of children because of her shared life with you. Even when all supposed friends leave the sinking ship, the wife remains: she follows her husband even to the doors of prison as a dog follows its master, if the need arises.'[372] The expression 'guardian of the hearth' even takes up an old pagan honorific title which expresses the special and dominant role of the woman in the home. It clearly refers to the old tradition of venerating Hestia, the goddess of the hearth, home and family, at the domestic hearth and entrusting the care of this cult place to the housewife. This detail shows how Christians almost took for granted the status of the Roman wife as 'mistress of the house'.

Sexual intercourse

Given the widespread, at least moderately critical, views of marriage among Christians (like those which Asterius sought to contest in his sermon), it is hardly surprising that the fundamentally more Puritanical attitude to marital sexuality to be found among most contemporaries who were in any way educated was accentuated further. Almost all Christian theologians of antiquity agree in advising intercourse only 'in due order and at the appropriate time', i.e. for the purpose of procreating children.[373] Augustine recommends to a couple at the beginning of the fifth century that they should mature in such a way that they can learn to dispense with sexual intercourse as early as possible – that would be in keeping not with physical compulsion but with a 'premature praiseworthy attitude'. Sex which serves procreation 'is innocent; if it serves only to satisfy lust . . . it is a venial sin'.[374] In any case, only those should marry who thought that they could not get by without a spouse. Paul had already said the same thing: 'It is better to marry than to be consumed with passion' (I Cor. 7.9). The increasing importance of the monastic movements in the fourth century (see 148–53 below) reinforced similar tendencies in the Christian marriage ethic which were present from the start. Peter Brown has spoken of a 'democracy of sexual shame' at this time, i.e. a requirement to avoid sex which was binding on all – religious functionaries, specialists and lay people.[375]

Mixed marriages

What further impressions do we get of everyday marriage? First of all that the problem of mixed marriages, to which Paul had already alluded (see 128 above), always played a prominent role. For in a pagan marriage in antiquity, the shared practice of the household cult was as much regarded as the heart of successful married life as the confession of Christ in a Christian union. Thus there were important objections to mixed marriage on both sides. But since for a long period in antiquity there was a surplus of Christian girls ready and willing to marry, total prohibitions of mixed marriages could not stand for long. The Synod of Carthage nevertheless prohibited at least the sons and daughters of bishops from marrying pagans or schismatics (AD 397). In Asia Minor, such marriages were completely forbidden.[376] Then in the fourth or fifth centuries the emperors completely banned marriage with sectarians. In two books, Tertullian at the beginning of the third century described to his wife the difficulties which had arisen in practice for such families earlier. Mixed marriage first leads to the problems of different festal calendars – one is fasting while the other is arranging a banquet. But one should not share any festivals together with non-Christians. According to Tertullian the Christian partner is troubled with all kinds of religious practices which he can regard only as the utterly blasphemous worship of demons. Moreover in the end it cannot remain a secret from one's spouse if one signs oneself and one's bed with the cross and gets up at night to pray. 'Who,' he writes, 'can allow his wife, for the sake of visiting the brethren, to go round from street to street, to other men's and indeed to all the poorer huts? Who will willingly bear her being taken from his side by nocturnal assemblies, if the need be?'[377]

Women's dress

In addition to these remarks, which praise the value and importance of housewives in their domestic functions, there are of course also many testimonies which correspond more closely to the distribution of roles between the sexes traditional in antiquity and therefore accentuate the domination of the husband: for example Clement of Alexandria advises his readers, an educated public and not without means, that 'women ought to dress neatly, and bind themselves around with the bond of chastity and modesty, lest through frivolity they slip away from the truth.'[378] Even if he is quoting these instructions almost word for word from Plutarch, i.e. a popular philosophical writer who lived just under a century previously, the delight in detail with which patriarchal anxieties are depicted here is surprising. If the husbands do not put any reins on their wives or do not clip their wings (another image from Plutarch), then, Clement fears, the women will give themselves airs around the place, deck themselves with excessive jewellery, and seek pleasure with strange men. Plutarch and Clement are also agreed that husbands are always threatened with the danger of being put under the thumb of rich and prominent wives and thus having to lose their pride and courage. Conversely, there are also women who are seriously humiliated and subjugated by up and coming men from the lower class. So both pagan and Christian call for a reciprocal process of education for the couple: both are gradually to reduce their 'unreasonable drives and desires'. The more moral life is the more reasonable life, and at the same time the simpler life and the 'worthy way of living' generally.[379] As in modern books of etiquette, Clement of Alexandria applies these widespread maxims of contemporary Cynic-Stoic ethics in the style of popular philosophical instruction (*diatribe*) to almost all spheres of daily life: eating, drinking, sleeping, clothing and sex. Thus women are to wear a golden signet ring on their finger joints, men their signet ring at most on the bottom half of their little fingers. Clement recommends that the husband's hair should be 'cropped, and the beard should be washed'; he advises the wife to have smoothly combed, long hair which she 'binds up simply at her neck with a plain clasp'.[380] Wigs are completely forbidden. The list is enough to show how far this 'Christian' marriage ethic simply represents the counterpart of corresponding pagan models, despite the biblical verses which are occasionally quoted, not always appropriately. Marriage is a battleground on which above all the husbands can learn self-control: 'to be uninfluenced by joy and sorrow in marriage and in bringing up children and in care of the household'.[381]

Children

The view that the procreation of children was the central purpose of marriage united Jews, Christians and non-Christians. Whereas the first two groups could refer to the commandment of the very first *pronuba* (to use Asterius's term), 'Be fruitful and multiply' (Gen. 1.28), in pagan marriage contracts this purpose of marriage was sometimes even put down in writing. At any rate an extant copy of a Roman marriage contract stipulates this;[382] in particular it corresponds to a requirement of Stoic ethics and also of the legislation of the early empire: procreating children is an obligation and a contribution to the prosperity of the commonwealth. At the beginning of the fifth century Augustine not only writes that marriage between man and woman is a good thing but defines the purpose of marriage as 'the procreation of children' and 'the communion of the different sexes given by nature'.[383] If children are procreated, sexuality, which otherwise has somewhat negative connotations because of the element of lust, still bears 'a good fruit': 'Bodily desire glows in a more moral way when the sense of parenthood orders it.'[384] By contrast John Chrysostom in an address to his community in Syrian Antioch claimed that the earth was sufficiently populated for this reason for marriage now to lapse.[385] Nevertheless, in a writing of his own he gave advice on bringing up children and complained about the general indifference on this topic. Chrysostom formulated the main motive of Christian nurture like this: 'Bring up a warrior for Christ, and from his earliest youth teach him to fear God, even if he lives in the world . . . You first delight in good behaviour if you have a good son, and then God rejoices. You work for yourself.' 'The stamp of a holy man is to be put on the child generally.'[386] There follow very concrete instructions about the child's language, about the prohibition against telling pagan fairy tales, and about the form of punishment: first a strict look, then hurtful words, and only as a last resort the strap, and then with restraint: 'He should not constantly be given blows.'[387]

Concubinage

Since even according to a pagan Roman view the purpose of marriage consisted in the procreation of descendants, and there were also strict legal penalties for adultery, during the period of the Roman empire many men from the upper classes shunned marital responsibility. They chose a form of life together which bears the misleading designation 'concubinage' – for this is not an association alongside a marriage but one instead of a marriage. *Concubinatus* is a way of evading the strict marriage laws of the early period of the empire: for example, a man could live permanently with a woman of a lower class and in so doing avoid having children, but still have sex. Concubinage was therefore a comparatively everyday affair which, within certain limits, was even recognized by the church. For example, Augustine lived for a long time in such a union with a woman and only left her in 385, to become engaged to a young and rich heiress. Later he criticized such dealings with concubines and forbade it to the men in his community. Moreover his own past was evidently so painful to him that he does not once mention the name of his consort anywhere in his writings. Later he condemns concubinage because here he sees two people joined together, 'not to procreate children but merely to enjoy the sexual encounter with one another; here each promises the other that they will not go elsewhere in the meantime': a 'temporary wife'.[388]

Adultery

That the reality of marriage did not always correspond to the lofty description of it as an indissoluble promise of loyalty and harmony under God's blessing is evident from the regulations of the various synods at which as a rule the bishops assembled. A first adultery on the part of the wife is already sufficient reason for divorce,[389] but it can still be atoned for by the instrument of penance. Moreover remarriage is forbidden. According to the decisions of the Synod of Elvira, a second adultery leads to life-long exclusion from the sacrament of the eucharist, as does adultery and subsequent remarriage. An exception is made only in the case of serious illness. Strict Christian regulations about obstacles to marriage at such synods corresponded to Old Testament and Roman legal practice: marriage to kinsfolk by marriage was not allowed; infringements were punished by the exclusion of those concerned from eucharistic communion for five years. Similarly, the marriage of a stepdaughter to her step-father was felt to be incest.[390] On the other hand, the instructions of the synods in times of a flourishing ascetic movement also leave no doubt about the institution of marriage and its significance. A synod in Gangra in Paphlagonia (today the Turkish Çankiri) in the last third of the fourth century stipulates: 'Whoever rejects marriage and claims that a women who sleeps with her husband and also believes and is pious cannot enter into the kingdom of God, let him be excluded.'[391] The Greek word *anathema* which occurs here indicates that the person concerned is publicly cursed and expelled from the church, in other words is abandoned to destruction. Wives who leave their husbands for such reasons and parents who neglect their children because of them are similarly anathematized. Of course here too there were divergent voices.

Marriage and Christ

The little medallion on the Syrian wedding girdle from Byzantine times could also be interpreted in quite a different way, namely as a kind of 'marriage threesome', as an association between bride, bridegroom and Christ as a further marriage partner. In this special *ménage à trois*, Christ stands between husband and wife and orders their relationship in the sense described. Though explicit mention of the 'marriage threesome' probably occurs for the first time in Søren Kierkegaard and therefore in Europe in modern times, the views about marriage held by the ancient Christian theologians often come very close to this. They were prepared for by the Letter to the Ephesians, from the school of Paul, which – perhaps in the footsteps of Paul (II Cor. 11.2) – at the same time also applied the image of marriage to the relationship between Christ and his church: 'The two become one flesh' (Matt. 16.9); 'Great is this mystery; but I am speaking of Christ and the church' (Eph. 5.32). Here the letter bases the triumphal procession on a metaphor from marriage which could be developed in particular in commentaries on the biblical Song of Songs – from the beginning of the third century this Old Testament book was interpreted in terms of the marital love between Christ and the church. For example, in the early third century the Roman theologian Hippolytus interpreted the verse 'Let us hasten: the king leads me into his bedchamber' as follows: 'Who is the king? Christ. What is the bedchamber? The church.'[392] After the two interpretations of the Song of Songs by the Alexandrian theologian Origen, who around the middle of the third century wrote on it in the form of sermons and a multi-volume learned scholarly commentary, the focal point shifted to an individual use of these metaphors. Origen interpreted the entry into the bedchamber as follows: the human soul is attached to the word of God because Christ leads it to understand his meaning.[393] The relationship of love spoken of by the Old Testament book is presented as that between Christ and the believing soul, so that the reader or hearer of such a text who is ideally married lives in a kind of double marriage: for the duration of this world age he is married to an earthly wife, but his real indestructible relationship is the heavenly one. Interpretations like these led to the retention of the primitive Christian evaluation of marriage as a provisional institution even in later centuries. Although there was no longer any expectation of an immediate or imminent end to the world, which would put a definitive end to any earthly marriage, the 'marriage with Christ' already set limits to the relationship on earth in the present. Of course, conversely, this widespread notion could also be used to demonstrate the special value of earthly marriage as a parable of the heavenly link between Christ and his church: for Augustine at the beginning of the fifth century, marriage is a sign of this eternal covenant, in the reality of which it participates.[394]

Slaves

Slaves posed a special problem within a Christian community and family; here the simple distinction between 'free' and 'slaves' can easily lead us astray in the period of the empire. First, slaves were principally a family phenomenon: in the extended family, slaves, like children and grandchildren and occasionally also the wife, were subject to the domestic authority (*patria potestas*) of the father of the house (*pater familias*). However, the different legal status of *pater familias* and slaves by no means implied a difference in social status: 'Depending on the state of the civilization, intellectual or personal capacities or special training, slaves could fulfil the most varied tasks in the city or in the country, working with freemen on the land, in businesses as administrators or bookkeepers, as the agents of great merchants, or as servants in confidential positions in the household, as readers, musicians, actors, or as craftsmen, physicians, elementary teachers and in other professions.'[395] But of course even elementary 'human rights' like sex, the chance to have children and to bring them up, could be refused to slaves, so that in some circumstances they had to live an extraordinarily unsatisfactory life. However, many slaves must have cherished the well-founded hope that they would be released into the freedom of Roman citizenship in the lifetime of their owner or after his death. Moreover their legal status was improved and humanized. Thus in the case of the killing of a slave by his owners without adequate reason, Antoninus Pius was able to lay a charge of murder against the perpetrators; however, corporal punishment continued to be allowed as an ultimate means of discipline. In the most favourable instance the dependent relationship during a lifetime turned into a relationship of patronage: obedience, small obligations and respect for the patron's protection. However, there is no doubt that the Christian community essentially took over slavery as an 'important structural principle of the economic and social order in antiquity'.[396] We can already see this in the case of Paul, who advises everyone to remain in the state in which he is called (I Cor. 7.21). Already in the second century the freeing of slaves at the community's expense was explicitly rejected.[397] The frequent designation of Christians as 'slaves of God' (Luke 2.29) or as 'slaves of Christ' (thus for example Paul of himself in Rom. 1) does not imply any criticism of this structural principle, but was an expression of a pious simile: just as the father of the house can require respect and obedience from his slaves (and in the ideal case can offer them protection and lodging in exchange), so God requires respect and obedience of those who as his creatures are within his sphere of rule. Christian demands for gentleness in dealing with slaves then arise against the background of what initially was an extraordinarily strict law for slaves, with its right to chastisement and other physical violence. However, as has been said, this happens without the institution being fundamentally put in doubt. Ernst Troeltsch coined the expression 'a Christian patriarchalism of love'[398] for this attitude, which *mutatis mutandis* corresponds to the relationship between the sexes, and many examples of this can be collected: it has been worked out that, for example, the letter to the community in Colossae in Asia Minor which comes from Paul's school uses fifty-six words to admonish slaves to obedience, but only eighteen to call on their owners to be gentle.[399] And along these lines the first Christian church order quotes an earlier Jewish text: 'Do not give your male slave or your female slave, who hope in the same God, any orders when you are bitter, lest they cease to fear the God who is over you both . . . And you slaves, be subject to your master in reverence and fear as to God's representative.'[400] The Alexandrian theologians were comparative critical of slavery. They accepted the philosophical criticism of this legal form, but without pleading for its abolition. Origen wrote: 'Why do I need to point out how reasonable is the law which prohibits any Jew from being the slave of a fellow believer for more than six years, and how this harms neither master nor slave!'[401] Of course it was easy for Origen to say that. He did not need any slaves, since a rich patron financed an opulent private scriptorium with seven stenographers, seven copyists and seven calligraphers.[402] If we leave aside small groups like the Circumcellions, which in part consisted of runaway slaves, circulated in Numidia in North

Africa between 340 and 420,, and forcibly compelled masters to free slaves,[403] we can sum up the Christian attitude in the words 'an invitation to moderation along with a fundamental affirmation'. However, the Christians could not escape a degree of 'rebrutalization' of slavery in late antiquity.[404] The Synod of Elvira stimulated that if a mistress killed her slave girl in anger, the mistress should be excluded from communion for seven years (in cases of murder) or for five (in cases of manslaughter). The case presupposed is flogging which leads to death within three days. In the middle of the fourth century, the synod of Gangra anathematized those who instructed slaves not to 'serve their master loyally and honourably', but led them astray into 'despising them under the semblance of fear of God and into leaving their service'.[405] John Chrysostom put forward the view that, like the first Jerusalem Christians, a Christian should really have no slaves at all, or at most one or two. After all, God did not make any slaves for Adam. Slaves were to be trained in useful occupations and then set free: 'If you strike them and cast them into prison, this is not an expression of your brotherly love.'[406] He advises the slaves: 'For the sake of Christ, let us serve our masters', after previously consoling them: 'Slavery is only an empty name. The domination merely extends to the body, is transitory and of short duration.'[407] Chrysostom several times explained his basic maxim as meaning that 'Christ did not give his laws to overthrow the state order, but to improve it, and to teach us that we should not wage superfluous and useless battles against it.'[408] Moreover the preacher's criticism of slavery is less strict than that of the misuse of riches.[409]

For all the gentleness, probably most well-to do Christians agreed with the pagan conviction that if slaves were not punished, they were led astray into evil-doing. Lucius Caelius Lactantius, born in Africa and at the beginning of the fourth century state teacher of rhetoric in the residence cities of Nicomedia and Trier, writes this in a treatise 'On the Wrath of God'. His advice to rulers is first of all to moderate their wrath and only then to chastize. Nevertheless he thinks it natural that people are enraged when they see 'sins in the house . . . for the sight of sin is itself enough to put one into a rage'.[410]

The status of women

This basic tendency to affirm a particular social order while at the same time attempting to mitigate its harshnesses also applies to the way Christians dealt with the status of the woman – though here there are clearer divergences from the majority norm than in the case of slavery. Jesus' open way of dealing with women met with a greater response among different movements on the periphery of the church than in the majority church. However, grotesquely false results are obtained when occasionally a rule is derived from this that the movements excluded from the majority church were in principle more friendly to women that the majority church, and that the fact of their exclusion was connected with the different way in which they deal with women. If one may sum up their extremely different tendencies in this respect at all, movements like 'Gnosticism' were just as friendly or hostile to women as the rest of the church.

Women played a major role in the dissemination of Christianity, as is already evident from the New Testament. For example, house communities in Rome, Corinth and Ephesus gathered around a Prisca/Priscilla (I Cor. 16.19; Rom. 16.3); she may have had the status of a teacher and community leader there. At the beginning of the second century a number of prominent women evidently played a role in the Christian community in Smyrna in Asia Minor, since they are given a special greeting in the letters of bishop Ignatius of Antioch: Alce and Tavia/Gavia or the wife of the governor.[411] Just as in the early period of the empire women could develop a considerable degree of autonomy as those who ran the house, so here women were in charge of house communities. In any case Asia Minor seems to have been a region of early Christianity which was comparatively 'woman-friendly': in the second half of the second century a number of prophetic women put their stamp on a Phrygian movement, though it was named 'Montanism' after a man called Montanus. However, they already reported resistance to their preaching – thus a statement by the prophetess Maximilla: 'I am driven away as a wolf from sheep; I am not a wolf, I am word and spirit and power.'[412] One of their messages corresponded entirely to the proclamation of the majority church and ran: 'Do not listen to me, but listen to Christ!'[413] Pliny the Younger, the governor of the province of Bithynia in Asia Minor between AD 111 and 113, had two slave girls tortured in accordance with current legal practice, 'who were called deaconesses, but I discovered nothing else than a perverse and extravagant superstition'.[414] Some names of women who were patronesses of theologians or ascetics have also been handed down over a period from the second to the fourth centuries; but similar activities on the part of pagan women were already not uncontroversial in the first century, as is shown by the divided reaction to them on the part of Livia, the emperor's consort (58 BC–AD 29). All these references to the domination of women in the communities can be related not only to the impulses of Jesus and the first generation but also to an emancipatory tendency in the life of women in the early empire, though this had ebbed away by the fourth century at the latest.[415] A reflection of this development is the increasing marginalization of women, which stands out when we compare the church history of Origen's pupil Eusebius (four editions between AD 295 and 325) with the church histories of the fifth century (Socrates, Sozomen and Theodoret).[416] However, already in Paul (I Cor. 11.5f. or 14.33–36) and then again in other late New Testament writings (I Tim. 2.11–15) we find harsh invectives against women who speak prophetically or teach otherwise in public worship. An 'exchange of roles' between men and women was in any case never debated in Christian antiquity, as a remark by John Chrysostom shows: '(A woman) gives her spouse complete security, frees him from all household cares, looks after money, wool-working, the preparation of food and the right clothing. She deals with all these matters, which it is not fitting for her husband to engage in, nor could he carry them out satisfactorily, should he put his hand to them – even if he made an honest effort.'[417] So on this point too, almost from the beginning, for the most part the Christian community did not succeed in implementing Jesus' intentions with real consistency in the face of over-powerful gender roles. Whatever in actual fellowship between women and men in the early communities touched on or removed the restrictions imposed by gender and social status took the form of offices reserved for women (see 194f. below), and whatever broke the dominance of the male priesthood fell short of what would have been possible – or rather, what may seem to us today to have been possible.

Asceticism and monasticism

Asceticism

In its basic form, the Greek word *askesis* means to work carefully or 'behave virtuously in order to strengthen the character'. Only in the popular philosophical lectures of the early period of the empire is the term narrowed down to mean 'continence' and the renunciation of every possible pleasure and enjoyment.[418] Asceticism now means separation from the world, or more precisely the separation from the body which provides the link with society and the world. In this case the founder certainly does not stand at the beginning of the development towards a Christian form of asceticism: Jesus of Nazareth evidently did not continue the ascetic tendencies of John the Baptist. His disciples did not fast (Mark 2.18f.), and his practice of sharing meals with groups which were on the periphery or outside religion and society aroused criticism (Matt. 11.18–20). Nevertheless, already in the New Testament there are the beginnings of a morality of the 'better righteousness' which can be read, and indeed have been read, in the sense of a two-level ethic: whereas according to Mark Jesus further advised the well-to-do young man to sell his possessions with the words 'one thing you still lack' (Mark 10.21), in Matthew the invitation runs: 'If you want to be perfect . . .' (Matt. 19.21), so that here one could now distinguish between a simpler morality (namely the Ten Commandments: Matt. 19.18–20) and a more perfect morality, which implies the complete renunciation of possessions and riches. It is clear that the historical Jesus did not intend a legal schematization of this kind; he evidently tolerated very different forms of discipleship around him – provided that each person in his or her situation took the confession seriously. The separation of a specifically ascetic ethic is initially a phenomenon of the acculturation of the Jesus movement, since society in antiquity was familiar with different forms of ascetic life, both in the Jewish and in the pagan spheres. Moreover Christianity participated in tendencies which were latently hostile to the body, and which in the most varied forms permeate ancient texts, as some random examples can show. A contemporary of Cicero, the Latin grammarian Gavius Bassus, associated the Latin word *coelebs* (unmarried) with *caeles* (heavenly) and the Greek term for young companion (*eïtheos*) with the term for God (*theos*)[419] – historically a quite untenable etymology but an interesting indication of a mood of the time. Examples of this kind pile up in the fourth century: the Neoplatonic philosopher Porphyry began the description of the life of his teacher Plotinus (died AD 270) with the statement: 'Plotinus the philosopher . . . was the kind of man who was ashamed to be stuck in a body.' In another work the same author wrote: 'Sexual intercourse pollutes'.[420] Another Neoplatonic philosopher, Iamblichus, reported at around the same time with great sympathy on the communism of possessions among the Pythagoreans: 'Pythagoras . . . completely banished from the lifestyle of his pupils the tie to private property . . . This extended to the least of possessions, as these could foment discord and confusion.'[421] At present there is much talk about Jewish ascetic movements of the early empire like the community of Khirbet Qumran in the Jewish wilderness; its monastic-type settlement, its strict disciplinary rule, its scholarly work, to which we owe the extensive library of texts that has been discovered, and its life-style (communism of goods, obedience to the leaders, study of the law and manual work) seem to be a kind of anticipation of life in the various Christian monastic foundations which came to be established around four hundred years later, also in the Judaean wilderness and no great distance away. The Alexandrian Jewish philosopher of religion Philo described a comparable group, the 'Therapeutae' (servants). Here too the

Pagan parallels

Jewish parallels

parallels to later Christian institutions are striking: 'The interval between early morning and evening is spent entirely in spiritual exercises (*askesis*): they read the holy scriptures . . . They do not confine themselleves to contemplation but also compose hymns and psalms to God in all sorts of metres and melodies which they wrote down.'[422] The same goes for their meals: 'At this meal . . . no wine is brought, but only water of the brightest and clearest, cold for most but warm for such of the older men who live delicately. The table too is kept free from the flesh of animals; the food laid on it is loaves of bread with salt as a seasoning . . . When the guests have laid themselves down arranged in rows . . . then a general silence falls . . . Then their leader discusses some question arising in the holy scriptures or one that has been propounded by someone else.'[423] Scholars over the years have given very different answers to the question whether the amazing similarities also indicate historical dependence. However, here as elsewhere convergences have been confused with causalities.

Beginnings

The beginnings of a wider Christian ascetic movement might still lie in the second century – at any rate, for example, we have such texts in the form of the anonymous Syriac letters, originally written in Greek, *On Virginity*, which date from the Syria-Palestine of the third century. These groups still had a number of similarities with the itinerant primitive Christian teachers, those engaged in the early mission in the first century and who are now called 'itinerant radicals'.[424] They too still went around preaching, teaching, offering intercessions and doing miracles. In the letters *On Virginity* a two-level ethic is developed which grounds the 'virginity' of men and women (the term is applied to both sexes) in 'for the sake of the kingdom of heaven' (cf. Matt. 19.12): 'Whoever is in truth righteous, his works bear testimony to his faith.'[425] 'For the mere name without works does not lead us to the kingdom of heaven.' 'Whoever desires greater and better things, renounces the whole world and separates himself from it, so that he goes on to lead a godly, heavenly life like the holy angels, in pure and holy service and in the holiness of the Spirit of God, and so that he may serve God, the Almighty, through Jesus Christ, for the sake of the kingdom of heaven. Therefore he has detached himself from all desires of the body and has not just renounced that "Be fruitful and multiply" (Gen. 1.28).' Thus the goal of those ascetics is an angelic life in the greatest possible conformity to Christ: 'Unless he or she is like Christ and those who are Christ's in every respect, no virgin can be saved.'[426]

These early ascetic movements not only propagated continence (*encrateia,* hence partly also the Encratites) in questions of food (no alcohol, dietary requirements), but also expressed the sharpest criticism of sexuality and marriage. Thus for example an account of the actions of the apostle Thomas which was similarly written in Syria at the beginning of the third century foisted a radical criticism of marriage, sex and the family on Jesus himself: 'If you abandon this filthy intercourse you become holy temples . . .' The unknown author warned against children: for the most part they are possessed by evil spirits, 'lunatic or half-withered or crippled or deaf and dumb or paralytic or stupid'. And healthy children commit adultery, murder or theft and thus afflict their parents.[427] The author advised the unmarried to remain unmarried; the married to refuse themselves to their partner, for example in the following way: 'But she cried, "Henceforth you have no place with me, for my Lord Jesus who is with me and rests in me is greater than you."'[428] The Encratites (the 'Continent') legitimated these views by a special exegesis of the biblical creation story: they interpreted sexuality as a consequence of the Fall, which made the first human beings like the beasts. Adam and Eve did not yet have sexual intercourse with one another in the innocence of paradise. This harsh view, critical of marriage, would of course have resulted in completely breaking and finally destroying the cycle of birth and death, indeed the functioning of the economy, the state and society generally. In view of these truly gloomy prospects it is not surprising that Christian theologians emphasized the sanctity of marriage, in order also to keep the positive tone of the primitive Christian statements on this form of life.

Monastic asceticism

Out of this pre-monastic Syrian asceticism, as depicted for example in the letters *On Virginity* and the Acts of Thomas, which in a sense still remained within the community, real monastic asceticism outside the community developed in the course of the third century. Its characteristic may be seen as a clear departure from the community, physical separation from the rest of the world around. That is already clear from the term 'monk', which is derived from the Greek *monachos* – originally it means 'alone'.[429] Evidently in Syrian Christianity it became established as a term for ascetic life devoted to spiritual perfection. It is hardly possible to demonstrate more completely why such movements came into being in the third century in particular. Simply to explain the phenomenon as a protest against the increasing secularization of the church corresponds to a modern Protestant tradition of digging deep ditches between piety and the official church.[430] Ancient sources speak of the need for the monk to flee above all from bishops and women (thus John Cassian, who lived in Egypt for a long time and became an important figure in the dissemination of monasticism in the West of the empire[431]); these texts point more to motifs which are critical of the hierarchy and of sexuality. Moreover we cannot overlook the fact that at least in the fourth century the ascetic model of life also gained considerably in plausibility in pagan circles, among philosophers and more ordinary people. On the other hand, many biographies of founding fathers – both from Egypt and from Syria – show that reasons so to speak intrinsic to asceticism led these people to retreat into solitude: at the beginning of the fifth century, Simeon, the pillar saint (see above, 108f.), first climbed a hill in order to set himself apart from the less strict monastic ascetics; then a pillar which was raised three times, so that he was not disturbed by the excessive throng of pilgrims. Antony, the real founder of eremitical asceticism (anchorite monasticism), began asceticism in the second half of the third century first of all in his own house. Only later did he follow the example of an anonymous hermit and 'began to stay in places outside the village'.[432] The catalyst was apparently one of the central proof-texts for a two-level ethic in the New Testament, 'If you would be perfect . . .'[433] His preaching again 'persuaded many to embrace the solitary life. And thus it happened in the end that cells arose even in the mountains, and the desert was colonized by monks who came forth from their own people and enrolled themselves for the citizenship in the heavens.'[434] After the death of her betrothed, Macrina, the first person to have left tangible traces in literature, who founded a convent, refused betrothal a second time because she still felt bound to this 'absent bridegroom in a strange land'. According to her brother Gregory of Nyssa, in his description of her life, at the age of twelve (i.e. in AD 339) she resolved 'to remain single. And this decision was stronger than her age (viz. might have suggested).'[435] Gregory describes the way from this decision to the foundation of a convent for women as a consistent and coherent development in several steps. According to information from various intrinsically consistent accounts of his life, Pachomius, who founded a monastery in Tabennisi ('The Palms of Isis', in Upper Egypt, 100 kilometres south of Sohag on the Nile), became the ancestor of 'coenobite monasticism' after hearing a voice and seeing a vision which called him.[436] Even such trivial and non-religious motives as the flight of people from the land in an attempt to avoid the extraordinarily harsh conditions of agricultural work, the increasing burden of taxation or the rising financial obligations for curials, those who qualified for councils of state, played a role in the increasing significance of monasticism in Christianity in late antiquity. In 365 the emperor Valens even prohibited the acceptance into monasteries of curials seeking to avoid the sponsorship now increasingly imposed on them by law.[437]

The 'stars' of asceticism in late antiquity who gained the most publicity were to be found in Syria;[438] they did not live deep in a hostile desert beyond cultivated land (like many Egyptian monks), but on its periphery. Their monasteries and hermitages stood up and down the hills which run through the limestone massif of north Syria – they rose, clearly visible, above the fertile area which was used above all for growing olives. Of course this exposed position was chosen quite deliberately: thus the pillar on which St Simeon stood served as a kind of 'lighthouse' for the surrounding area.[439] The hordes of seasonal workers engaged for the harvest, craftsmen attached to projects, and also travellers found here an orientation in their unstable life. But at the same time, as we already saw, the ascetics took over the role which the patrons in village communities overwhelmingly exercised for prosperous farmers.

Harshness

We should have no illusions about the quite inhuman harshness of the asceticism. Antony is said often not to have slept at night, and to have eaten only once during the day, after sunset; often, though, he ate only after two, sometimes even only after four, days. His whole diet is said to have consisted of bread, salt and water. Nevertheless, 'he began to debate with himself how he could get used to an even harsher regime'.[440] Each ascetic sought to outdo the other in strictness: when Macarius of Alexandria heard of other monks who during the forty days fast before Easter ate nothing cooked but only raw stuff (so-called 'homophagy', Greek for 'eating raw'), 'he resolved for seven years to eat nothing that had been through the fire'.[441] 'Another time Macarius wanted to dispense with sleep and therefore, as he himself related, remained in the open air for twenty days, scorched by the sun during the day and shrivelled up with cold by night. He said (viz. after the end of this torture): "Unless I had soon gone under a roof and got some sleep, my brain would have so dried up as to drive me into delirium for ever after. And I conquered as far as depended on me, but I gave way so far as depended on my nature that had need of sleep."'[442] This competition over fasting had absurd consequences – at least for present-day taste: worms crept out of the teeth of the hermit Batthaeus of Edessa after he had fasted for a very long time.[443]

Simeon Stylites

In the biography of his friend Simeon, the pillar saint, Theodoret reports that in a forty-day fast Simeon 'lay as if lifeless on the ground. He could not speak and could not move. Then he (viz. Bassus, the leader of the country priests) asked for a sponge, moistened and thus cleansed his mouth and gave him the form of the divine mysteries (viz. bread and wine). Thus strengthened, he arose and took some food, lettuce, endives and the like. Without chewing much, he swallowed it down.'[444] Theodoret also relates that the pillar saint stood day and night on the small platform on the top of his pillar and prostrated himself. 'Once one of my companions counted one thousand two hundred and forty four (prostrations). But then he grew tired and stopped counting. When he bows, he always lowers his head to his toes. Only once a week does his body receive food, and that very scanty. Thus his back maintains its easy mobility.'[445] Already in his first monastery Simeon had stood out by virtue of his abnormal tendency towards asceticism – and for that reason had been expelled by his fellow brothers: he struck his back with ropes until blood came, fasted for months, fought against the tendency to sleep by constantly standing, and once had himself bricked up for ten years. He spent thirty years on the platform, barely four metres broad, on his pillar, around twenty metres high, with no roof, protected from sun, wind and rain only by a hood and a sheepskin over his garment. Once a week he was brought food on a ladder; a channel provided for the simplest hygiene.[446] Once when a pilgrim from Ravenna in northern Italy asked him whether he was human or an incorporeal being (i.e. an angel), Simeon showed him the suppurating wound which he had caused himself by constant standing. Theodoret's account ends: 'With amazement the man beheld the terrible sore and learned that the saint took nourishment.'[447]

The detailed account of Simeon's life in Syriac, probably the official Life produced by his monastery,[448] raised a question which is still interesting today. With a few changes it could be addressed to a great many ascetics: 'Perhaps there is someone who says, "What drove him?" or "Was it necessary for him to put himself on a pillar? Could he not have pleased God on earth or in this corner?" . . . Wherever a person calls on God in an upright way, there he finds him . . . But in the case of the lord Simeon it pleased his Lord to put him on the pillar in those days and in the last times, for he saw that humankind had so to speak gone to sleep. Through the torment of his saint he wanted to awaken the world which was sunk in deep sleep.'[449] The ascetic as the amazing example of special, tormenting piety, with which God wants to shake sleeping humankind awake – this theological interpretation of a radical ascetic individual neutralizes the threat which such lives pose to those members of the community in town and country who live in families and are bound up in a profession, and completes the integration into society which Simeon himself had in fact made above all through his activity in counselling.

The expectations which the 'ordinary' members of the community had of ascetics and monks were high, as a more or less chance example can show. A letter by a Christian named Justin to a monk named Paphnuthius has been preserved from fourth-century Egypt. From it we can reconstruct that a brother of Justin's took this letter to the monk with a 'small amount of oil' as a gift of thanks. The author asked Paphnuthius, whom he addresses as 'Master', 'to think of me in your holy prayers', in other words for the service of intercession. The layman evidently attached great importance to the prayer of the religious professional, since he regards the outcome of the last judgment as being already decided for the monk whom he is addressing: 'We believe in your citizenship in heaven,' he says, alluding to Paul (Phil.3.20): 'Therefore we regard you, the Master, as a new man.' The monk has put off the old man with its body marked by transitoriness: as such his intercession with God may do more than that of an 'old man'.[450] There are many parallels to this formula in the letter: a late one, from the sixth century, comes from a woman called Kyra: she reminds the monks of the duty of intercession and beseeches them 'by the mysteries of Christ which are being performed in these days', i.e. by the eucharist.[451]

Ancient criticism of asceticism

But ascetic attitudes also incurred criticism. For example, an anonymous but well-informed pagan critic ironically asked how it was that if Jesus had given no commandment about virgins (thus Paul in I Cor. 7.25), 'some people boast of their virginity as if it were a great thing and say that they are filled by the Holy Spirit in the same way as she who bore Jesus' (viz. Mary).[452] A Phrygian inscription from the beginning of the fourth century reports on an Ammia who to the great grief of her parents refused to marry; it gives us an insight into the family drama of a Phrygian country family.[453] Only after her early death did a vision lead her parents to acknowledge her way of life – in it they wanted to see their daughter as she declared : 'My saviour Jesus Christ has made me righteous.'[454] And this perceived authority clearly convinced the desperate parents.

The Community

In a way which cannot be derived either from the contemporary rabbinate or from apocalyptic prophecy, Jesus of Nazareth gathered around himself a community of people who were closely bound together and evidently already had an internal hierarchy. These people followed him. Just as according to the testimony of the Old Testament, prophets were called by God (e.g. Isa.6.8–10), so in the place of God Jesus called people to follow him.[455] Whereas the first disciples (men and women) sometimes broke radically with their origin, their calling and their place of abode, from the beginning there were also supporters (again both men and women) who remained where they were in their particular occupation and environment. From the beginning, conversion to Jesus Christ was also bound up with a change (Greek *metanoia*, in English also 'repentance'). Those who attached themselves to the community at least in part departed from their previous attitudes and modes of action; they confessed these as 'sin' and experienced forgiveness. However, both Gospels and Acts describe in a comparatively matter-of-fact way how despite repentance and the confession of sins, from the beginning this community was endangered by disputes over rank (Matt. 18.1–5 or 20.20–28), by selfishness (Acts 5.1–11) and by fear (John 20.19). Above all both the apostle Paul and the evangelist John understood Christian life and Christian sonship as communion with God or Christ (also with Christ's suffering and death: Rom. 6; I Cor. 10.14–22), but also as a fellowship of believers which is to be marked by mutual concern and respect for the weak (Rom. 12–14). That corresponds to Jesus' 'community' ethic of brotherhood and sisterhood. For Paul, discipleship of Jesus takes shape in the community as the 'body of Christ' (Rom. 12.5/I Cor. 12.27).

The idea

The idea of community was also an influential social concept in pagan Graeco-Roman culture; that has left its mark on the sociability of the people of the ancient world. Epictetus, who taught Stoic philosophy in Western Greece at the end of the first and beginning of the second century, accordingly called human beings 'social beings';[456] the organizational expression of such views is to be found in the rich development of associations at this time. Thus members of associations of merchants, tradesmen and tenants – we can imagine these as a parallel to our limited partnerships – usually called one another 'friends'. However, at the latest by the end of the first century, the Christians, whose form of community organization may have reminded pagan contemporaries of such an association, excluded themselves from the special right to form a religious community which had been granted to Judaism (Tertullian calls this a 'permitted religion', *religio licita*[457]). Thus the mere confession of Christianity could become the basis of a charge and a death sentence. Only after the great persecutions in the middle of the third and beginning of the fourth century was the practice of the Christian religion tolerated (see 28f. above), and more: in the course of Constantine's religious legislation, from 320 on the clergy also formed a corporation or body acknowledged by the state.[458] The comparison between the Christian community and the civil community was an obvious one: Origen made it in the middle of the third century in the form of an antithesis: 'The Church of God, say, at Athens is meek and quiet, since it desires to please God. But the assembly of the Athenians is riotous and in no way comparable to the Church of God there. You may say the same of the Church of God at Corinth and the assembly of the people of the Corinthians, and of the Church of God, say, at Alexandria and the assembly of the people of Alexandria.'[459]

Terminology

A look at the terminology of Christian community in antiquity allows us to make interesting inferences to the theology of community. In early Christianity the Greek word for 'community', *koinonia,* is almost never used as a designation for pure 'community' or 'fellowship' of believers among one another, but, in a continuation of Pauline conceptuality (I Cor. 10.16), was transferred to the sacrament of the eucharist and understood in the light of it.[460] In order to demonstrate the incompatibility of Christian and pagan worship the apostle wrote: 'The cup which we bless, is it not the communion *(koinonia)* of the blood of Christ? The bread which we break, is it not the communion (*koinonia)* of the body of Christ? We being many are one body, because we all partake of the one bread' (I Cor. 10.16–17). For Paul, through the eucharistic food people are thus incorporated into the 'body of Christ', and to this degree come into a 'communion' with God. Of course the theologians of antiquity were not unaware that a community assembled for this purpose, but like the apostle they interpreted this assembly as a divine work by relating themselves to the Pauline notion and talk of the 'body of Christ'. Thus, for example, Chrysostom in his sermons on I Corinthians: 'For what do I mean by *koinonia*? . . . We are ourselves the body. For what is the bread? The body of Christ. And what do they become who partake (viz. of this sacrament)? The body of Christ. Not many bodies but one body. For we are all partakers of that one bread. For just as the bread consisting of many grains is made one, so that the grains nowhere appear; they exist indeed but their difference is not seen by reason of their conjunction, so we are conjoined with one another and with Christ: there not being one body for you and another for your neighbour to be nourished by, but the very same for all. Wherefore he also adds, "For we are all partakers of the one bread." Now if we are all nourished by the same and all become the same, why do we not also show forth the same love?'[461] The believers are designated such a community with other terms, for example through the expressions 'assembly' (*congregatio)* or 'community' (*communitas*). At the latest from the beginning of the third century the Latin expression *communio* denotes a relationship, 'namely the community of its members, produced by the church in respect of the faith, the confession, and of course also the sacraments. The use of the word can also be narrowed down by church law. It then means the church communion existing between the bishops on the basis of reciprocal recognition of orthodoxy and orthopraxy, but never the totality of bishops.'[462]

Norms

From the end of the second century the community described in this way was stabilized and safeguarded by three basic criteria – rule of faith, canon of scripture and church ministry – designated the 'three apostolic norms'.[463] The old idea that the disordered early life of the community in the Spirit was fixed in this way in a kind of legislative act more than 150 years after the origin of Christianity, and thus at the same time also distorted, corresponded more to the current needs of liberal Protestant theology at the end of the nineteenth century than to the historical reality of the age of the Roman empire. Short, succinct formulations of the faith which varied in detail ('rule of faith' or 'canon of truth') were based on the substance of Christian faith as it was alive in the communities and betrayed the specific theological views of the authors who formulated them in action. A normativity was not imposed, but arose. Nor should the origin of a canon of biblical writings, the nucleus of which was normed, be interpreted as a sudden normative action with a concern alien to primitive Christianity. Rather, it was an organic development from the authoritative self-awareness of Jesus (see above 84); despite all the development we should see a similar continuity to the beginnings in the case of the ministry (see below, 183–95). Of course we must not overestimate the capacities of these three 'norms';[464] the theological and organizational problems of the Christian communities in the third century were resolved, on the basis described, by independent theological and social developments.

Community life

Size of communities

In the early pre-Constantinian period many details of community life remain obscure, because it is not until the great cycles of sermons in the fourth and fifth centuries that we have information about the everyday life of the Christian churches.

Thus it is almost impossible at this period to get any concrete information about the size of communities. We are first given firm figures for the urban Roman community, at any rate the Christian church of the imperial capital, in a letter from 251. But since for understandable reasons the metropolis had a particularly high proportion of pagans in its population until well into the fourth century, and at least the Christian Roman community was particularly important for the church as a whole, we should not in any case generalize from this individual piece of information. Bishop Cornelius of Rome is writing to his colleague Fabius of Antioch: a bishop, he says, presided over the Roman community 'in which there are forty-six priests, seven deacons, seven subdeacons, forty-two, fifty-two exorcists, readers and doorkeepers, and more than fifteen hundred widows and persons in distress, all of whom are supported by the goodness and loving-kindness of the Lord.'[465] The number of people fed by the community through its finances remains impressive. But as long as we cannot discover how many of the approximately 700,000 inhabitants of Rome were Christians, it is just an isolated fact. Granted, attempts have been made to calculate the number of Christians as 7,000 church members from the proportion of the needy to the population as a whole,[466] but that presupposes that there were not more needy in the Christian communities or that not more of them were supported than in the rest of society. And in view of the underdeveloped system of social welfare during the time of the Roman empire, that would be the more improbable assumption. For the period after Constantine we have the extremely interesting information from Gaza (above, 115 f.), but of course the authenticity of that is disputed.

Level of education

Nor should we have any illusions about the level of education of many Christian communities, despite the many reports of prosperous and educated members of the community which have constantly been quoted in this account. Here is a single example. Above Lake Genessaret in a south-easterly direction lies the town of Gadara (present-day Umm Qeis, directly on the frontier between Israel and Jordan). Excavations of baths both on the hill and at sea level (the latter near hot springs which are still used today) attest the comparative prosperity of the town. We must not underestimate the favourable climate to education in the town and the educational level achieved: Menippus, the inventor of satire (third century BCE) came from there, as did the epigrammatist Meleager (second/first century BCE) – he wrote the lines 'Gadara was my home/ that new Athens in the Assyrian land'.[467] Somewhat later, according to Suidas, Theodoros was born there; he was the son of a slave and between 33 and 30 BC taught Tiberius, later to become emperor (so well, that Tiberius was able to give a funeral oration for his physical father Tiberius Claudius Nero at the age of nine[468]). Finally, at the beginning of the second century AD the town was the home of the Cynic Oinomaus. In view of this proud list, which is not even complete, it is not a little surprising that in the fifth century the bishop of the Christian community in this town could not even write: in the acts of the Council of Ephesus the chief pastor Theodorus, who was personally present in this metropolis in Asia Minor, did not sign in person, but through his archdeacon Aetherius. And twenty years later, at the great council in the imperial summer residence of Chalcedon, Bishop Theodorus had still not learned to write. Aetherius signed again for him: 'I, Theodorus, Bishop of Gadara, have signed by the hand of another, namely that of the archdeacon Aetherius.'[469] Evidently the bishop was one of the two-thirds of the population of the empire at this time who have been calculated to have been illiterate.[470]

Worship

Right from the beginning, community life centred on the assemblies, on worship and the shared meal. The celebration of the Lord's Supper, i.e. the action named 'eucharist', 'thanksgiving', from the second century on, is the specific and central worship of Christians at the latest from the third century.[471] At the beginning of the development stands Jesus' last supper before his execution in Jerusalem. The so-called 'words of institution' which report the foundation of a memorial meal by the historical Jesus (I Cor. 11.23–25 or Matt. 26.26–29; Mark 14.22–25 and Luke 22.15–20) may themselves already have been formulated as sections of liturgical texts, i.e. as passages intended to be recited in worship. At any rate, Christian cultic forms developed from the normal 'liturgical' course of the Jewish meal on the basis of this last meal of Jesus and the communal meals held by the primitive community. Initially, full meals with a liturgical order (*agape*) and a sacramental, i.e. eucharistic, meal were not yet separated. Christian brotherly and sisterly love (*agape*) was made concrete in shared meals in which the more prominent were meant to make it possible for their poorer fellow Christians to fill themselves (I Cor. 11.21f.). Presumably around the middle of the second century the meal proper and the cultic meal were finally separated completely.

Eucharist

Remarkably, we find the first extensive account of the course of the independent cultic meal in a text intended for non-Christians, the *Apology* by the Roman theologian Justin. The author describes how the eucharist was preceded by a communal prayer of intercession and the brotherly kiss which introduced the celebration proper. 'Bread and a cup with water and wine' were brought to 'the president of the brethren';[472] it was in accord with ancient practice never to drink wine undiluted. 'He, taking them, sends up praise and glory to the Father of the universe through the name of the Son and of the Holy Spirit, and offers thanksgiving (*eucharistia*) at some length that we have been deemed worthy to receive these things from him. When he has finished the prayers and the thanksgiving, the whole congregation present assents, saying, "Amen" . . . When the president has given thanks and the whole congregation has assented, those whom we call deacons give to each of those present a portion of the consecrated bread and wine and water, and they take it to the absent' (the so-called *apophoreta* = gifts).[473] Justin also explains that this food is called 'eucharist', and that the unbaptized are not allowed to partake of it. 'For we do not receive these things as common bread or common drink; but as Jesus Christ our Saviour being incarnate by God's word took flesh and blood for our salvation, so also we have been taught that the food consecrated by the word of prayer which comes from him, from which our flesh and blood are nourished by transformation, is the flesh and blood of that incarnate Jesus.'[474] The New Testament account of the institution was thus recited at the celebration of the eucharist in the urban community in Rome in the second century, at least in nucleus and perhaps in that liturgical short form which Justin himself reports; moreover the eucharistic elements were evidently understood by analogy with the theories of nourishment in antiquity: according to Justin, like any food consumed they were transformed into the flesh and blood of the one who ate them. So what was claimed was not a transformation of the elements but a transformation of the one who consumed them. Not everyone was admitted to the sacrament of the eucharist; the Didache already prohibits the consumption of the wine and the bread of the eucharist by those who have not been baptized: 'For about this too the Lord has said, "Do not give the holy to the dogs."'[475] The doors were guarded by deacons or subdeacons. The calls for self-examination which John Chrysostom addressed to his community, along with warnings about celebrating Christian feasts in purity, also take this line: 'We should not act as we do now, approaching because of the season rather than from any earnestness of mind. For we do not consider how we may approach prepared, purged of the ills that were within us . . . but how we may come on festivals, when all do so. No one ought to be compelled to approach by reason of the festival if indolently disposed and reluctantly, nor should anyone prevent him because it is not a festival if he is penitent and prepared.'[476]

The analogies between this sacred meal and the various similar meals in other pagan cults of antiquity already struck contemporaries, who made their comments on them. For example, Justin defended himself against the charge that in their eucharist Christians were imitating features of the mysteries of Mithras by simply reversing it: 'The evil demons in the Mithras mysteries have also imitated this custom.'[477] That could indeed be the case if the genuine Roman Mithras mysteries together with their (initiation?) meal of bread and water in fact came into being later than Christianity;[478] in any case a historical derivation of one practice from the other remains quite improbable. Moreover the clientele of the two cults had nothing in common: the Mithras mysteries flourished above all between AD 140 and 312 in Rome and on the military frontiers of the Roman empire, and were particularly widespread among officers and officials from the *equites* on the one hand and slaves and freemen of the emperor on the other.

Agape

After the agapes had been separated from eucharistic worship, their character changed and they became an instrument of the communal meal concentrated on the welfare of the poor. By a detailed description, in his *Apology* Tertullian attempted to remove pagan suspicions and prejudices against this form of Christian meeting: 'Our feast explains itself by its name. The Greeks call it agape, i.e. love. Whatever it costs, our outlay in the name of piety is gain, since with the good things of the feast we benefit the needy. If the object of our feast is good, in the light of that consider its further regulations. As it is an act of religious service, it permits no vileness or immodesty. The participants, before eating, taste first of prayer to God. As much is eaten as satisfies the cravings of hunger: as much is drunk as befits the chaste. After washing of hands and the bringing of lights each is asked to stand forth and sing, as he can, a hymn to God, either from one of the Holy Scriptures or one of his own composing – a proof of the measure of our drinking.'[479] That Tertullian is depicting the ideal case for apologetic reasons is evident from his roughly contemporaneous colleague Clement in Alexandria, with his polemic against degeneracy. After a long and malicious enumeration of sweetmeats and other delicacies which the Christian in-people of the metropolis spread on their table ('birds from Phasis, the Egyptian snipe and the Median peafowl . . . These gluttons, surrounded with the sound of hissing frying-pans, and wearing their whole life away at the pestle and the mortar, cling to matter like fire'[480]). Clement, a theorist with a moderate appetite, comes to the point: 'They dishonour the good and saving work of the Word, the consecrated agape, with pots and pouring of sauce; and by drink and delicacies and smoke not deserving that name they are deceived in their idea.'[481] However, a form of agape under the direction of the clergy was held down to the fourth century, sometimes even in the church. Thus for example a synod in Laodicea in Phrygia stipulated 'that one must not hold so-called agapes in church buildings or churches, and eat and set up sofas for food in the house of God'.[482]

Liturgy of the word

In his Apology in the middle of the second century Justin also gave an account of the Sunday liturgy of the word. On this day 'there is a meeting in one place of those who live in the cities or in the country, and the memoirs of the apostles or the writings fo the prophets are read out as long as time permits. When the reader has finished, the president in a discourse urges and invites [us] to the imitation of these noble things.'[483] Thus the worship has a fixed order of reading (perhaps a continuous reading in sections, as in the synagogue) with passages from the Gospels of the New Testament, in process of formation, or the prophetic writings of the Old Testament. This combination of a reading from scripture, a homily and a concluding prayer comes from contemporary synagogue worship, and along with some details of prayer language shows how much Christian worship owes to the Jewish synagogue.

Further development

The further development of the Christian liturgy in the third and fourth centuries is stamped on the one hand by a great variability and geographical multiplicity. The reason for this is that up to the middle of the third century the bishops had had the freedom to improvise a substantial part of the liturgy of sacramental worship (in particular the main eucharistic prayer). Only in the fourth century did a tendency 'from freedom to formula',[484] which had already been present for some time, finally establish itself. Nevertheless Christian worship remained indebted to its model, Jewish synagogue worship – which preserves a certain unity of structure despite all the differences. Moreover the different liturgies can be put into families, and these in turn can be roughly divided according to the different patriarchates (see below, 175 f.). As a rule (the disputes over the date of Easter formed the characteristic exception), the local liturgical divergences were not felt to be a danger to the unity of

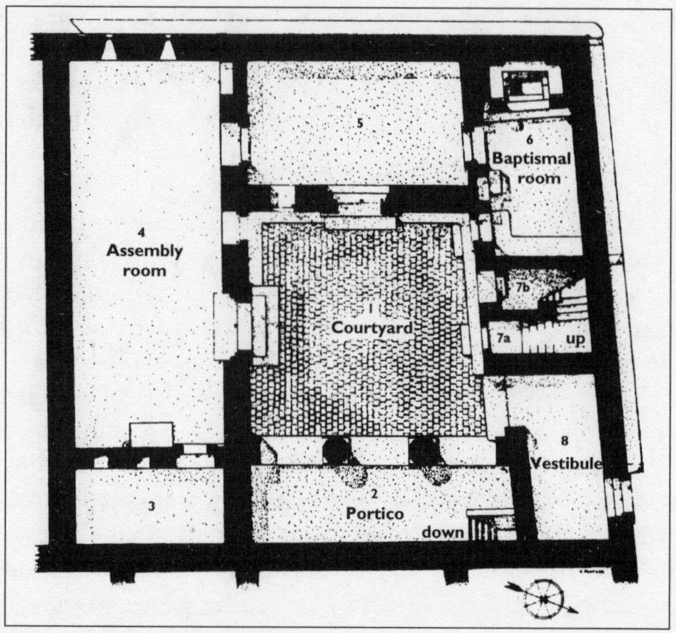

C. *House church at Dura Europos (Syria)*

the church as a whole; this is documented by a bishop from Asia Minor in the middle of the third century: 'Just as in very many other provinces also many things are varied because of the difference of the places and people. And yet on this account there is no departure at all from peace and unity of the catholic church.'[485]

House churches

In the early period of the Christian communities, of course there were still no fixed church buildings to which the public had access; meetings were held in the private houses of well-to-do members of the community. Fortunately, such house churches have been preserved in Syria. The most famous example is in the Roman frontier garrison of Dura Europos on the Euphrates; a less well known one is in Qirqbize (near Qalb Lhose) in Belus, a fertile area east of Antioch in which mainly olives and wine were produced by substantial agricultural businesses, then to be transported to the capital of the province.

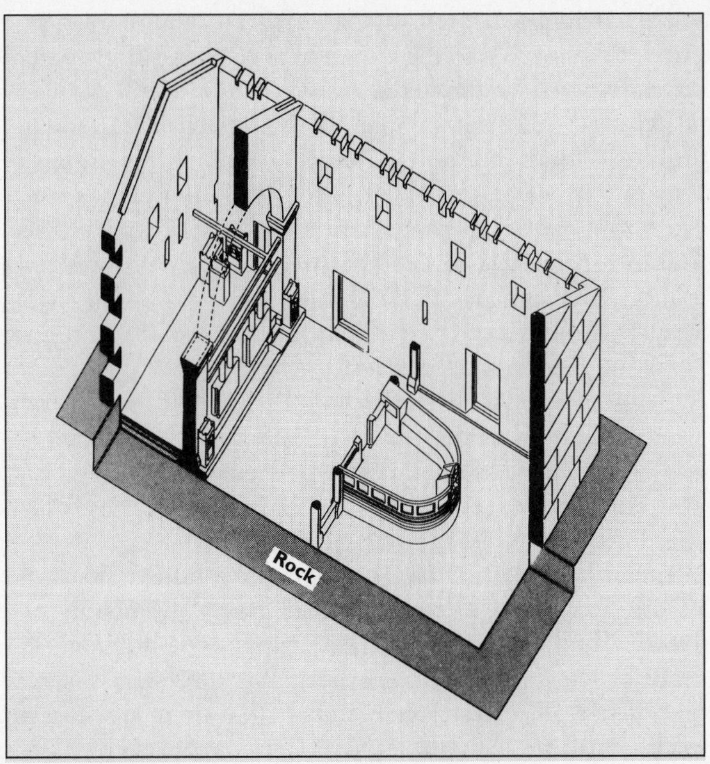

D. House church at Qirqbize (Syria)

If we compare the two lay-outs, many common features become evident, although the house church in Dura came into being more than fifty years earlier. In both places a house typical of the place is transformed into a church. In Dura this is a normal town house with an atrium (no agreement has yet been reached over its date: first to second/third century); the house in Qirqbize is a third-century Roman country house (see above). In both places a church room has been created by joining the main living room to a neighbouring room. Both 'churches' are orientated on the east, and in both 'community centres' we can note a gradual growth of rooms: these rooms were made in the 330s in Dura, whereas the room in Qirqbize was successively given a podium (= *bema*) at the east end for the altar and clergy, a triumphal arch and a further podium west of the centre of the room – so the church was further differentiated by an area reserved for the clergy and a room for the laity. The fact that around fourteen people would fit on the podium of Qirqbize allows interesting inferences about the number of clergy in this village settlement. If they were not monks from an adjacent monastery, perhaps here the laity too were allowed to stand in a privileged place. The size of the two rooms for the assembly are similarly comparable: the main room in Dura measures around 15m by 5m, in Qirqbize 15m by 7.5m; since the layout there provided space for between sixty and seventy people, we may assume similar numbers in Qirqbize (however, the incorporation of the western bema reduced the number of places available). The numbers are particularly amazing because the size of the two settlements to which the churches belonged is hardly comparable: according to the plan of Qirqbize, this settlement hardly comprised more than ten households, whereas Dura was a real urban settlement consisting mainly of the military and their families. We can explain the difference quite simply by the fact that in the north Syrian village essentially more, if not all, of the inhabitants at the point of time when the church came to be used were Christians. By contrast, the artistic decoration of the house church of Dura (we need only compare it with other cultic rooms, like the Jewish synagogue or the Mithraeum) indicates that the Christians of Dura represented a somewhat insignificant minority. At all events, we can attempt to make inferences about the social status of the community from the peripheral location of the house, directly against the town wall and a few minutes by foot from the centre of the town. In Qirqbize the Christian community centre dominates an open space in the middle of the village. However, since a Greek papyrus fragment of the Gospel harmony in use in Syria at that time (Tatian's Diatessaron) was found by the excavators in Dura a considerable distance from the house church, we should not draw over-hasty conclusions here either. Moreover the community evidently continued to be tolerated despite the empire-wide persecution under emperor Decius (AD

250); at all events there are no traces of deliberate damage, say, to the frescoes. Only a presumably completely uncontroversial but unavoidable defensive measure in the city destroyed the church building: a glacis was built against the town wall to prevent its being undermined and destroyed by the advancing Persian troops in AD 256 (though without success).

Furnishing

The furnishing of a 'village' church like that of Qirqbize allows further inferences about the liturgical course of the worship that was held here: in the centre of the podium towards the west was a throne for the priest, specially decorated with rosettes on the armrests; it had a little compartment which we may probably imagine to be a place for keeping liturgical books or lectionaries with the most important texts for worship. In the northern part of the podium, in the apse platform at the east end, we can still find three reliquaries for oil. Here oil could be poured down into a stone sarcophagus; it then flowed over the bones of venerated martyrs and saints and could conveniently be caught at the bottom, on the side, in an ampoule. We tend to see such reliquaries above all in relation to the cult of particular saints, on pilgrimages and the like – such ampoules with decorations specifically related to the place could be taken away as souvenirs. But the example of Qirqbize shows that this was probably a widespread form of piety in a simple village community. Here, as in the whole region, oil played a role in economic life which is not to be underestimated. Here as elsewhere in Syria, a normal table-top of the kind customarily used in fairly well-to-do households served as an altar. As such table-tops were in the form of a letter C (an early form of the Greek letter S) on its side, they are called 'sigma tables'. The adaptation of this ordinary kind of table-top for Christian worship – instead of the normal pagan forms of altars, usually blocks of stones with spiral decorations or the like – has been explained as indicating that while Christians were still meeting in houses, they naturally had the same kind of furniture and utensils as the people around them. Finally, right down to the sixth century it was customary in normal Roman households to recline by the sigma tables on couches which were shaped in a similar form.

The sigma tables in private houses and churches had a slightly elevated rim, since only in the late empire did tablecloths become customary; the rim prevented scraps of food from falling or liquids from dripping from the table.

Penance

Penance was also very important for the structure of the Christian community in antiquity, although it was slow in developing – however, it is impossible to describe in detail here the origin of an ordinance of the church's 'authority of the keys' (i.e. the authority to bind and loose), which was accompanied by battles and theological debates.[486] By the third century the original possibility of a single repentance and forgiveness of sins at baptism (see above, 69f.) had developed into a regular church procedure for penance, with the help of which in the end even major offences against the church's moral code could be atoned for. One of the presuppositions of this process was the theological way of coping with the constantly recurring experience that the 'holiness' of Christians, once converted, was endangered in the everyday world. 'Sin' was now perceived more markedly as a permanent phenomenon of the Christian life and no longer a characteristic of a pagan way of life which could be and was to be laid aside. On the other hand, the community exercised its right to forgive sins, as a representative of Jesus Christ and in the authority of the Holy Spirit (cf. John 20.22f.), with increasing enthusiasm. So-called 'deadly sins' like apostasy from Christianity (for example in persecution), the worship of strange deities ('idolatry'), murder and certain sexual practices had long been excluded from forgiveness. Here the original rigour of penitential discipline was first changed as a result of the problems caused by the large number of the so-called *lapsi* who had turned their backs on Christianity in the great persecutions in the middle of the third century and the beginning of the fourth (see above, 28f.), and who sought contact with the church again when state pressure died down. Rather more mildness was shown even to people who had committed capital crimes. At a relatively early stage, already in the second century, the practice had become established in the West of people appearing publicly before the community at worship in a penitential garment and with ashes poured over them (in 'sackcloth and ashes', cf. already Matt. 11.21), to confess their transgressions and ask for forgiveness. The clothing corresponded to the usual mourning garments. A first sign of the increasing legalization of the process of penance is represented by the four 'stages of penance' which developed in the East after the third century: 'weepers' (*prosklaiontes),* who stood in the forecourt and begged those going to church for their intercessions; 'hearers' (*akroomenoi*), who were at least allowed to take part in the liturgy of the word; 'kneelers' (*hypopiptontes*), who in addition received a special blessing from the bishop; and finally the 'standers with' (*systantes*), who could also take part in eucharistic worship but without receiving communion. A further sign of legalization is represented by the fixing of the three classic acts of penitence (prayer, fasting and alms) in concrete canons of the synod. In the church of bishop Basil of Caesarea in Cappadocia in the last third of the fourth century, the period of penance, i.e. exclusion from the eucharist, lasted thirty years for pederasts, sodomites and murderers, and eleven years for manslaughter.[487] It is hard to overestimate the significance for the life of a specific Christian community of this form of dealing publicly with both smaller and larger transgressions and also with serious crime.

Fellowship

Everyday community life was stamped with a particular form of fellowship which differed considerably from that of comparable organizations by its particular linguistic phrases, gestures, forms and institutions. Thus for example normally only professional colleagues, i.e. people of the same social stratum and intellectual interests, were member of associations. Although the Christian community represented a gathering ordered and limited by the 'patriarchalism' of the men and the leading classes, in antiquity there were very few similarly colourful associations with such a broad social spectrum.

Initially, 'brother' and 'sister' as a form of address was one of the distinctive ways of talking that stamped this community which transcended class. However, at the same time this form was also used in pagan institutions: for example, members of the professional societies and numerous Mithras mystics are called 'brother' on inscriptions, and 'sisters' are also mentioned at least once.[488] The practice of Jesus may have been an important motive for this form of address in the Christian communities. In a key statement critical of relatives, Jesus said: 'Whoever does the will of God is my brother and my sister and my mother' (Mark 3.35). Moreover Jesus' ethic of love of enemy allowed the linguistic integration of people who were not numbered in the Christian community: Tertullian distinguished a universal relationship of brotherhood to non-Christians from the special brotherhood of those 'who have been led to the knowledge of God as their common Father, who have drunk in one spirit of holiness, who from the same womb of a common ignorance have been raised into the same light of truth'.[489] But at the latest from the fourth century on, the old form of address within the community was used only between bishops and clergy and among monks: 'with brothers. i.e. monks', we read in a pilgrim report from the late fourth century.[490]

The holy kiss

The gestures within the community included the so-called 'holy kiss' (*philema hagion*), with which the community gave visible and tangible expression to its special fellowship; this stands alongside the various other gestures of kissing by the individual (see above, 96f.). Paul already asks at the end of letters, 'Greet all the brothers with the holy kiss' (I Thess. 5.26; similarly I Cor. 16.20; II Cor. 13.12; Rom. 16.16). The context of these requests shows that the apostle saw the gesture as the visible expression of the cohesion of the community, steeped in prayer and personal dedication, and a fixed part of the ritual of greeting. The adjective 'holy' continues to make it clear that the gesture does not belong in the sphere of secular rituals or even of intimate tenderness but – at any rate according to the self-understanding of the Christians of antiquity – in the divine sphere. From these passages in the letters we can reconstruct the place of the 'holy kiss' of the members of the community, before the celebration of the Lord's Supper. It is similarly attested by the later accounts of the liturgy in Justin (middle of the second century)[491] and the extended liturgy of the so-called Clementine mass formula, which comes from the fourth century and shows certain precautions against the abuse of a good occasion: 'And the bishop shall greet the community and say, "The peace of God be with you all!" and the people shall answer "And with your spirit!" And the deacon shall say to all, "Greet one another with a holy kiss!" And the clergy shall kiss the bishop, the male laity the laity, the women the women.'[492]

Support of the poor

The support of the poor, almsgiving, continued to play a great role in community life (see above, 113–17). However, in the fourth century a tendency developed towards privatizing this task which fell on the community as a whole; this was connected with the rise of powerful episcopal figures in the cities. They took the place of patrons for the common good and accordingly felt themselves responsible. For example, in Ancyra (Ankara) a host of sick people gathered together, 'both married and single, who lay in the narthex of the church and waited for their daily ration of food'.[493] The 'family' or the 'clientele' of the bishops was recruited from such people. Community life was also stamped by ready financial support and visits for those who had been arrested and were in prison. The accounts of the martyrdom of a Carthaginian matron named Vibia Perpetua and her slave girl Felicitas from the beginning of the third century contain similar reports and references to the bad state of the prisons in the African provincial capital: pitch darkness, very cramped quarters and tormenting heat because of overcrowding.[494] But two deacons of the Christian community managed to get better places in prison for the women through bribery: the supervisor of the institution allowed many Christians in to visit. Constantine's last rival on the way to sole rule, his brother-in-law Licinius, accordingly decreed among his anti-Christian measures (like mass arrests) a law 'that no one should treat those in prison humanely by distributing food, or have pity on those who were perishing of hunger in bonds'.[495] In Jerash in present-day Jordan, the ancient Gerasa, at the beginning of the sixth century Bishop Paulus even built a prison to make conditions for the inmates easier.[496]

Finally, mutual help and protection had a very important place. Chrysostom put it like this: 'If someone goes to the market and there meets just one friend, his sorrow often disappears completely. Now we do not go to the market, but to church. There we meet not just one friend, but so many, and thus come together with so many brothers and sisters. How then should we not lay aside our despondency and reap all joy?'[497] Especially from the fourth century on, those classes which had previously given money for public buildings and other communal projects were active within the Christian community: now they funded mosaic floors for churches and other institutions. In the nave of one of the ten churches so far excavated in Madaba in Jordan (south of Amman), the Church of the Apostles, it is still possible to see a broad mosaic with parrots arranged in pairs and a central medallion with a personification of the sea (Plate 6). The inscription on this mosaic, which was made at the end of the sixth century, mentions the donors and the craftsman: 'O Lord, you who have made heaven and earth, give life to Athanasius, Thomas and Theodora, and Salamain the mosaic artist.'[498] In addition to this, the church building had three side rooms in all, each with mosaics; their inscriptions document the religious dimension of such gifts: 'O Lord, accept the sacrifice of those who have borne fruit and bear fruit for the temple of the holy apostles in memory of the priest John through the zeal of the deacon Anastasius.' 'In the time of the most holy bishop John this place was given mosaics by the zeal of the most pious monk John.'[499] Theodoret, the bishop of the pilgrimage town of Cyrrhus in Belus in northern Syria, who has been already mentioned several times, took care to collect tax arrears in the place and had the town's aqueducts and bridges restored.[500]

Structures and forms of communication extending beyond the community

In the early period the distinction between the local community and the church as a whole did not as yet have any special significance. The one church was felt to be the indivisible body of Christ, which nevertheless had local units. Paul writes to 'the church of God which is in Corinth' (I Cor. 1.2). Initially any local community, i.e. as a rule the Christian community of a city, was an independent structure. It was led by people who had usually come from its midst. Initially there was no authority over the church, so that with the common features, major local differences developed, in respect both of church customs, worship and liturgy, and also of theological characteristics and the precise demarcation of the canon of biblical writings. At the latest after the end of the primitive Christian community in Jerusalem as a result of the Jewish rebellion, the custom of communities in Asia Minor – like the Jewish Diaspora from the time of the Maccabees – making a collection for it lapsed: Paul had been involved in bringing such a collection (I Cor. 16.1f.). However, we must not misinterpret such a lack of higher structures as a general lack of relations. Thus already at the end of the first century, in the case of a dispute within the church, there seems to have been the custom of calling on another community for an opinion or an arbitration, either because it was nearby or because it was important. This other community might indeed feel an obligation to express its view. At any rate, at this point in time the Roman community approached its Corinthian sister community with a request for clear advice in resolving a conflict. Regular meetings of delegates to solve church conflicts ('synods', from the Greek '*synhodos*', 'the meeting') appeared for the first time in connection with controversies over a prophetic movement in Phrygia: 'For when the faithful throughout Asia had met frequently and in many places in Asia for this purpose, and on examination of the new-fangled teachings had pronounced them profane and rejected the heresy, these persons were thus expelled from the church and excluded from its communion.'[501] In connection with the disputes over the date of Easter (see 35–8 above), such synods met in Palestine around AD 190 under the presidency of Theophilus of Caesarea and Narcissus of Jerusalem; in Ephesus under Polycrates; in Rome under Bishop Victor; in Amastris in Pontus under Palmas; in Gaul under Irenaeus, and in Osrhoene – almost a 'general council', though it did not meet in one place and did not arrive

Synods

at a common result. A new quality of synodical assemblies was achieved when the emperor Constantine began to summon bishops' meetings to resolve disputed matters in the church, and imperial commissioners followed the event (with varying success) and occasionally attempted to dominate it. The assembly of Nicaea, already described by contemporaries as an 'ecumenical' (i.e. empire-wide) synod, represented a first climax. It was held in June 325 in the imperial palace of the imperial summer residence in Bithynia (Iznik), which had an attractive location by a lake. After his victory over his rival Licinius in September 324, the emperor Constantine wanted to crown his political work by a 'synod of union' at which the last conflicts that disturbed the unity of the church were to be removed. However, success was achieved only during the meeting and shortly afterwards; soon afterwards the theological conflict broke out again. During the synod the monarch housed and fed the bishops 'in rich abundance'; he himself entered with a procession, and attended the meeting, sitting on a small golden throne. At the end the emperor celebrated his twenty years on the throne with the bishops and gave them rich presents.[502]

Metropolitans

The structures going beyond the community also included the development of the metropolitan constitution, the rise of the primacy of Rome and the papacy. Tendencies towards bringing Christian communities together in accordance with regional perspectives and the Roman provinces possibly begin very early: Paul wrote to the Christians of the region (or, as another interpretation would have it, the province) of Galatia. At the end of the second century, Bishop Dionysus of Corinth wrote both to individual urban communities and to whole regions.[503] The communities of the neighbouring cities of Lyons and Vienne in Gaul corresponded at roughly the same time with the 'brothers in Asia and Phrygia'. The marked concentration of the Christian communities on the urban metropolises of the Roman empire which at the same time were provincial capitals (Carthage, Alexandria, Caesarea, Antioch, Ephesus, Corinth, Lyons and Milan) similarly had an effect. Such a form of disseminating Christianity at the same time formed the nucleus of a very close but initially unconscious association with the organizations of the state. In the course of the third century this pattern of inter-church relations, concentrated on the provinces and their respective provincial capitals (metropolis), was introduced – hence its name, the 'metropolitan constitution'. A synod which met in Antioch, probably at the beginning of the 330s, illustrated the purely pragmatic motivation of this aspect of the early church's constitution when it stipulated: 'It is fitting for the bishops in every province to acknowledge the bishop who presides in the metropolis and who has to take thought for the whole province; because all those with business come from every quarter to the metropolis. Therefore he shall have precedence in rank, and the other bishops shall do nothing without him, according to the canon already established in the time of our fathers, except what pertains to their own dioceses and the districts subject to them. For each bishop has authority over that . . . But let him undertake nothing further without the bishop of the metropolis, nor the latter without the consent of the other bishops.'[504] Another close tie with the political order came about in the late fourth century. In the course of the reform of the empire by Diocletian shortly before the end of the third century, on the one hand there was decentralization through an increase in the number of provinces, but on the other new central authorities were created. The four or five praetorian prefects and twelve or fifteen diocesan vicars took up residence in cities which for the most part had long been large (or smaller) Christian metropolises, sometimes theological focal points: Trier, Milan, Rome, Carthage, Constantinople, Ephesus, Caesarea in Cappadocia, Antioch, Alexandria. Towards the end of the fourth century the church adopted this model and developed the 'supermetropolitan constitution'. An imperial council which met in the Eastern capital Constantinople in 381 stipulated that the bishops of a diocese should form a higher administrative unit, but in synodical decisions should not make pronouncements beyond the limits of their particular diocese. At the very next empire-wide gathering of bishops in the imperial residence of Chalcedon, the bishop of Constantinople was allowed to consecrate the supermetropolitans of three Eastern diocese on the explicitly political grounds that the seats of the 'emperor and the senate' were there. By contrast, the system of the five patriarchates of Rome, Constantinople, Alexandria, Antioch and Jerusalem, which finally became the norm in the seventh century, is a later attempt to 'spread the veil of ecumenical unity over the rivalries between Rome, Byzantium and Alexandria'.[505]

The primacy of Rome

However, from the fourth century on, the Bishop of Rome resisted all attempts to bring his *cathedra* into line with the other great episcopal sees by such models. Here he could, for example, appeal to a decision of the Council of Constantinople, already mentioned (381), that the 'Bishop of Constantinople shall have the primacy of honour after the Bishop of Rome, because it (viz. Constantinople) is the new Rome'.[506] Granted, the council elevated the place where it met, hitherto an insignificant suffragan see, to high honour simply because of its great political significance (against which Rome also promptly protested), but it also recognized a pre-eminence which at the latest by the middle of the third century made itself felt in the self-confidence of the Roman bishops, and from the middle of the fourth century went virtually unchallenged. This heightened self-awareness goes back to corresponding self-awareness in the Roman community. Evidently even before the formation of a monepiscopate in the second century (see below, 189), it gloried in the martyrdom of the two apostles Peter and Paul (I Clement 5.3–7); towards the end of the second century Irenaeus also spoke of the 'very great, the very ancient, and universally known church founded and organized at Rome by the two most glorious apostles, Peter and Paul',[507] in so doing putting forward a historical fiction. However, Irenaeus did not as yet assent to any precedence of Rome over the whole church, but admonished apostolicity, i.e. the continuity of particular churches with the apostolic tradition.[508] Even if in the following period for a long time Roman bishops who claimed precedence alternated (with great energy, but not always successfully) with others who maintained a lower profile in this respect, we can say that once a bishop of Rome had appealed to his succession to Peter in order to establish a theological position in the middle of the third century, and at around the same time Cyprian, bishop of Carthage, had collected biblical arguments which were later used to support, against his original intention, a Roman claim to leadership, from the middle of the fourth century the legal and church political precedence of Rome was cemented. At least in Protestant church historiography it has become the established custom to call the Roman Bishop Damasus (366–384) the first pope, because around 365/377 he is addressed by a Latin theologian as the holder of a specific Roman 'Petrine office' (and is acting accordingly): 'I am speaking with the successor of the fisherman and a disciple of Christ. In that I recognize no other leader but Christ, I am bound to your holiness, that is, to the cathedra of Peter. For I know that on this rock the church is founded.'[509] In general it is the case that this claim fundamentally anticipates the reality of the papacy up to the Middle Ages; its actual influence on developments in church politics and theology was limited in late antiquity by the emperor of the time and the extremely agile supermetropolitans of Alexandria and Constantinople.

Communication

Inter-church communication was an essential precondition for the rise of these more comprehensive church structures. From the days of the apostles the various parts of the one church, the diverse communities in the different regions of the Roman empire, were in lively contact. There was a good deal of travelling and just as many exchanges by letter; as a rule, in pagan antiquity these were sent by special messengers whom the sender chose from his slaves or freemen. In their travelling habits the Christians adapted to the custom of philosophers, physicians and high state officials, who sometimes led what to present-day tastes would seem a restless itinerant life. For example Pertinax, who later became emperor (he was born the son of a freeman in Liguria in AD 126), began his career as prefect of a cohort in Syria, went as a military tribune to England, then to Upper Moesia, Cologne, then to the central Danube region, northern Italy, the upper Danube, Syria and finally to North Africa and Rome. There he was the first soldier to be proclaimed emperor by the military, in 192; he was murdered the very next year. By his own account, the Alexandrian theologian and philosopher of religion Clement studied at the end of the second century with two teachers in Greece who for their part came from Syria and Egypt, and also 'in the East' with an Assyrian and a Jewish teacher from Palestine. Lastly he mentions his Alexandrian master (probably Pantaenus).[510]

Since the energetic fight against the pirates in the eastern Mediterranean and the different road- and bridge-building programmes, travelling had become considerably easier. Even if the network of roads with staging posts for changing horses and inns primarily served military communication, it was also used by general traffic. The imperial post (*cursus publicus*) could be used for communication only by the authorities and such persons as were allowed to travel by it because they had good connections with high officials or because they had limited time for their task. Because of such connections, Gregory the Miracle Worker, bishop of the community of Amasea in Pontus, could travel to Berytus (Beirut) by the state post to take up his legal studies. He had enough of the coveted passes (*diploma*). By contrast, in AD 160 Pertinax had to travel the 150 kilometres from Antioch to his first posting on the Syrian frontier of the empire on foot, because he had no permission to use the state post.[511] The emperors succeeding Constantine then allowed the bishops to use the state post; it was this that first made possible the great empire-wide synods of the fourth and fifth centuries, with several hundred participants from all parts of the empire. At the end of the fourth century the pagan historiographer Ammianus Marcellinus commented spitefully on this development: 'Throngs of bishops hastened hither and thither on the public post-horses to synods, and while he (viz. emperor Constantius II) sought to make the whole ritual conform to his own will, he cut the sinews of the courier service.'[512] However, in all parts of the empire a network of private transport for passengers and goods was available, which as a rule could serve all needs, provided that there were the financial means to meet their costs. Commercial corporations organized and financed transport for merchants; alongside this, during the period of the empire a kind of health tourism developed among the well-to-do classes, along with pilgrimages to holy places. Usually people travelled only by day, and in sections between two rest stations (*mansiones*), as a rule distances of between seventy and ninety kilometres. Many travellers will also have gone on foot. Travelling by ship was possible only between March and late autumn; moreover people avoided sailing too far from the coast and going, say, straight across the Mediterranean. It is of course difficult to get details of the duration of journeys on the ancient ship routes; wind and current often led journey times to differ from the average (e.g. from Alexandria to Puteoli at least nine, more likely fifteen, at most twenty days; Caesarea in Palestine to Ostia at least twenty days; Carthage to Ostia between three and five days). The importance of the sea routes should not be underestimated; the great mass transportation of goods in ancient commerce took place between Rome and Alexandria. As there were no special passenger ships, freight ships had to be used – so the traveller had no influence on the route. Sometimes up to 600 passengers travelled on the great voyages; journeys were often interrupted by shipwrecks.[513]

Hospitality

The degree to which from the beginning Christians took part in this 'world travel business' is shown by the rapid expansion of Christianity in the metropolises of antiquity (see above, 5 f.).That may also have been connected with the professions which Christians practised. Thus for example the Letter of James in the New Testament attacks Christian merchants who made plans governed by the needs of their business without heed to divine plans and guidance, and said: 'Today or tomorrow we will go into this or that city and will spend a year there and engage in trade and make profit' (James 4.13). Christians were called on to receive one another: the earliest extant church order stipulates: 'Everyone who comes to you in the name of the Lord must be welcomed. Afterwards, when you have tested him, you will find out about him, for you have insight into what is right and left (i.e. right and wrong). If it is a traveller who arrives, help him all you can. But he must not stay with you more than two days or, if necessary, three. If he wants to settle with you and is a craftsman, he must work for his living. If, however, he has no trade, use your judgment in taking steps for him to live with you as a Christian without being idle. If he refuses to do this, he is trading on Christ. You must be on your guard against such people!'[514] Authentic prophets and teachers must, however, be supported. Christians usually travelled with letters of commendation; at the beginning of the second century Bishop Polycarp of Smyrna adds one of these in his letter to the Philippians: 'I am sending you this letter by Crescens, whom I recently commended to you and now commend him again. He has lived with us blamelessly and I believe he will do so among you.'[515] Some texts of this kind have also been preserved on papyrus: thus at the end of the third or beginning of the fourth century a certain Sotas somewhere in Upper Egypt asked 'beloved brother Peter', 'to accept our brother Heracles as is the custom. Therefore I ask you and all the brothers who are with you, I and those who are with me.'[516] Evidently there were also problems with this procedure. At the beginning of the fourth century, the Synod of Elvira dealt with the practice of confessors sending out such letters of commendation and showing these letters to others to impress them. The assembly of Spanish bishops stipulated that these should be exchanged in a simple communal document which did not mention the confessor by name, in order to avoid misuse.[517]

The mines

A form of more involuntary but no less warm contact arose when Christians were condemned to work in the mines, the worst punishment after the death penalty. Those who were condemned to such forced labour, for example in the mines of North Africa, were treaded as penal slaves of the state and branded. With their heads shaved, as a rule they worked chained and under military supervision. Occasionally those who after ten years were no longer capable of work were 'given back' to their relatives. The work in marble quarries like the one in Chemtou/Simitthus (in present-day Tunisia) was strenuous –

simply because of the extreme fluctuations of temperature; tremendous slag heaps even now show that the volume of waste corresponded to that of the material obtained. The workers were housed in a walled camp; there is also evidence of Christians among the workers who broke the famous 'Numidian marble'. Some of these men came from a long way away, which meant that Christians from all over the empire met. Four Christian sculptors who were condemned to forced labour in the quarries of Pannonia under Diocletian at the beginning of the fourth century found a bishop of Antioch there.[518] However, such prisoners were not abandoned: around AD 170, Bishop Dionysius of Corinth thanks Soter, Bishop of Rome, for financial gifts intended to support the 'brothers living in the mines'.[519]

Correspondence

A bibliography of Christian epistolary literature published recently[520] shows the still impressive remains of the rich literary communication between the communities in the first three centuries; 100 pages are needed for the Greek sphere alone: at the end of the first century the Roman community wrote to the community of Corinth (I Clement); Bishop Ignatius of Antioch (or an anonymous author in his name) wrote seven letters to communities in Asia Minor and to his colleague Polycarp on his prison transport to Rome. Polycarp in turn wrote a letter to the community in Philippi; Polycrates of Ephesus corresponded in the second half of the second century with his Roman colleagues. The communities of Lyons and Vienne reported a persecution of their fellow Christians in Asia in AD 177: the community in Smyrna in Asia Minor had written some years earlier about the martyrdom of their bishop Polycarp. Bishop Alexander of Jerusalem wrote at the beginning of the third century to the community of Antioch; Bishop Dionysius of Alexandria – a diligent correspondent – wrote in the middle of the third century to the bishop of Antioch and to a number of Roman colleagues. As well as this, there is the sometimes extensive correspondence with which the bishops of Alexandria made known the date of Easter. The concentration of letters to the Roman community is striking and documents the central importance of the community in the capital already in these early times. If we add the extensive official and private correspondence of well-known Latin bishops like Cyprian of Carthage and church teachers like Origen, the picture drawn here becomes even more colourful and fuller. Origen's correspondence was collected only a generation after his death (253/254); a catalogue of the late fourth century distinguished five groups:[521] two miscellaneous collections of eleven volumes in all, the correspondence with a friend and a pupil, and two collections of excerpts each in two volumes, made later (for reasons of church politics, to defend the author) – unfortunately this mass of material has been lost, apart from a few fragments and two complete letters. That is particularly bitter in the case of the letter written to the emperor Philippus Arabs (AD 244–249) and his consort Otacilia Severa: this is a private letter from a Christian to the monarchs of the Roman empire! The collection of letters of Cyprian went back to the author himself and today comprises sixty-five letters by the bishop of Carthage and thirteen letters addressed to him – almost as many letters of Cyprian again have been lost because they were not included in the collection, which moreover circulated in late antiquity in a substantially less extensive form. More than a quarter of the extant correspondence is addressed to Rome or comes from there; the rest is to correspondents in Carthage, North Africa, Sicily, Spain, Gaul and even Cappadocia.

The church's ministries

Origins

How does a church hierarchy of ministries develop anyway? This question arises not only for modern, possibly Protestant, historians who are consequently critical of the ministry. In his *Panarion*, an anti-heretical compendium which Epiphanius, the bishop of the city of Salamis on Cyprus, compiled between 374 and 377, there is a report on a group from Pontus which today is almost completely forgotten – theologians who in the fourth century were traced back (historically quite erroneously) to the Alexandrian presbyter Arius who had been condemned in AD

325 at the Council of Nicaea and had died in 336 after recanting his position. Epiphanius called this group 'Aërians', after a certain priest Aërius, and passed on remarkable literal quotations from its scriptures. Possibly they come from Aërius itself: 'How is a bishop worth more than a presbyter? The presbyter does not differ from him on any point. There is one (single) order, one honour, one dignity. The bishop lays on hands (e.g. within the framework of ordination, C.M.), in the same way so too does the priest. The bishop holds worship, the priest in the same way. The bishop sits on the throne, so also does the priest.'[522] In the fourth century it would probably have been difficult to find a stronger thesis than this to attack the reality of the constitutional church. Bishop Epiphanius, who was a zealous (not to say bigoted) heresiarch, also reacted in a correspondingly sharp way and rejected this criticism of the precedence of the episcopal office, which was unusual in the fourth century, with a somewhat ugly but customary literary motif of the polemic against heretics. He argued that Aërius had developed this 'crazy theory' because he himself would very much liked to have become a bishop, but had lost to a friend in an election. At the same time, however, the Bishop of Cyprus also handed down the historical argument with which Aërius evidently supported his questions and theses. He argued that the apostle Paul had written only 'presbyters and deacons', and not bishops – that is true if in Phil.1.1 we do not understand '*episkopoi* and deacons' as yet referring to the later episcopate. Of course Aërius and the Aërians were far too late with their exegetical and historical argument against the precedence in honour and high liturgical competence of the episcopal office, since according to the current general consensus of scholars, the three-level hierarchy of bishop, presbyters/priests and deacons had developed in essentials in the second half of the second century.[523] At the latest at the beginning of the third century a single bishop stood at the head of each Christian community; alongside him there were presbyters and deacons, and hardly anyone doubted that this order was right, in accordance with the divine will, and in accord with the tradition of the apostles.

To this degree the Aerians seemed an isolated group which was questioning after the event a development that hardly anyone was conscious any more of having been a development. Only the criticism of the churches in the late Middle Ages and modern times (in part also within the church) has once again brought the historical and theological problem of this development into sharper focus; the best known and at the same time the most succinct formulation comes from the French reform Catholic Alfred Loisy, who died excommunicated in 1940: 'Jesus preached the kingdom and the church came.'[524] Whether there is continuity between this church and the preaching of Jesus, at least in the form of an 'inner spiritual bond',[525] is in any case constantly disputed. The historical account of the origin of a ministry with a hierarchy division seems to be the key test for all theses on this topic, and of course is to a special degree dependent on the particular religious standpoint of the person undertaking this task.

First of all it is amazing that around one hundred and fifty years after Jesus and those whom he had personally called, such structures had already been developed. For during the lifetime of Jesus there was no segmented church organization which was differentiated horizontally into a variety of specific ministries and vertically into a hierarchy of these ministries. Nevertheless the 'Jesus movement' was not an amorphous anarchical mass of people who followed the Master through Galilee. From his considerably larger host of followers Jesus of Nazareth collected around him (Luke 8.2f.) a circle of twelve apostles as a kind of inner nucleus of the movement, probably as a symbol of the eschatological Israel of the twelve tribes, in the belief that he had been called to bring them together (Matt. 19.28). It has been claimed that this leading group came into being after Easter, but that is improbable. The term 'service' plays a central role for the 'ordering' of this inner circle: 'Whoever would be great among you must be your servant, and whoever would be first among you must be slave of all' (Mark 10.43f.). After the execution of Jesus, this order of an inner group of twelve, understood as a serving community, was preserved, roughly speaking, for only a short period. Individual figures quickly stood out from this group. On his first visit to Jerusalem (c.AD 35/36), the apostle Paul wanted to make the acquaintance of Cephas (Graecized as Peter), and already at the negotiations usually called the 'Apostolic Council' (c.AD 48) he still had dealings only with a body of three consisting of James the brother of Jesus, Simon Cephas/Peter and John the son of Zebedee. Thus less than twenty years after the death of Jesus, this body (Paul calls them 'those of note' and 'the pillars', Gal. 2.6,9) and no longer the Twelve, formed the inner nucleus, and probably also the hierarchical focus of the Jerusalem community. This reordering seems essentially to have been governed by the special status assigned to the so-called 'witnesses to the resurrection' (I Cor. 15.5–9). But the relatively rapid upheaval in the leadership of the community after Jesus also shows how strongly the form of organization of the earliest community had been stamped by the charismatic personality of Jesus; the relatively far-reaching freedom from all ties of bourgeois existence of course also implied an attitude which was more critical of institutions.[526] With the death of Jesus and the manifest failure of the end of the world to materialize, though this end had been expected as a matter of course, there was no important impulse for an itinerant missionary life and those of its features which were critical of institutions. The fact that blood relatives of Jesus then played a role in the leadership of the Jerusalem community, although during his lifetime Jesus had had a very critical attitude towards his family, was a normal phenomenon in acculturation (here into the oriental clan system). Nevertheless, the development of hierarchical structures did not take place everywhere with the same speed. The first church order from the second century still contained regulations for itinerant prophets – i.e. for a form of Christian existence relatively close to the primitive community. However, the tendency of the text is already critical: 'Let every apostle who comes to you be received as the Lord, but let him not stay more than one day, or if need be a second as well; but if he stays three days, he is a false prophet. And when an apostle goes forth, let him accept nothing but bread until he reaches his night's lodging; but if he asks for money, he is a false prophet.'[527] Thus there was more fear of frauds than hope for Christian missionaries and travellers with honest intentions. How much money one could earn in such an itinerant life with a religious motivation is shown by the account in an inscription of a slave of the Syrian goddess from Kefr-Hauwar at the foot of Mount Hermon, who is said to have brought back seventy begging bags from each of his begging trips.[528] At any rate it is striking that the prophetic-charismatic ordering of the primitive community in Syria survived for a long time after the death of Jesus.

Hierarchy and urbanization

One of the most decisive changes in early Christianity was probably that from a movement stamped more by country life to an explicitly urban religion. In these towns and communes, larger and smaller, there were of course hierarchically ordered offices, and there were all kinds of professional organizations and associations (for example burial associations). Christianity now established itself in this environment, and people streamed to it who took such hierarchical structures completely for granted. First of all the Christian communities developed a constitutional order which in principle resembled such associations and which finally almost formed a 'city in the city' – from the third century onwards it also increasingly took over tasks of the urban administrations (for example the care of the poor). Once this course had been adopted, it is not surprising that the communities finally took on the provincial constitutions, established structures which went beyond the community, and in the fourth century also created empire-wide structures of communication, 'always half-denying, half assenting'.[529]

Presbyteral constitution

The form of constitution which now began its triumphal progress is usually called a 'presbyteral constitution'; it comes originally from Palestine. Already in the 40s, as the Acts of the Apostles shows, in the Jerusalem community there was a council of elders on the Jewish model (*presbyterion* – a term which moreover is also attested in the world of the Greek associations).[530] However, at first the mission communities founded or dominated by Paul did not have this constitution, but still followed the charismatic model of the primitive community – albeit in a varied form. In the 'undisputed authentic Pauline letters there is no mention anywhere of presbyters, although there was also an order and specific offices in the Pauline communities . . . In Paul's thought, therefore, the congregation is not just another constitutional organization with grades and classes, but a unitary, living cosmos of free, spiritual gifts, which serve and complement one another. Those who mediate these gifts may never lord it over one another, or refuse to have anything to do with one another.'[531] Nevertheless, in the prescript of Paul's letter to the Philippians, for the first time two of the 'ministries' which were central to subsequent development, '*episkopoi* and deacons', are mentioned by name. The title *episkopos* as the designation of an office is not a Christian invention; in Athens *episkopoi* were determined by lot and exercised the function of governors in the subject cities of the Delian and Attic Leagues; the title also occurs in the associations of the time of the empire (without the single fixed demarcation of an office). Remarkably, in the early period the title *episkopoi* appears only in the plural – for that reason, among others, the convention has developed of translating one and the same Greek word *episkopos* still with *episkope* (and not with 'bishop') up to the rise in the second century of the church constitutions concentrated on one bishop as leader (*episkopos*) of the community. This is in order to make the difference clear: in one case we have one community office among others, and in the other the office of community leadership. As was customary, for example, among rabbis in Judaism, the *episkopoi* of the early period were appointed to office by the laying on of hands; clearly they stood out as a result of a particular gift for administration (I Cor. 12.28f.), and at that time they still represented a sub-group of presbyters. As the Greek term *diakonos* already shows, the 'office of deacon' may already have developed from table service; care of the poor in the community will have been their responsibility – at any rate this would have corresponded to the practice in Jerusalem (Acts 6.1–7).

Episkopos/ diakonos

The second century

The structure of ministry and constitution which became established in the second century consisted of a combination of the Jerusalem model of presbyteral order and the more Gentile-Christian model of Pauline mission communities. The first evidence of this constitutional situation is an official letter from the Roman community to the Corinthian community from the end of the first century. It is clear from this letter that in Corinth there were now similarly presbyters, and alongside them, or rather above them, also 'the leaders' (Greek *hegoumenoi,* I Clem. 1.3). They are also called *episkopoi* and 'deacons' (42.4f.; 44.1/4) – the function of the *episkope* was essentially cultic. Interestingly, the Roman senders of this letter derived this order theologically along a line (which of course is theologically inaccurate) leading from God the Father through Christ to the apostles: these had appointed the first *episkopoi* and deacons, and had given instructions that after their death 'other tested men should take over their service' (I Clem. 44.2). The appointment of these *viri probati* was now to be followed by 'other respected men with the assent of the whole community' for life. Therefore with its letter the Roman community was also protesting against the deposition of those holding office in Corinth. The terminology and notions of the letter correspond very closely to the Hellenistic style of office as this appears, for example, in the documents about appointment to office and respect for office; however, the letter also shows continuity with the Old Testament cultic institutions. It documents the fact that in the urban communities an 'office', in the sense of a 'position of leadership clearly laid down by law and recognized socially, with dignities and means of power',[532] had developed; it is not fortuitous that here too we have the first evidence of the terminological distinction between priests and 'laity' (I Clem. 40.5). From the end of the second century, first with Clement, Tertullian and Origen, the complementary Greek term clergy (*kleros*) also appears for the liturgical offices. The term really means 'lot'; evidently it denoted those of the bishop's circle of fellow-workers who had been chosen by him. However, it is striking that the terms 'priesthood' and priest (*hierateuma* and *hiereus)* hardly appear at all in this context to begin with. The Christian communities wanted to distinguish themselves energetically (and also terminologically) from the pagan cult, which they regarded as idolatry. Nevertheless the title 'presbyter' already indicates an office which, from a phenomenological perspective would have to be regarded as 'priestly office'; therefore at the latest in the fourth century the Greek word presbyter *(presbyteros)* can be rendered by the English word 'priest', as it is then also used explicitly as a synonym of the corresponding Greek term.

The monepiscopate

Quite evidently at this time both the Roman and the Corinthian communities still had collegial leadership; the specialization of offices – there seem to have been some ministers who were specifically responsible for external relations – was not the basis for a hierarchy or subordination of persons in the collective community leadership. Therefore the propagation of the so-called 'monepiscopate' by letters to communities in Asia Minor represented at least just as decisive a revolution in the constitution of ancient Christianity.[533] 'Monepiscopate', with the Greek word for 'only, alone' (*monos*), denotes the fact that now a single bishop leads the community – the expression 'monarchical episcopate' which used to be customary inappropriately introduces the circumstances of the third and fourth centuries into the second.[534] In this early period no one claims a monarchical rule over the presbyters which no longer leaves room for the collaboration of presbyters and deacons in leading the community. Moreover, this type of church government was not very widespread; as we saw (above, 12f.), in the middle of the third century Gregory the Miracle Worker became bishop in a town with seventeen Christians. Ignatius (or the anonymous author who wrote under his name) at any rate worked very energetically to impress this model of the monepiscopate on the communities to which he wrote. In all probability we may take this intensity as an indication that the constitutional order which he commended was not established in these places, and that its introduction was not even considered. 'For when you are in subjection to the bishop as to Jesus Christ it is clear to me that you are living not after men, but after Jesus Christ . . . Likewise let all respect the deacons as Jesus Christ, even as the bishop is also a type of the Father, and the presbyters as the council of God and the college of apostles.'[535] 'See that you all follow the bishop, as Jesus Christ follows the Father, and the presbytery as if it were the apostles. And reverence the deacons as the command of God. Let that be considered a valid eucharist which is celebrated by the bishop, or by one whom he appoints. Wherever the bishop appears, let the congregation be present; just as wherever Jesus Christ is, there is the catholic church. It is not lawful either to baptize or to hold an agape without the bishop; but whatever he approves, this is also pleasing to God, that everything which you do may be secure and valid.'[536] Whether the underlying typology here which connects God with the bishop and the apostles with the presbytery initiated or supported this energetic propagation of the monepiscopate or only legitimated it after the event can no longer be decided with any certainty. But since at the same time Ignatius emphasized the character of the episcopal ministry as service, we may not use the letter to make anyone a completely solitary figure within the development of the office. For lack of further sources, there are only hypotheses to explain the development away from the collegial constitution: some scholars refer to natural developments within collegially structured organs,[537] others to the need to oppose heretical movements in the second century with a leader who could speak with complete authority.[538] Most recently, the notion of the community as a 'house of God' has also been used. The ancient household used to be headed by a figure acting in a sovereign way in the person of the master of the house, so that the development towards a monepiscopate would be consistent within the framework of this picture of the church.[539] Early Christianity itself was hardly aware of the phenomenon of development, and therefore only very rarely attempts to offer explanations. The Antiochene theologian Theodore, bishop of Mopsuestia in Cilicia at the end of the fourth century, wrote: 'The apostle Paul in I Timothy 3 (here only *episkopoi* and deacons are mentioned, C.M.) did not forget the presbyters, but the same persons in office initially bore both the name "presbyter" and also the name "bishop". Those who had the authority of consecration (of ministers by the laying on of hands, C.M.) and are now called "bishops" did not preside over a church but over a whole province and bore the name "apostles" . . . Thus in that ancient time those who are now called "bishops" were for a whole province what those consecrated (as bishops) now are for an individual town and an individual village area. That was how the church constitution was at that time. But when the religion had spread powerfully, and not only towns but also villages were full of believers, and the blessed apostles had died, those who later were appointed to the leadership of the whole (viz. the whole province) were no longer equal to those former men, nor could they give testimony through miraculous gifts as they did . . . Therefore they felt it a burden to bear the name "apostle"; they divided out the other designations: they gave the name "presbyter" to the presbyters, and assigned "bishop" to the one who was to be competent to consecrate, so that he was now entrusted with the leadership of the whole.'[540]

This form of monepiscopate began to establish itself in Rome around the middle of the second century; the presbyter entrusted with relations with outside communities clearly became better known and had greater authority than his colleagues. That form was introduced at the latest in AD 189;[541] the introduction of a dating by bishops is a not unimportant sign of this. This chronology was made possible by the compilation of lists of bishops, which by means of a catalogue without gaps projected the new constitutional order back into the apostolic period. Probably the revolution in the understanding of the term 'presbyter' also dates to this time; now linguistically, too, it became a synonym for the term 'priest'. In the West, Tertullian already speaks quite happily of 'priestly tasks' and calls the bishop 'the high priest'.[542] The eucharistic action is called a 'sacrifice' and the altar a place of sacrifice (*thysiasterion*). The original office of elder had thus clearly been transformed into a priestly office; the earlier honorific office had been clericalized, and the gap between the community and church office, between priests and laity, had clearly widened. One reason for this change in the image of the presbyter, and at the same time a further element in the stablization of the mon-episcopate, may have been the variant, customary above all in the West, on the Eastern typological relationship between Christ and the bishop propagated by Ignatius, the model of 'representation'. The idea is called 'vicariate' after the Latin term for a representative *(vicarius)*.[543] Christ, it was taught, appointed heads of communities as successors to the apostles, and thus the bishop (and the priest as his representative) held office as a representative of the apostles or a successor to them in office. In particular Cyprian, bishop of Carthage, had supported such notions strongly in the middle of the third century. He concluded from the Lukan 'Whoever hears you, hears me' (Luke 10.15): 'The bishop is in the church and the church in the bishop; whoever is not with the bishop is not in the church.'[544] And at a synod in Carthage in 256 over which Cyprian presided, another bishop (named Clarus, from Mascula, present-day Khenchela in Algeria) explained along precisely the same lines: 'The view of our Lord Jesus Christ is clear: he sent out his apostles and transferred to them alone the authority which had been given him by the Father. We are their successors, who guide the Lord's church with the same authority and baptize in the faith of the believers.'[545]

Bishops

It is surprising that – if we leave aside the Aërians and movements like the Gnostics, which were critical of the majority church – hardly any reports of resistance to the introduction of this episcopal constitutional order have come down to us. A certain conclusion in the development of the office had already been reached in the third century, as the *Apostolic Tradition* shows. It is disputed whether this writing describes circumstances in the city of Rome or whether it does not rather have the custom of the church of Alexandria[546] in view. All that is certain is that it is to be dated before the great persecutions in the middle of the third century. In this text a clear distinction is now made between clergy and laity, and also between a higher and a lower clergy. The higher clergy are divided into bishop, presbyter and deacon – these entered office through the laying on of hands and a prayer for the Holy Spirit. It is not entirely fortuitous that immediately after the preface the work begins with the regulations about bishops. Around the middle of the third century, the only possible candidate for bishop was someone who had already commended himself by his career in the church's ministry – accordingly, deviations like the election of a lay person, which nevertheless still happened, were matters of special note. Bishops were initially chosen by the whole people, but some bishops of neighbouring communities and the presbytery were also involved in the election. The *Apostolic Tradition* stipulated: 'Let the bishop be ordained being in all things without fault, chosen by all the people. And when he has been proposed and found acceptable to all, the people being assembled on the Lord's day, together with the presbytery and such bishops as may attend, let the choice be generally approved. Let the bishops lay hands on him and the presbytery stand by in silence.'[547] It is no longer possible to reconstruct the precise procedure of election, but the 'democratic' element of the popular election was in fact limited by the need for the election to be confirmed by the laying on of hands by the bishops of surrounding churches. However, the restriction was given a theological basis: the laying on of hands was said to communicate to the candidate the divine spirit, the handing on of which was not thought to be safeguarded by an electoral procedure. The bishop was consecrated on a Sunday; the laying on of hands by the other bishops (who represented the community of the churches) made the election valid. The presbytery and the community prayed in silence for the descent of the Holy Spirit, but stood silently ('epiklectic silence') on the periphery of the ceremony. In the ordination prayer God was asked for the gift of the Spirit, and then the prayer continued: 'Father, grant that this . . . your servant, whom you have chosen for the episcopate to feed your holy flock and serve as your high priest, may minister blamelessly by night and day, that he may unceasingly propitiate your countenance and offer to you the gifts of your holy church, Give him authority . . . to forgive sins according to your command, to assigns lots according to your bidding . . . and to loose from every bond.'[548]

Presbytes

In the church order mentioned there is an essentially shorter account of how the members of the college of presbyters are to be appointed. Their prayer of consecration also proves shorter. The presbyters helped the bishop in individual liturgical actions; for example they spoke the prayer of thanksgiving at the eucharist. Presbyters and deacons are to be at a designated place daily to teach the community. Finally, the deacon is not ordained to the priestly office but to serve the bishop. This distinction is represented in the ordination: the presbyters were ordained by the bishop and the other presbyters, the deacon by the bishop alone.[549]

Lower clergy

Below this the *Apostolic Tradition* puts a 'lower clergy' as a series of further offices: the 'confessors', community widows, readers (they were appointed without ordination by being given the book), virgins, subdeacons and those who possessed the gift of healing. Hands were not laid on the holders of these offices,[550] so they were not ordained and are thus clearly distinguished from the representatives of the 'higher clergy'. Remnants of the old pneumatic charismatic view of the ministry which had shaped the structure of the Pauline mission communities and represented a legacy of the primitive community and the historical Jesus are still preserved in this developed hierarchical stage of development of the Christian ministry. That is evident above all from the prayers of consecration reported in detail for all three higher offices (bishop, presbyter/priest, deacon), in which the Holy Spirit is always invoked to support the person holding office.

Women

It is striking that here two substitute offices (community widow or virgin) are reserved for the women, since the threefold ministry of the majority church was closed to them. Above all recently, it has been pointed out that in the primitive Christian period women were still conceivable as dominant figures in house churches (e.g.Phoebe in Cenchreae: Rom. 16.1, or Lydia in Philippi: Acts 17.15,40) and as holding church offices like that of the diaconate (cf. Rom. 16.7 and the discussion over the gender of Junias), because this was in keeping with their position in the households of this time. In general at this point we can see the deep dependence of early Christian theology on the picture of women, above all in the middle class, which was constructed by society. Women exercised public priestly functions in the real sense only in some groups on the periphery of the church. Within the majority church, no reason at all was given for the exclusion of women from the threefold ministry; this indicates that it was taken for granted. Nor did women hold office as priests in the Jerusalem temple. Interestingly, however, there were attempts to elevate the substitute offices mentioned, above all that of widows. Thus, according to the evidence of a Syrian church order from the third century, evidently widows taught theologically in the framework of the conversion of non-Christians, performed lesser liturgical actions (prayer and the laying on of hands) independently, and perhaps even baptized. However, the author of the church order attempted to combat this practice as misuse and to restrict such women to household activities; in addition he expressed his disapproval of women appearing in public: 'A widow shall not run around and wander to and fro between the houses.'[552] Nor, of course, were the laity a negligible factor as community members: their designation as people' (Latin *plebs)* was probably not meant to be disparaging. The significance that the laity still had, at least theoretically, is evident from the procedure for the election of bishops, for which the acclamation of the 'people' by the cry 'Worthy' *(axios)* was still necessary.

Theology of the ministry

There is an interesting piece of evidence for the developed theology of ministry in the fourth century in a writing of John Chrysostom, which he possibly composed four years after his own ordination as priest around 390,[552] 'On the Priesthood'. Both in antiquity and in the early modern period it had a considerable influence; here one can speak somewhat anachronistically of a 'vocational picture' of the priest. The author presented ideas about the personal requirements for being a priest and the right way to exercise the priestly office which claimed general validity. He contrasted this 'vocational picture' with an unsatisfactory 'vocational reality' and composed a 'reform writing'[553] which sought to reform the reality of the calling by the picture. According to Chrysostom, one is really called to this office by Christ, but at the same time there are high demands on those who aspire to it: because so many souls are entrusted to them, those who hold it must stand out from the crowd by the quality of their souls to the degree that human beings stand out from animals. 'For they have been conducted to this dignity as if they were already translated to heaven, and had transcended human nature, and were released from the passions to which we are liable.'[554] On the basis of the two-level ethics – and thus with ascetic and monastic arguments – the author called on those holding office to show a special love of Christ and self-surrender. He was clearly opposed to the mass entry into church office of the urban strata of the decurions which was already beginning in the third century, and which led to a takeover of originally communal tasks by the church. When the author castigates his colleagues in office for 'desire of honour', 'doctrines designed to please' and 'paying court to the rich',[555] he is simply exposing the psychological degeneration in the beneficence of the highest urban authorities, who might expect public recognition for their giving, say for religious and sporting festivals. Thus John Chrysostom is implicitly disputing that the tasks of decurions and the church are comparable by referring to the other preconditions for the office of the clergy. To this end he defines the 'calling' of the priest in a very exclusive sense, in respect both of the particular qualities of those who exercise it and also of the particular intrinsic characteristics of this calling: 'For the priestly office is indeed discharged on earth, but it ranks among heavenly ordinances, and very naturally so: for neither man, nor angel, nor archangel, nor any other created power, but the Paraclete (viz. the Holy Spirit) himself instituted this vocation and persuaded men while still abiding in the flesh to represent the ministry of angels.' Without this ministry it is not possible for Christians 'to obtain our own salvation or the good things that have been promised to us':[556]

they help in the baptism to new life and communicate salvation in the eucharist and the forgiveness of sins. Therefore priests, quite distinct in category from other worldly callings, deserve more honour than magistrates and kings. Chrysostom's writing is not only a testimony to the 'renewal of the church ministry in the fourth century'; it is also an extremely interesting piece of evidence about the reception of Pauline (and Deutero-Pauline) theology. Paul is the ideal model of the true priest by virtue of his tremendous dedication and readiness for sacrifice: 'No man loved Christ more than Paul; no one exhibited greater zeal; no man was counted worthy of more grace.'[557]The author's theology of ministry corresponds to that of the Pastoral Letters, which see themselves as the tradition of the Pauline school: in the end of the day, the advice on the method of exercising office goes back to the historical Paul, who led his communities with great missionary sensitivity (cf. I Cor. 9.20) and at the same time great strictness (I Cor. 5.5). That explains the marked pastoral tone and impulse of the work, which preserves the massed theology of the ministry from being one-sided. Thus, for example, according to Chrysostom 'it is not possible for anyone to cure a man by compulsion against his will';[558] persuasion is to take the place of strictness. Not only the deeds but the attitude of those who do them must be taken into account.

Celibacy

The requirement that priests may no longer marry, i.e. should live celibate lives, can also be put in this very clear tendency to distinguish the priestly ministry from the lay state. Priestly sexuality was felt to be unclean and a stain on the purity of the sacrificial action. From the early period of the empire, the term *caelibatus,* unmarried state, itself really designated a morally reprehensible rejection of the obligation of the citizen to procreate children. From the time of the Republic on this could result in proceedings before a moral court with a declaration of dishonour, and under Augustus the penalties were further increased. The church requirement of the celibacy of priests developed in the course of the third century, initially as a minority opinion. Here, too, we must not underestimate the influence of the ascetic movements, which were growing steadily. Already in the first years of the third century in Rome a theologian protested against married priests; however, the Synod of Elvira at the beginning of the fourth century still accepted married ministers. It prohibited only the 'bishops, priests and deacons and all clergy (generally) who have a function in serving (the altar) . . . from having intercourse with their wives and begetting children; those who do so nevertheless shall lose the dignity of the clergy . . .'[559] By contrast, the first empire-wide council of Nicaea (AD 325) forbade bishops, presbyters and deacons already living celibate lives to have a strange virgin with them 'unless this is, say, a mother or a (physical) sister . . . or some other person who is above all suspicion'.[560] It was in keeping with this development that after Constantine all the strict pagan laws against celibacy were abolished. That evidently happened at least to take into account those Christians who lived unmarried lives – at any rate that is how the Palestinian bishop Eusebius reports the emperor's motivation: 'Others continue childless, not from any dislike of posterity, but because their ardent love of philosophy renders them averse to the conjugal union. Women too, consecrated to the service of God, have maintained a pure and spotless virginity, and have devoted themselves soul and body to a life of entire chastity and holiness. What then? Should this conduct be deemed worthy of punishment, or rather of admiration and praise?'[561] The obligation to celibacy as a presupposition for any priestly ordination is a mediaeval institution; however, for example a canon of a synod at the end of the fourth century deals with members of the community who did not want to receive the eucharist from the hands of married priests. At that synod the position was still anathematized.[562]

Dress

In the fourth century clergy still hardly differed from the laity in respect of their clothing and hair-style, as we can see from the famous mosaic portrait of Bishop Ambrose of Milan which is still in the San Vittore chapel in Ciel d'Oro, immediately beside the bishop's tomb. The bishop is wearing a white tunic with broad sleeves that have two blue stripes on them, and below it – as we can see clearly from the position of his hands – a further tunic (the *tunica interior*) with narrower sleeves. The left arm is carrying the fold of a convenient purple cloak, the *paenula*, on which there is a golden cross. Apart from the *stola*, the narrow linen band round the neck, this is the only sign of clerical dignity. Ambrose presumably did not as yet have a tonsure; rather, his hair-style is due to incipient baldness. Otherwise, on the mosaic we see a somewhat lean aristocrat of the end of the fourth century. Accordingly, it has also been conjectured that the basis for this portrait, which was made shortly after the death the bishop in AD 397, was a picture from his time as governor of the province of Liguria Emilia, before he entered church office.[563] The mediaeval tonsure was not yet usual: on the contrary, so that Christian priests could not be confused with the worshippers of Isis and Serapis, priests were to grow their head long enough for the skin (of their heads) to be covered.[564]

Conclusion

'Between two worlds' – the history of early Christianity between its beginnings in small Galilean villages and its amazing rise to the imperial court and its dissemination to the last corners of the empire is held together by the fact that in quite different ways people attempted to live as citizens of two worlds. As Augustine once declared in a sermon: 'They really loved this life, but they disparaged it: they thought how much they should love the eternal things if they were capable of such a great love of things that are transitory.'[565] For all the differences, existence between two worlds links Christianity before and after Constantine; it provided opportunities but also caused problems for Christian existence.

At the end of our survey of the structures of early Christianity, the question nevertheless remains *why* Christianity exercised such a great power of attraction. The question remains *why* it developed from a small movement in a hardly noticed province to the state religion of the declining Roman empire. After all, it required of people a comparatively radical break with the past and the pagan environment, and also with family and friends, who had now to be classed as idolaters – the practical problems in everyday life alone must have been immense, when we think of the ritualized appearances before household altars in families in which there were both Christian and non-Christian members.

Adolf Harnack attributed this amazing effect of the preaching of Jesus of Nazareth to a mixture of simplicity and breadth. He said that the Christian mission preaching had been so simple 'that one could experience it in a great inner upheaval and describe it with a few short words'.[566] If one understands 'simple' merely in this sense, does not confuse it with 'simplistic', and keeps in view the tremendous claim of the Christian message to explain and shape individual life and the whole of society, one can still agree with Harnack today. In turn he used 'breadth' to characterize the great achievement of this religion in bringing about integration (Harnack speaks of *complexio oppositorum*): on the one hand this is a new movement, but on the other many features of Jewish religion are taken over. Here was a retelling – at any rate by the criteria of antiquity – of a myth of the incarnation of a pre-existent son of God and yet a concern – again by the criteria of antiquity – to penetrate this myth in a rational and scientific way. The church claimed that God was at work in all things and yet at the same time taught human free will (if we leave aside Paul, Alexandrian theologians like Augustine and his pupils). As well as scholarly theology and preaching, through 'sacraments' it offered the ceremony and emotional depth of mystery; it taught simultaneously the resurrection of the flesh and an earthly mortification of this flesh or a fight against it. Alongside the radical ethical demands stands the institution of penance and the forgiveness of sins. In summary it has recently been remarked: 'Christianity: a radical and a moderate religion.'[567] The church founded a religious fellowship which transcended the constraints of nation, gender and social position and with the hierarchical authority of the ministry again set up such constraints. Alongside the harsh criticism of the state stood loyalty to the state; alongside polemical criticism of cultural, economic and social life stood integration, reshaping and affirmation of the realities of the imperium Romanum.

Of course this catalogue must not be understood to indicate that Christianity simply offered something for everyone; that would be wrong. It is better to take it as evidence that as a great synthesis the new religion finally also integrated a large number of people. There was nothing comparable in antiquity to this utterly comprehensive religious institution – critics like Julian saw that particularly clearly. Moreover the New Testament already offers theological approaches which can be divided into the pairs of opposites mentioned above: 'narrowness – breadth' or 'radical – moderate'. On this basis a Christianity could develop which was in many respects pluralistic and colourful: the Christian church 'was simply more complex and was economically and intellectually better equipped than the stereotype of uneducated manual workers and foolish women would have it'.[568] This cliché in essence goes back to the pagan polemic of antiquity: the Platonic philosopher Celsus, who lived in the middle of the second century, said disparagingly of Christians that among them there were no 'educated, no wise, no understanding'.

Great care is also called for over all accounts which simply want to explain the rise of Christianity with reference to the political, religious, social or even ethical decline of the Roman empire.[569] Neither the popular Marxist view that the 'economic impoverishment of the masses' reinforced 'the longing for a life of bliss in the beyond' nor the slogan about a 'universal religion for the universal empire' are satisfactory. To say that Christianity encountered a philosophy which had become 'authoritarian, and too credulous over revelation and miracles' ignores the fundamentally religious character of ancient philosophy. Nor will a psychologizing variant of this model do: at least for the beginning and middle of the second century, it is simply not true that people lived in an 'age of anxiety' (*pace* E. R. Dodds[570]). 'Anxiety' and 'a sense of homelessness' are to be rejected as key words for describing this economically favourable and politically peaceful 'golden age' of the second century. They catch better the mood of the crisis of the empire in the third and fourth centuries – but these feelings were shared by both pagans and Christians. One of the central proof-texts for the hypothesis of the 'age of anxiety' accordingly does not come from the second century but from the second half of the fourth:

'The world is a stage and life a game
dress up and play your role
but banish any serious thought
otherwise you risk breaking your heart.'[571]

Remarkably, the reasons for the attractiveness of Christianity mentioned here are backed up by statements from antiquity. The Platonist philosopher Alexander from Lycopolis in Upper Egypt began a knowledgeable refutation of the Manichees at the end of the third century with some remarks about Christianity: 'The Christian philosophy (i.e. Christian doctrine) is described as simple. But it takes most care over ethical education, and in respect of exact reports about God it makes only hints . . . For even in the ethical questions they avoid the rather more difficult problems, like what is ethical and what is rational virtue (i.e., a traditional philosophical distinction) . . . therefore they devote themselves particularly to ethical admonition. Many people observe these precepts and, as you can see with your own eyes, they make great progress in respect of virtue, and an impression of piety is well established in their behaviour.'[572]

The rise of Christianity in antiquity will go on being a riddle precisely because the sources that have been handed down are so sparse or completely lacking: there are hardly any accounts of conversions which can be assessed psychologically. Only a careful stocktaking of characteristics of Christianity in antiquity will bring together the many features which are responsible for the comparatively rapid expansion and amazing privileges of this religion: as the special strength of Christianity, these certainly include the totality which embraces and regulates the whole of life, the simplicity of its dogma and the precision of its ethical rules, and the offer of a formal kind of piety. In addition, clearly the consistent monotheism, which nevertheless was able to integrate a human existence into the life of God, the guarantee of a connection to this God through prayer, worship, sacrament and the intercession of religious specialists were also impressive. However, the element of astonishment at the upright attitude of the martyrs; the life of ascetics, rich in deprivation; and the development of the splendour of the church as an organization after the fourth century must not be underestimated either. Finally, mention should be made of the miracles and exorcisms or the reports of them; the attractiveness of martyrs and holy men and women; certainly the way in which Christians stuck together, within their communities and indeed all over the empire, their care of widows and orphans, their hospitality – all this was unparalleled in antiquity. To be a Christian brought more protection and help for everyday life than one could ever get as a pagan *civis Romanus*. A further occasion for becoming a Christian in all probability lay in the openness of the movement to all classes and to both sexes. Whether in fact Christian worship (because of the abolition of blood sacrifices) was cheaper for people than pagan religion must be doubted in view of the obligation to give alms.[573] The question whether social reasons were also decisive for a conversion, which can hardly be resolved, needs further, careful investigation; but it can hardly be disputed that more ordinary people simply followed the example of the better-off, for example that of their patrons.

To describe the rise of Christianity one could initially use a modern interpretative concept and speak in a summary form of a 'reduction of complexity' (to use a phrase of Hermann Lübbe's) and an 'unburdening of the soul': early Christianity reduced the complexity and diversity of the world. It reduced it because it declared the world to be a good creation of God in which life according to God's commandments made sense. With a simple ethic and few precepts, people were told what they had to do. In Jesus Christ the distant God came near to them again. Instead of an almost confusing multiplicity of divine figures with all kinds of more or less convincing myths, Christianity preached just the one creator of the world who walked on the earth in the form of his Son, a true human being. The institution of the forgiveness of sins and the perspective of an ongoing existence in heaven relieved believers' souls of a burden, as did the exemplary life and intercession of the holy women and men. But at the same time Christianity made into a theme that 'mythical remnant', that desire for 'more' which does not end in this world: and this way of straddling two such different worlds evidently appeared to large masses of people.

Notes

1. R. M. Grant, *Early Christianity and Society*, London 1978.
2. C. Andresen, *Die Kirchen der alten Christenheit*, Stuttgart 1971.
3. Namely in Paul, Phil.3.20.
4. I have made a series of detailed studies on this, for which see the Bibliography.
5. W. Bauer, *Orthodoxy and Heresy in Earliest Christianity*, Philadelphia 1971 and London 1972.
6. See in the meantime my brief contributions 'Alte Kirche' and 'Christentum, geschichtlich', in *Die Religion in Geschichte und Gegenwart*[4] (1, 1998, 344–60 and 2, 1999, forthcoming; English translation in preparation).
7. *Panegyrici Latini* V 20, 2f.
8. Cf. Matt. 9.1; 11.20; and John 1.44.
9. Julian, *Contra Christianos,* p.199,1–6 Neumann.
10. Justin, *Dialogue with Trypho* 40,4.
11. Theophilus, *To Autolycus* III 26.
12. Bauer, *Orthodoxy and Heresy in Earliest Christianity* (n.5), 48–53.
13. A. M. Ritter, 'Das frühchristliche Alexandrien im Spannungsfeld zwischen Judentum, "Frühkatholizismus" und Gnosis – zur Ortsbestimmung clementinisch-alexandrinischer Theologie', in id., *Charisma und Caritas,* Göttingen 1993, 117–36.
14. Dio Chrysostom, *Oratio* XXXII 51.
15. Socrates, *Church History* VII 5.
16. Melito of Sardes, *Homily on the Pasch* 2, 6 and 8.
17. Dio Cassius, 67, 14, 1f.; Suetonius, *Domitian* 15,1; Eusebius, *Church History* III 18, 4.
18. Thus at any rate Tertullian, *Against Marcion* IV 4, 3/ *Trial speeches* 30,2. The sum represented a moderate but at the same time quite ordinary amount for someone from the provinces; however, in Rome to be a senator one needed capital of at least one million sesterces.
19. G. Schöllgen, *Ecclesia Sordida?*, Münster 1985, 268f.
20. Thus Jerome in the fourth century in his biographies of the church fathers, *De viris illustribus* 53, 1.

21. In Eusebius, *Church History* III 20, 1–3.
22. Eusebius, *Onomastikon*, p.112.
23. R. MacMullen, *Christianizing the Roman Empire,* New Haven 1984, 109f.
24. Gregory of Nyssa, *Life of Gregory,* Gregorii Nysseni Opera X/1, p.16, 3f. Heil; cf. also 20,20f.
25. A.von Harnack, *Mission und Ausbreitung des Christentums*, Leipzig [4]1924, 381.
26. R. Merkelbach, *Mithras*, Königstein im Taunus 1984, 153–88.
27. Berliner Griechische Urkunden, I 27.
28. Thus Theodor Nöldecke, *Die Chronik von Arbela,* trans. P. Kawerau, Corpus Scriptorum Christianorum Orientalium 468, Leuven 1985, 5f.
29. W. Wischmeyer, *Von Golgatha zum Ponte Molle*, Göttingen 1992, 21–62.
30. Abercius inscription, lines 8–13 (text and German translation in T. Klauser, 'Aberkios', *Reallexikon für Antike und Christentum* 1, Stuttgart 1950, 13f.).
31. Pliny the Elder, *Natural History* XXVII 3.
32. W. Dittenberger, SIG[3] 685.
33. K. Wengst, *Pax Romana,* London 1987, 13.
34. F. Vittinghoff, 'Arcana imperii – Zur politischen Integration sozialer Systeme in der hohen römische Kaiserzeit', in id., *Civitas Romana*, Stuttgart 1994, 272–81: 274.
35. W. Dittenberger, OGIS 613.
36. Berliner Griechische Urkunde, I 27; CIL VIII 10570.
37. Thus P. Brown, *Society and the Holy in Late Antiquity*, London 1982, 169.
38. A. Alt, 'Bischofskirche und Mönchskirche im nördlichen Ostjordanland', *Palästinajahrbuch* 33, 1937, 89–111.
39. John Chrysostom, *Catecheses* III/7 4.
40. Brown, *Society and the Holy in Late Antiquity* (n.37), 173.
41. A. von Harnack, *Kleine Schriften zur Alten Kirche*, Opuscula IX/2, Leipzig 1980, 200–26 (= Sitzungsberichte der Berliner Akademie der Wissenschaften 1913, 157–83).
42. Firmilian of Caesarea in Cyprian, *Letter* 60.
43. Hymn to the Cherubim in the so-called Liturgy of St Chrysostom.
44. Thus at any rate K. Holl, 'Die religiösen Grundlagen der russischen Kultur', in id., *Gesammelte Aufsätze* II, Darmstadt 1964, 418–32: 419f.
45. Orosius, *World History* VII 43, 19 or VII 1, 3.
46. Aelius Aristides, *Oratio* III 26, 64 and 10.
47. Ibid., III 109; cf. Virgil, *Aeneid,* I 279: *imperium sine fine.*
48. Augustine, *Sermo* 105, 7–10; similarly 81,9.

49. Tertullian, *Apology* 32.
50. Hippolytus, *Daniel Commentary* IV 21.
49. Melito of Sardes, Fragment 1.
51. Eusebius, *Church History* I 2, 23 and IV 27, 7.
53. Prudentius, *Against Symmachus* II 634–6.
54. Orosius, *World History* VII 7,10; 10,5; 12,3; 15,4; 17,4; 19,2; 21,3; 22,3; 23,6; 25,13; 27, 14 and 28,1. For the years of the reigns of the emperors mentioned see the chronological table on 241 f.
55. Orosius, *World History* VII 26,2.
56. Augustine, *City of God* XVIII 3.
57. Lactantius, *On the Deaths of Persecutors* 34, 4.
58. Ibid., 48,2–12 or Eusebius, *Church History* X 4, 2–14, 15–17.
59. *Codex Theodosianus* I 27,1; ibid., II 8, 1.
60. Eusebius, *Life of Constantine*, III 64,1–65, 3.
61. *Codex Theodosianus* XVI 10,2 or 10,4.
62. Ibid., XVI 1, 2.
63. Mark the Deacon, *Life of Bishop Porphyry* 41.
64. A. Schindler, 'Catholicus, -a', in *Augustinus-Lexikon* I, Basel 1986–94, 815–20.
65. Tertullian, *Apology* 1,7.
66. Thus at the end of the second century Hegesippus in his *Reminiscences*, preserved in Eusebius, *Church History* II 23,6f.
67. Ignatius, *To the Magnesians* 9.2.
68. Eusebius, *Life of Constantine* IV 18, 3.
69. Pseudo-Eusebius of Alexandria, *Sermo* XVI.
70. Eusebius, *Sermo* XVI 1,4 and 8.
71. Thus D. Lohse, *Das Passafest der Quartadecimaner*, Gütersloh 1953, 101–3.
72. W. Huber, *Passa und Ostern*, Berlin 1969, 25–31.
73. Differently ibid., 31–3.
74. Thus Eusebius, *Church History* V 24, 16.
75. Ibid., V 24, 9–11.
76. Letter of Bishop Irenaeus of Lyons and further bishops of Gaul to Victor in Eusebius, *Church History* V 24,13.
77. Thus Huber, *Passa und Ostern* (n.72), 64–8.
78. Eusebius, *Life of Constantine* III 18, 2/3.
79. There is a table of the Roman festival calendar in H.Lietzmann, *Petrus and Paulus in Rom. Liturgische und archäologische Untersuchungen*, Arbeiten zur Kirchengeschichte 1, Berlin and Leipzig 1927, 72–83.
80. G. Bardy, *Menschen werden Christen*, Freiburg 1988, 17.
81. H. Dessau, ILS no. 1264, CIL VIII 1025.
82. Prudentius, *Peristephanon* X 1036–40.
83. Syrian Baruch 41, 4.

84. A. Deissmann, *Light from the Ancient East*, London [2]1911, 446f.
85. Justin, *Dialogue with Trypho* 3,1–8,1: quotation from 8,1.
86. Plato, *Letter* 7 (341 C): '. . . it (viz., the understanding) arises suddenly, like a light that is kindled by a jumping spark, in the soul'.
87. Gregory, *Panegyric on Origen* 6,83: more recent objections to the attribution to Gregory are not convincing.
88. Ibid., 6, 74–80.
89. Ibid., 7, 93–15, 183 or 5, 50 (quotation).
90. Thus at any rate Jerome, *Chronicle of the Year of Abraham* 2343 = AD 327.
91. Cyprian, *To Donatus* 3 or 4.
92. G. Alföldy, 'Der heilige Cyprian und die Krise des Römischen Reiches', in id., *Die Krise des Römischen Reiches, Geschichte, Geschichtsschreibung und Geschichtsbetrachtung*, Stuttgart 1989, 295–318.
93. Origen, *Against Celsus* III 55, cf. also III 50.
94. Tatian, *Against the Greeks* 33,2.
95. Origen, *Against Celsus* III 55.
96. Augustine, *Confessions* VII 9,13.
97. Ibid., VIII 12, 29.
98. Ibid., VIII 12, 30.
99. H. Dessau, ILS 6091 = MAMA VII, 305: *quod omnes ibidem sectatores sanctissimae religionis habitare dicantur.*
100. Augustine, *On the True Religion* 16, 31–83.
101. Augustine, *Retractationes* I 13, 7 or *Letter* 93, 5 = Luke 14.21–23.
102. Augustine, *Letter* 93, 17, 5,14 and 16.
103. There are controversial positions on this in F. R. Trombley, *Hellenic Religion and Christianization c.370–529*, I, 246–82, and J. Hahn, *Gewalt und religiöser Konflikt*, Heidelberg 1992/1993, 313–63.
104. Mark the Deacon, *Life of Porphyry* 19 or 21.
105. Ibid., 31.
106. Ibid., 61, 66 and 72
107. Ibid., 72 or 74.
108. Ibid., 76.
109. Trombley, *Hellenic Religion* (n.103), II, 66–73.
110. Mark the Deacon, *Life of Porphyry* 93.
111. P. Brown, *The Cult of the Saints*, Chicago 1981 and London 1983, 29.
112. Symmachus, *Relatio* III 3.
113. Ibid., III 8–10.
114. Anonymous poem, lines 93f.
115. This letter was included in the corpus of the letters of Jerome as no. 93 and has been so preserved.

116. Mark the Deacon, *Life of Porphyry*, 17.
117. Origen, *Homilies on the Book of Joshua* VIII 4.
118. Cyprian, *Letter* 67, 6.
119. Canon of Elvira II.
120. Ibid., LV and I.
121. Ibid., III.
122. Julius Africanus, Fragment from Book VII, no.I 2 in Thee.
123. VII 14: the attribution of the chapter to Julius Africanus is disputed.
124. Tertullian, *Apology* 18,4.
125. According to Eusebius, *Church History* VI 19,6.
126. Harnack, *Mission und Ausbreitung des Christentums* (n.25), 437.
127. Eusebius, *On the Palestinian Martyrs* 11, 8.
128. J. Jeremias, *Infant Baptism in the First Four Centuries*, London 1960, 34f.
129. Theodoret of Cyrrhus, *Healing of the Greek (i.e. Pagan) Sicknesses* VIII 55.
130. Juvenal, *Satires* VI, 592–7.
131. Didache 2.2 (perhaps composed in Syria in the middle of the second century).
132. Ethiopian Apocalypse of Peter 8/ Greek Apocalypse of Peter 26.
133. Canon of Elvira LXIII, Canon of Ancyra XXI and Canon of Lerida II.
134. Methodius of Olympus, *Symposium* II 6, 46.
135. Didache 5.2 and Apocalypse of Peter 8.
136. Clement of Alexandria, *Eclogae Propheticae* 50,1.
137. Tertullian, *On the Soul,* 37, 1.
138. Clement of Alexandria, *Instructor* I 48, 1.
139. Ibid., II 82,4–5.
140. P. Brown, *The Body and Society: Men, Women and Sexual Renunciation in Early Christianity*, New York and London 1988, 130f.
141. Clement of Alexandria, *Instructor* II 91,1/ 93,1 or *Miscellanies* VII 71, 5 and III 72, 1–4.
142. Clement of Alexandria, *Instructor* II 91,2 = Plato, *Laws* VIII 841d.
143. Julius Africanus, Fragment IX 4 Thee.
144. A. M. Kropp, *Zaubertexte* III, 198–203.
145. Thus John Chrysostom in his *Sermons on I Corinthians* XII 7.
146. Ambrose, *On the Virgins* I 25/26.
147. Brown, *The Body and Society* (n.140), 343.
148. M. Meslin, *Les Ariens d'Occident 335–430*, Patristica Sorbonensia 8, Paris 1967, 51.
149. Palladius, *Lausiac History* 36.
150. Gerontius of Jerusalem, *Life of St Melania* 61, 69.

151. Aelius Aristides, *Oratio* XXX 1 and 19.
152. Tertullian, *On the Soldier's Garland* 3, 3.
153. Origen, *Commentary on Matthew* X 22; the unnamed interpreter is the Jewish exegete and philosopher of religion Philo of Alexandria, who was active in the first half of the first century.
154. Augustine, *Sermo* 301,1.
155. Pseudo-Augustine, *Quaestiones Veteris et Novi Testamenti* 127,10–23.
156. Ambrose, *On the Virgins* III 1.
157. Ammianus Marcellinus, *Roman History* XXI 2, 5.
158. Pseudo-Cyprian, *De Pascha computus* 18/19: 'Therefore the prophet Malachi already said rightly to the people, "The Sun of Righteousness will dawn upon you" (Mal.3.20/4.2)'.
159. H. Rahner, *Greek Myths and Christian Mystery*, New York 1971.
160. Clement of Alexandria, *Miscellanies* I 145, 5/6.
161. *De solstitiis et aequinoctiis,* PLS I, 557–67(fourth century at the earliest, quotation 567).
162. Jerome, *Homilia de nativitate domini,* 214 and 217.
163. W. Dittenberger, OGIS 458.
164. G. Bornkamm, 'Baptism and New Life in Paul (Romans 6)', in *Early Christian Experience*, New York and London 1969, 71–86: 78.
165. Justin, *Apology* I 61, 4.
166. Irenaeus of Lyons, *Refutation of the Gnostic Heresy* II 22, 4.
167. Jeremias, *Infant Baptism* (n.128).
168. K. Aland, *Did the Early Church Baptize Infants?*, London 1963.
169. Babylonian Talmud, Tractate Yebamoth 48 b [Bar.], etc.
170. Didache 7.1–4.
171. Thus G. Schölgen in his bilingual edition, Fontes Christianae 1, 46.
172. Irenaeus of Lyons, *Demonstration of the Apostolic Preaching* 99/100.
173. A. Bouley, *From Freedom to Formula. The Evolution of the Eucharistic Prayer from Oral Improvisation to Written Texts*, Studies in Christian Antiquity 21, Washington 1981.
174. Cyprian, *Letter* 70,2 and 68,7; 75, 11.
175. Cf. Christoph Markschies, 'Wer schrieb die sogenannte Traditio Apostolica? Neue Beobachtungen und Hypothesen zu einer kaum lösbaren Frage aus der altkirchlichen Literaturgeschichte', in W. Kinzig, C. Markschies and M. Vinzent, *Tauffragen und Bekenntnis. Studien zur sogenannten 'Traditio Apostolica', zu den 'Interrogationes de fide' und zum 'Römischen Glaubensbekenntnis'*, Arbeiten zur Kirchengeschichte 74, Berlin and New York 1999, 1–37.
176. *Apostolic Tradition* 21.

177. Canons of Hippolytus 17; cf. F. J. Dölger, 'Der Exorzismus im altchristlichen Taufritual', in *Studien zur Geschichte und Kultur des Altertums* 3/1–2, Paderborn 1909, 112f.
178. *Apostolic Tradition* 16.
179. Ibid., 17.
180. Ibid., 20.
181. *Pilgrimage of Egeria* 46.2.
182. *Apostolic Tradition* 19.
183. G.Kretschmar, *Die Geschichte des Taufgottesdienstes in der Alten Kirche,* Kassel 1970, 141f.
184. Basil, *Homily* XIII 1.
185. Ibid., XIII 3 or 7.
186. Thus J. Gribomont – bibliography in P.Rousseau, *Basil of Caesarea,* Berkeley, etc. 1994, 178 and 194.
187. John Chrystostom, *Catecheses* I 1.
188. Ibid., I 6, 10 and 14.
189. Ibid., III/3 24–26 or II/116.
190. A. Effenberger, *Frühchristliche Kunst und Kultur,* Leipzig 1987, 125f.
191. CIL V 617, 2 = E.Diehl, ILCV 1841.
192. P. Veyne (ed.), *A History of Private Life, 1. From Pagan Rome to Byzantium.*
193. *Agricola* 46, 1.
194. Seneca, *Letters to Lucilius* 63, 15–16.
195. Papyus Oxyrhynchos 115.
196. Tertullian, *On the Resurrection of the Flesh* 1,4.
197. Lucian, *On the Syrian Goddess* 6.
198. Tertullian, *On the Resurrection of the Flesh* 1,1.
199. Ibid., 2, 2 or 2, 8.
200. In Origen, *Against Celsus* V 14.
201. W. Schneemelcher and R. McL. Wilson, *New Testament Apocrypha* 2, 269f.
202. U von Wilamowitz-Moellendorff, *Alexandrinische Inschriften*, 1098.
203. Acts of the Scillitan Martyrs 14.
204. Cyprian, *On mortality* 26.
205. Augustine, *Confessions* IX 12, 32.
206. Syrian Didascalia 26.
207. Cyprian, *On mortality* 20.
208. Cyprian, *Letter* 67,6.
209. Augustine, *The Care of the Dead* 4,6.
210. *Apostolic Tradition* 40.
211. E. Diehl, ILCV 3759.
212. Paulinus, *Life of Ambrose* 45,2.

213. Gregory of Nyssa, *Life of St Macrina,* 984A.
214. Ibid., 992C.
215. E. Diehl, ILCV 1549.
216. Andresen, *Die Kirchen* (n.2), 86–91.
217. Letter of Barnabas 10,11.
218. Andresen, *Die Kirchen* (n.2), 87.
219. Letter of Diognetus 4,6 – 5,12.
220. Brown, *Society and the Holy in Late Antiquity* (n.37), 144.
221. John Chrysostom, *Homilies on the Gospel of Matthew* V 1.
222. H. Lietzmann, 'Wie wurden die Bücher des Neuen Testaments heilige Schrift?', in id., *Kleine Schriften* II, Texte und Untersuchngen zur Geschichte der altchristlichen Literatur 68, Berlin 1958, 15–98: 15.
223. Canon of Laodicea LIX.
224. Thus above all W. G. Kummel, 'Notwendigkeit und Grenze des neutestamentlichen Kanons', in E. Käsemann (ed.), *Das Neue Testament als Kanon*, Göttingen 1970, 62–97: 84.
225. M. Hengel, *Die Evangelienüberschriften*, Heidelberg 1984, 47–51.
226. A. von Harnack, *Die Briefsammlung des Apostels Paulus und die anderen vorkonstantinischen christlichen Briefsammlungen*, Leipzig 1926, 26.
227. Irenaeus of Lyons, *Against the Heresies* III 11, 8. The figure is of course historically fortuitous, but cf. Ezek.1.5–28a and Rev.4.6–10.
228. Thus H. Freiherr von Campenhausen, *The Formation of the Christian Bible*, Philadelphia and London 1972, 206f.
229. B. M. Metzger, *The Canon of the New Testament*, 287–90.
230. A. von Harnack, *Über den privaten Gebrauch der heiligen Schrfiten in der Alten Kirche*, Leipzig 1912 – the author builds on a little known work which has even fuller material, C. W. F.Walch, *Kritische Untersuchung vom Gebrauch der heiligen Schrift unter den alten Christen in den vier ersten Jahrhunderten*, Leipzig 1779.
231. Origen, *Commentariorum Series* 134 on Matthew 27.45.
232. Eusebius, *Church History* VI 3,9; cf. now H. Y. Gamble, *Books and Readers in the Early Church. A History of Early Christian Texts*, New Haven and London 1995, 152–8.
233. Acts of the Scillitan Martyrs 12.
234. Harnack, *Über den privaten Gebrauch* (n.230), p.48; Origen, *Homilies on Numbers* II 1.
235. John Chrysostom, *Homilies on the Gospel of Matthew* I 6, 13 or V I.
236. Ibid., V I.
237. Ibid., II 9; cf. also *Lazarus Homily* III 3.
238. John Chrysostom, *Homilies on the Letter to the Romans* I 1.
239. Zeno of Verona, *Treatise* I 24 = II 38.

240. Augustine, *Lectures on the Gospel of John* VII 12; cf. also John Chrysostom, *Homilies on the Gospel of Matthew* LXXXII 2.
241. Eusebius, *Church History* VIII 2,1.
242. *Gesta apud Zenophilum consularem* 3–4 = J. L. Maier, *Le Dossier du Donatisme* I, Texte und Untersuchungen 134, Berlin 1987, 217–22.
243. C. Courtois, *Les Vandales de l'Afrique,* Paris 1955, 108.
244. Rev.22.18f.: p.88 Maier, cf. also p.116 Maier.
245. Eusebius, *Life of Constantine* IV 36, 1–4.
246. Cyprian, *To Quirinus* II 6.
247. Papyrus Michigan Inv.3718, pp.79–81 Froehlich.
248. Eusebius, *Church History* VI, 2,8.
249. Palladius, *Lausiac History* 26.
250. Basil, *Homily to the Youth about the Beneficial Use of Pagan Literature* 2.
251. Justin, *Dialogue with Trypho* 7, 2.
252. Augustine, *Confessions* III 5,9.
253. Jerome, *Letters* 29, 7, or 31, 1, etc.
254. J. Jeremias, *Jesus und seine Botschaft,* Stuttgart [2]1982, 30–2.
255. Cyprian, T*he Lord's Prayer* 8.
256. Ignatius, *To the Romans* 4.2.
257. Brown, *Society and the Holy in Late Antiquity* (n.37), 11–13; id., *Cult of the Saints* (n.111), 12–20.
248. Papyrus Erzherzog Rainer no. 19931.
259. Papyrus Oxyrhynchos 925.
260. *Apostolic Tradition* 41.
261. Nicene Canon XX.
262. E. Peterson, 'Das Kreuz und das Gebet nach Osten', in id., *Frühkirche, Judentum und Gnosis*, Darmstadt 1982, 15–35: 15.
263. Tertullian, *On the Soldier's Garland* 3, 4.
264. Nilus of Ancyra, *Letter* 3, 287: formulation following Cyril, *Catechesis* XIX 4–8.
265. Dadisho of Bet Qatraje, *Treatise on Solitude*, p.139 Mingana.
266. Pliny the Elder, *Natural History* XI 45, 103; but cf. also Ovid, *Amores* I 4, 27; id., *Metamorphoses* VII, 631f.; Cicero, *Second Speech against Verres* IV 94 and Tibullus, *Elegies* I 2, 83–6.
267. Papyri Graecae Magicae IV, 656–60.
268. Marianus, *Life of Proclus* 31.
269. Pseudo-Melito, *Apology* 9.
270. John Chrysostom, *Homilies on II Corinthians* XXX 2.
271. *Apology against Rufinus* I 19.
272. Prudentius, *Peristephanon* IX 99f.
273. Sulpicius Severus, *Life of St Martin* 18,3.

274. Eusebius, *Sermons* XVI 6 and 9.
275. *Apostolic Tradition* 37.
276. Cyprian, *Letter* 63.14.
277. Theodore of Mopsuestia, *Catechetical Homilies* XV 20/21.
278. Ammianus Marcellinus, *Roman History* XXI 14, 3.
279. Ignatius, *To the Trallians* 5.2.
280. Anonymous in Macarios Magne, *Apokritikos* IV 21 = Porphyry, *Against the Christians*, Fragment 76 Harnack.
281. PAES III A 3, nos. 245–68.
282. W. Wischmeyer, *Griechische und lateinische Inschriften*, Gütersloh 1982, no.39.
283. Laodicea Canon XXXV.
284. Sozomen, *Church History* II 3,9.
285. Eunapius, *Life of Sophists* 472.
286. Basil, *Homily* XIX 8.
287. P. Maravel, *Lieux saints et pélérinages d'Orient,* Paris 1985, 374 or 407.
288. Basil, *Homily* XIX 8; for the dating cf. Rousseau, *Basil of Caesarea* [n.183], 4ff.
289. Quotations from Basil, *Homily* XIX 8, 2 and 4.
290. *Martyrdom of Polycarp* 18,2–3; it is improbable that this is a secondary addition to the original letter.
291. J. Jeremias, *Heiligengräber in Jesu Umwelt*, Göttingen 1958, 22f.
292. Pilgrim of Piacenza 47.
293. Cyprian, *Letter* 12, 2.
294. C. Andresen, 'Altchristliche Kritik am Tanz – ein Ausschnitt aus dem Kampf der alten Kirche gegen heidnische Sitte', *ZKG* 72, 1961, 217–62.
295. *Apostolic Tradition* 9.
296. In E. Diehl, ILCV 2333.
297. E.g. in Brown, *Society and the Holy in Late Antiquity* (n.37), 103–52; id., *Cult of the Saints* (n.111), 86–105.
298. Letter of the priest Cosmas to Simeon, p.186 Hilgenfeld.
299. Theodoret of Cyrrhus, *Historia Religiosa* 26, 23.
300. Ibid., 26, 1 or 11.
301. *Acts of Cyprian* 4,3.
302. Thus Wolfgang Wischmeyer in a 1996 lecture in Oxford, *Acts of Cyprian* 5, 3–4.
303. V. and E. Turner, *Image and Pilgrimage in Christian Culture. Anthropological Perspectives*, Oxford 1978, 1–34.
304. W. Wischmeyer, 'Von einem, der wallfahren wollte, ohne aufzubrechen. Unterschiedliche Perspektiven von Wallfahrten', in H. R. Seeliger (ed.), *Kriminalisierung des Christentums? Karlheinz*

Deschners Kirchengeschichte auf dem Prüfstand, Freiburg 1993, 279–88: 285f.

305. Pilgrim of Piacenza 4.
306. Brown, *Cult of the Saints* (n.109), 42.
307. Pierre Maraval's lexical description of the places in the East of the empire alone amounts to 150 pages: Maraval, *Lieux saints* (n.287), 251–389.
308. Theodoret of Cyrrhus, *Historia Religiosa* 26,1.
309. Ibid., 26, 11 and 12.
310. Ibid., 26, 11.
311. M. Restle, 'Kalaat Seman', *Reallexikon zur byzantinischen Kunst* III, Stuttgart 1978, 853–92.
312. Cf. ibid., 861–86.
313. Papyrus Vindobonensis G 16685.
314. Gregory of Nyssa, *Life of St Macrina*, 990D.
315. John Chrysostom, *Homilies on Colossians* VIII 5.
316. *Canon of Laodicea XXXVI.*
317. *Historia Monachorum in Aegypto* VIII 36/37 = VIII 9, 2–3.
318. Brown, *Society and the Holy in Late Antiquity* (n.37), 122: 'The Syrians were notable cursers'.
319. Origen, *Against Celsus* I 68.
320. Berliner Griechische Urkunden III/9, no.954.
321. Thus Wolfgang Faith in a 1986 lecture in Tübingen, orally.
322. Canon of Laodicea XXIV.
323. CIG 9792.
324. Ps-Chrysostom, *Prayer* (PG 64, 1061 B/C).
325. Didache 4.6 or 1.6; cf. Sirach 12.1.
326. Didache 4.7f.
327. Tertullian, *Apology* 39, 6f.
328. Julian, *Letter* 84c, 430 D.
329. Ibid., 89b, 305B.
330. Ibid., 89b, 305 B/C.
331. John Chrysostom, *Homilies on the Gospel of Matthew* LXVI 3.
332. John Chrysostom, *Homilies on I Corinthians* XXII 7.
333. Mark the Deacon, *Life of Porphyry* 94.
334. K. Thraede, *Soziales Verhalten und Wohfahrtspflege in der griechisch-römischen Antike*, Heidelberg 1990, 52.
335. Cyprian, *On Good Works and Alms* 10/11 or 18.
336. Ibid., 15.
337. John Chrysostom, *Homilies on the Gospel of Matthew* LXXXV 3.
338. Didache 8.1.
339. *Apostolic Tradition* 36.
340. John Chrysostom, *Catecheses* III 4, 2.

341. Ibid., I 21.
342. Papyrus Erzherzog Rainer no.19889 recto.
343. Tertullian, *Apology* 9, 14.
344. BHO 22, 19.
345. John Chrysostom, *Homilies on the First Book of Moses* XXVIII 5.
346. H. Freiherr von Campenhausen, 'The Christian and Social Life according to the New Testament', in id., *Tradition and Life in the Church*, London 1968, 141–59.
347. Tertullian, *Apology* 42, 1–3.
348. Tertullian, *On Idolatry* 23,1–7/ Cyprian, *Letter* 41, 1.
349. *Apostolic Tradition* 16.
350. Tertullian, *On Idolatry* 7, 3.
351. A. von Harnack, *Militia Christi. Die christlichen Religion und der Soldatenstand in den ersten drei Jahrhunderten*, Darmstadt 1963 (= Tübingen 1905), 121.
352. H. Gülzow, 'Soziale Gegebenheiten der altkirchlichen Mission', in H. Frohnes and U. W. Knorr (eds), *Kirchengeschichte als Missionsgeschichte* I, Munich 1974, 189–226: 216–19.
353. E. Diehl, ILCV 414.
354. *Apostolic Tradition* 16.
355. Canon of Arles III.
356. *Apostolic Tradition* 16.
357. Tertullian, *On Idolatry* 17/18.
358. Canon of Elvira LVI.
359. John Chrysostom, *Homilies on St Julian* 4 (pp.672f.).
360. John Chrysostom, *On Empty Praise* 5.
361. John Chrysostom, *Catecheses* I, 20/22.
362. A. M. Ritter, 'Zwischen "Gottesherrschaft" und "einfachem Leben". Dio Chrysostomus, Johannes Chrysostomus und das Problem einer Humanisierung der Gesellschaft', in id.., *Charisma und Caritas*, Göttingen 1993, 309–30: 312–14.
363. John Chrysostom, *Homilies on the Gospel of Matthew* LXVI 3.
364. Ibid., LXVI 3 and 4.
365. John Chrysostom, *Homily IV on the Incomparability of God* 6.
366. See M. Rostovtzeff, *The Social and Economic History of the Roman Empire*, Oxford 1926, 427ff.
367. British Museum, Papyrus 713 = Grenfell II 73.
368. Papyrus Amherst 3a.
369. John Stobaeus, *Anthologium* IV 494, 513 and 524.
370. Claudianus XXXII 128–30.
371. Asterius of Amasea, *Homily* V 3,4.
372. Ibid. V, 5,3 and 5,5.
373. Thus e.g. Origen in his *Homilies on I Corinthians*, frag. 37, lines 34f.

374. Augustine, *On the Dowry* 3 or 6.
375. Brown, *The Body and Society* (n.140), 315f.
376. Cf. Canon of Carthage XII and Canon of Laodicea X.
377. Tertullian, *To his wife* II 78; cf. also Canon of Laodicea XXXIX.
378. Clement of Alexandria, *Instructor* III 58,1.
379. Ibid., III 57,4; cf. Plutarch, *Moralia* 47,9 p.754 A/B.
380. Ibid., III 57,1/ 59, 1 or III 62, 2.
381. Clement of Alexandria, *Miscellanies* VII 70,7.
382. H. A. Sanders, 'A Roman Marriage Contract', in *Transactions and Proceedings of the American Philological Association* 43, 1938, 104–15: 110,1–3; but cf. also Clement of Alexandria, *Miscellanies* II 140,1.
383. Augustine, *On the Dowry* 3.
384. Ibid.
385. John Chrysostom, *On Virginity* 19, 1.
386. John Chrysostom, *On Empty Praise* 19 or 80.
387. Ibid. 30.
388. Augustine, *On the Dowry* 5; cf. also *Sermo* 312, 2.
389. Thus Asterius, *Homily* V 11,1–3 and Canon of Elvira IX.
390. Canons of Elvira VII, LXI and LXVI.
391. Canon of Gangra I.
392. Hippolytus, Fragment of the *Commentary on the Song of Songs* 3, on Cant 1.4.
393. Origen, *Commentary on the Song of Songs* I 5, 1–5.
394. Augustine, *On Weddings* I 10(11)/21/(23).
395. F. Vittinghoff, 'Soziale Struktur und politisches System der hohen römischen Kaiserzeit', in id., *Civitas Romana*, Stuttgart 1994, 253–74.
396. Wischmeyer, *Golgatha* (n.29), 91.
397. Ignatius, Letter to Polycarp 4.3. However, I Clement 55.2 is evidence that there were clearly some Roman Christians who had contributed money for this very purpose at great personal sacrifice.
398. E. Troeltsch, *The Social Teachings of the Christian Churches* (2 vols), London 1930, 81.
399. Grant, *Early Christianity and Society* (n.1), 90.
400. Didache 4.10–11.
401. Origen, *Against Celsus* V 43.
402. Eusebius, *Church History* VI 23, 2.
403. Thus at any rate Augustine, *Letter* 185, 4, 15.
404. Wischmeyer, *Golgatha* (n.29), 102–8.
405. Canon of Elvira V and Canon of Gangra III.
406. John Chrysostom, *Homilies on I Corinthians* XI 5; cf. id., *Homilies on Acts* XI 3.

407. John Chrysostom, *Homilies on Ephesians* XXII 2 or 1.
408. John Chrysostom, *On Romans*, XXIV 1.
409. J. N. D.Kelly, *Golden Mouth*, London 1995, 99f. and 224.
410. Lactantius, *On the Wrath of God* 18, 2.
411. Ignatius, *To the Smyrnaeans* 13.2 or *To Polycarp of Smyrna* 8.2.
412. Eusebius, *Church History* V 16, 17; cf. John 10.12.
413. Epiphanius, *Refutation of all the Heresies* 48, 12, 4.
414. Pliny the Younger, *Letters* X 96,8.
415. K. Hopkins, 'Contraconception in the Roman Empire', in *Comparative Studies in Society and History* 8, 1965, 124–51.
416. A. Jensen, *Gottes selbstbewusste Töchter*, Freiburg 1992, 89–104.
417. *Which Women One Should Take as Spouses* 4.
418. H. Strathmann, 'Askese I (nichtchristlich)', *Reallexikon für Antike und Christentum* I, Stuttgart 1950, 749–58: 749f.
419. Gavius Bassus, Fragment in Quintilian, *Training of the Orator* I 6, 36.
420. Poryphyry, *Life of Plotinus* 1,1 or On *Continence* IV 20.
421. Iamblichus, *Life of Pythagoras* 168.
422. Philo, *On the Contemplative Life* 28–29.
423. Ibid., 73–74.
424. G. Theissen, *The First Followers of Jesus*, London 1978, 81ff.
425. Pseudo-Clement, *On Virginity* I 2, 2.
426. Ibid., I 3, 1; I 4, 1–2 and I 7, 2.
427. Acts of Thomas 12 (Schneemelcher and Wilson, *New Testament Apocrypha 2,* 344).
428. Ibid., 98 (Schneemelcher and Wilson, *New Testament Apocrypha 2,* 376).
429. A. Guillaumont, 'Perspectives actuelles sur les origines du monachisme', in *Aux Origines du Monachisme Chrétien*, Bégrolles en Mauges 1979, 215–27: 220f.
430. Thus rightly K. Heussi, *Der Ursprung des Mönchtums*, Aalen 1981, 110f. and n.2.
431. John Cassian, *De Institutis* XI 18.
432. Athanasius, *Life of Antony* 3, 3/4.
433. Ibid., 2, 3.
434. Ibid., 14, 7.
435. Gregory of Nyssa, *Life of St Macrina,* p.375 Callahan.
436. Thus the first Greek *Life of Pachomius* 12.
437. Codex Theodosianus XII 1, 65.
438. Brown, *Society and the Holy in Late Antiquity* (n.37), 107–30.
439. Theodoret of Cyrrhus, *Historia Religiosa* 26,13.
440. Athanasius, *Life of Anthony* 7, 6–7 and 7, 4.
441. Palladius, *Lausiac History* 18.

442. Ibid.
443. Sozomen, *Church History* VI 34, 3.
444. Theodoret of Cyrrhus, *Historia Religiosa* 26, 8.
445. Ibid., 26, 20.
446. H. Klengel, *Syrien zwischen Alexander und Mohammed*, Leipzig 1986, 54.
447. Theodoret of Cyrrhus, *Historia Religiosa* 26, 20/21.
448. Thus H.Lietzmann, *Das Leben des Heiligen Symeon Stylites*, Leipzig 1908, 215.
449. Syriac *Life of Simeon* 117, p.164 Hilgengeld.
450. Papyrus Heidelberg (Deissmann), 6.
451. Papyrus Heidelberg Inv.G.3850.
452. Macarius Magnes, *Apokritikos* III 36 = Porphyry, *Against the Christians*, Fragment 33 Harnack.
453. Wischmeyer, *Golgatha* (n.30), 115f.
454. W. M. Calder, 'Leaves from an Anatolian Notebook', *Bulletin of the John Rylands Library* 13, 1929, 254–71: 260–3.
455. M. Hengel, *The Charismatic Leader and his Followers*, Edinburgh 1989, 73–80.
456. Epictetus, Fragment 1.
457. Tertullian, *Apology* 21, 1.
458. Codex Theodosianus XVI 2, 3: *clericum consortium.*
459. Origen, *Against Celsus* III 30.
460. W. Elert, *Abendmahl und Kirchengemeinschaft in der alten Kirche hauptsächlich des Ostens*, Berlin 1954, 18f. and 166–9.
461. John Chrysostom, *Homilies on I Corinthians* XXIV 2.
462. Elert, *Abendmahl* (n.460), 168.
463. Thus probably for the first time A.von Harnack, *Dogmengeschichte*, [8]1991 (= ibid. 1922), 84f.: occasionally also, and even more unfortunate, 'three Catholic norms'.
464. A. M. Ritter, '"Orthodoxie", "Häresie" und die Einheit der Kirche in vorkonstantinischer Zeit', in id., *Charisma und Caritas*, 249–64: 251f.
465. Eusebius, *Church History* VI 43,11.
466. Grant, *Early Christianity and Society* (n.1), 6f.
467. *Anthologia Graeca* VII 417.
468. Suetonius, *Tiberius* 6, 57.
469. Conciliar Acts II 3/1 p.324.
470. Brown, *Society and the Holy in Late Antiquity* (n.37), 116, cf. also id., *Power and Persuasion in Late Antiquity. Towards a Christian Empire*, Madison WI 1992.
471. Kretschmar, 'Abendmahl III/1 Alte Kirche', *Theologische Realenzykopädie* I, Berlin 1977 = 1993, 59–89.

472. Justin, *Apology* I 65,3.
473. Ibid., 65, 3–5.
474. Ibid., 66,1.
475. Didache 9.5; cf. Matt. 7.6 and *Apostolic Constitutions* VIII 11,11.
476. *Homilies on I Corinthians* XXVIII 1.
477. Justin, *Apology* I, 66,4.
478. Merkelbach, *Mithras* (n.26), 189f.
479. Tertullian, *Apology* 39, 16–19.
480. Clement of Alexandria, *Instructor* II 3, 2.
481. Ibid., II 4,3.
482. Canon of Laodicea 67,3–4.
483. Justin, *Apology* I 67,3–4.
484. Bouley, *From Freedom to Formula* (n.173).
485. Firmilian of Caesarea, *Letter to Cyprian of Carthage* = Cyprian, *Letter* 75,6.
486. But cf. H. Freiherr von Campenhausen, *Ecclesiastical Authority and Spiritual Power in the Church of the First Three Centuries*, London 1969, 124–48, 238–64.
487. Basil, *Letter* 188,7 or 188,1.
488. H. Dessau, ILS 3051 (the founding of an altar by two mystics together with their 'brothers and sisters').
489. Tertullian, *Apology* 39, 9.
490. Egeria, *Pilgrimage* 10,3.
491. Justin, *Apology* I 65, 2.
492. *Apostolic Constitutions* VIII 11, 2.
493. Palladius, *Lausiac History* 68.
494. *Passion of Sts Perpetua and Felicitas* 3,5–7; cf. also 3,7 and 9,1.
495. Eusebius, *Church History* X 8,11.
496. P.-L. Gatier, 'Nouvelles inscriptions de Gerasa', *Syria* 62, 1985, 297–312: 297–9.
497. John Chrysostom, *Homilies on the First Book of Moses* V 3.
498. M. Picirillo, *Chiese e mosaici di Madaba. Studium Biblicum Franciscanum*, Collectio Maior 34, Jerusalem 1989, 105.
499. Ibid., 106.
500. Theodoret of Cyrrhus, *Letters* 42 and 81.
501. Quotation from an anonymous author from the second century in Eusebius, *Church History* V 16, 10.
502. Eusebius, *Life of Constantine* III 9 and III 15, 1–2 and 16. Constantine also paid the board and lodging for the bishops at other synods.
503. For example Crete and Pontus: Eusebius, *Church History* IV 23,9; cf. also *Church History* V 1,3.
504. Canon of Antioch IX.

505. Andresen, *Kirchen* (n.2), 377; cf. Canons of Constantinople III and Chalcedon XXVIII.
506. Canon of Constantinople III.
507. Irenaeus of Lyons, *Refutation of the Gnostic Heresy* III 3,2.
508. N. Brox, 'Rom und jede andere Kirche im 2.Jahrhundert', in *Annuarium Historiae Conciliorum* 7, 1975, 42–78; H. J. Vogt, 'Teilkirchen-Perspektive bei Irenäus', *Theologische Quartalschrift* 164, 1984, 52–8.
509. Jerome, *Letter* 15,2.
510. Clement, *Miscellanies* I 11, 1–3 = Eusebius, *Church History* V 11, 3–5.
511. Gregory the Miracle Worker, *Panegyric on Origen* 5, 69; Historia Augusta, *Helvius Pertinax* 1, 6.
512. Ammianus Marcellinus, *Roman History* XXI 16, 18.
513. Thus in the year AD 64 the Jewish writer Flavius Josephus, *Vita* 3, 13–16.
514. Didache 1.1–5; cf. also 13.1–2.
515. Ignatius, *To the Philippians* 14.
516. C. Wessely, *Les plus anciens monuments du Christianisme, écrits sur papyrus . . .*, Patrologia Orientalis XVIII/3, Paris 1924, 386f.
517. Canon of Elvira XXV.
518. *Passio Coronati Quattuor* 2,8.
519. In Eusebius, *Church History* IV 23,10.
520. *Epistolari cristiani (secc.I–V). Repertorio Bibliografico a cura di C. Burini* (3 vols), Rome 1990.
521. Jerome, *Letter* 33, 4.
522. Epiphanius, *Refutation of all the Heresies* 75,3,3.
523. E. Dassmann, *Ämter und Dienste in den frühchristlichen Gemeinden*, Bonn 1994, 225–30.
524. A. Loisy, *The Gospel and the Church*, London 1903.
525. A. von Harnack, *Enstehung und Entwickelung der Kirchenverfassung und des Kirchenrechts in den ersten zwei Jahrhunderten*, Darmstadt 1990, 3.
526. R. Bendix, 'Umbildungen des persönlichen Charismas. Eine Anwendung von Max Webers Charismabegriff auf das frühe Christentum', in *M. Webers Sicht des antiken Christentums*, ed. W. Schluchter, Frankfurt am Main 1985, 404–43.
527. Didache 11.4–6.
528. Cf. the reference in Deissmann, *Light from the Ancient East* (n.84), 109; *Bulletin de Correspondance Hellénique* 1897, 60.
529. Harnack, *Enstehung und Entwickelung* (n.525), 104.
530. H. Lietzmann, 'Zur altchristlichen Verfassungsgeschichte', in id., *Kleine Schriften* I, Texte und Untersuchungen 67, Berlin 1948,

141–86: 156–8.

531. Campenhausen, *Ecclesiastical Authority and Spiritual Power* (n.486), 63f.

532. J. Roloff, *Neues Testament*, Neukirchen-Vluyn [3]1982, 63f.

533. These seven letters possibly come from Ignatius, Bishop of Antioch, who was arrested in AD 115 in his Syrian metropolis, transported to Rome and executed there. However, their authenticity is again under discussion: a late dating to the second half of the second century is put forward with additional and weighty arguments by Reinhard M. Hübner, *Zeitschrift für antikes Christentum* 1, 1997, 44–72.

534. G. Schöllgen, 'Monepiskopat und monarchischer Episkopat', *Zeitschrift für neutestamentliche Wissenschaft* 1986, 146–51.

535. Ignatius, *To the Trallians* 2.1; 3.1.

536. Ignatius, *To the Smyrnaeans* 8.1–2.

537. Harnack, *Entstehung und Entwickelung* (n.525), 63f.

538. Bauer, *Orthodoxy and Heresy* (n.5), 62f.

539. E. Dassmann, 'Zur Entstehung des Monepiskopats', in id., *Ämter und Dienste in den frühchristlichen Gemeinden*, Bonn 1994, 49–73: 71–3.

540. Theodore of Mopsuestia, *Commentary on I Timothy* 3.1f. (pp.121–5 Swete).

541. Cf. P. Lampe, *Die stadrömischen Christen in den ersten beiden Jahrhunderten. Untersuchungen zur Sozialgeschichte*, Tübingen [2]1989, 340f. (however, Lampe considers a rather earlier dating).

542. Tertullian, *On Baptism* 17, 1: *summus sacerdos*.

543. Andresen, *Kirchen* (n.2), 132f.

544. Cyprian, *Letter* 66,4–8.

545. Synod protocol 79.

546. J. M. Hanssens, *La Liturgie d'Hippolyte. Ses documents – son titulaire – ses origines et son caractère*, Orientalis Christiana Analecta 155, Rome [2]1965, 343–493.

547. *Apostolic Tradition* 2.

548. Ibid. 3.

549. Ibid. 7, 39 and 8.

550. Ibid 1–14.

551. Syrian Didascalia XV.

552. Thus A. M. Malingrey in the Introduction to his edition of the text, SC 272, Paris 1980, 10–13.

553. H. Dörries, *Erneuerung des kirchlichen Amts im vierten Jahrhundert*, Tübingen 1973, 1–46.

554. John Chrysostom, *On the Priestly Office* 6, 13; 2, 2 and 3, 5 (quotation).

555. Ibid., 3, 9.

556. Ibid., 3, 4 or 3, 5.
557. Ibid., 3, 7.
558. Ibid., 2, 3.
559. Canon of Elvira XXXIII.
560. Canon of Nicaea III.
561. Eusebius, *Life of Constantine* IV 26, 3–4; cf. also *Codex Theodosianus* VIII 16, 1.
562. Canon of Gangra IV.
563. C. Bertelli, in *Milano capitale dell'impero romano 286–402 dc*, Milan 1990, 89.
564. Jerome, *Commentary on the Prophet Ezekiel* 44, 20.
565. Augustine, *Sermon* 344,4.
566. Harnack, *Mission und Ausbreitung* (n.25), 11 (cf. also 958). Of course this characterization is connected with the church historian Harnack's theological position.
567. D. Praet, 'Explaining the Christianization of the Roman Empire', *Sacris Erudiri* 33, 1992–1993, 71–3.
568. Harnack, *Mission und Ausbreitung* (n.25), 256.
569. As e.g. K. Heussi, *Kompendium der Kirchengeschichte*, Tübingen [16]1981, 92.
570. E. R. Dodds, *Pagans and Christians in an Age of Anxiety*, Cambridge 1965, passim.
571. *Anthologia Palatina* X 72.
572. Alexander of Lycopolis, *Critique of the Teaching of Manichaeus* 1.
573. Praet, 'Explaining the Christianization' (n.567), 54–6.

Abbreviations

ANF	Ante-Nicene Fathers, ed. Alexander Roberts and James Donaldson
BHO	Bibliotheca Hagiographica Orientalis
BiTeu	Bibliotheca Scriptorum Graecorum Romanorum Teubneriana
BKV	Bibliothek der Kirchenväter
CCSL	Corpus christianorum, Series Latina
CIG	Corpus Inscriptionum Graecarum
CIL	Corpus Inscriptionum Latinarum
CSEL	Corpus Scriptorum Ecclesiasticorum Latinorum
FChr	Fontes Christiani
GCS	Griechische christliche Schriftsteller
ILCV	Inscriptiones Latinae Christianae Veteres
ILS	Inscriptiones Latinae Selectae
LCL	Loeb Classical Library
MAMA	Monumenta Asiae Minoris Antiqua
NPNF	Nicene and Post-Nicene Fathers, Series I ed.Philip Schaff, Series II ed. Philip Schaff and Henry Wace
OGIS	Orientis Graeci Inscriptiones Selectae
PAES	Publications of the Princeton University Archaeological Expedition to Syria (Leiden 1907–29)
PLS	Patrologiae Cursus Completus supplementum (ed. A. Hamman, Turnhout 1990 = Paris 1959)
SC	Sources Chrétiennes
SIG	Syllogae Inscriptionum Graecarum
WUNT	Wissenschaftliche Untersuchungen zum Neuen Testament

Sources and Translations

Occasionally a more easily accessible but more usable edition is preferred to a critical edition where the latter is harder to get hold of. There are no independent entries for the volumes of J. P. Migne, Patrologia Graeca or Latina, Paris 1841–66 or easily obtainable classical authors like Homer, Juvenal, or Tacitus.

Aelius Aristides: *P. Aelii Aristidis opera quae exstant omnia*, ed. C. A. Behr and F. W. Lenz, Leiden 1976–1980; P. Aelius Aristides, *The Complete Works*, translated into English by C. A. Behr (2 vols), Leiden 1986/1981.

Alexander of Lycopolis: *Contra Manichaei Opiniones Disputatio*, ed. A. Brinkmann, Stuttgart 1979 (= Leipzig 1895); *An Alexandrian Platonist against Dualism. Alexander of Lycopolis' Treatise 'Critique of the Doctrines of Manichaeus'*, translated with an introduction by P. W. van der Horst and J. Mansfeld, Leiden 1974.

Ambrose of Milan: *Verginità e Vedovanza* (= On the Virgins; On the Widows) edited and translated into Italian with a commentary by F. Gori (2 vols, Opera Omnia Sancti Ambrosii 14/1 and 14/2), Milan and Rome 1989; selected writings of St Ambrose translated into German by F. X. Schulte, BKV 1, Series 32, Kempten 1871, 311–86.

Ammianus Marcellinus: *The Roman History,* translated by J. C. Rolfe, LCL, London 1935–39 (3 vols).

Amulets: A. M. Kropp, *Ausgewählte koptische Zaubertexte* (3 vols), Brussels 1930–1931.

Anonymous poem: 'Do we not all live under the same firmament?', German translation and note on the treatise *Contra Paganos* by C. Markschies, in *Die Heiden – Judische und christliche Identität durch ein Feindbild?*, ed. R. Feldmeier and U. Heckel, WUNT 70, Tübingen 1994, 325–77.

Apocryphal Acts of Apostles (e. g. Acts of Thomas): *Acta Apostolorum Apocrypha,* ed. R. A. Lipsius and M. Bonnet (3 vols), Darmstadt 1959 (=Leipzig 1891–1903); *New Testament Apocrypha,* ed. W. Schneemelcher and R. McL. Wilson (2 vols), Louisville, Ky and Cambridge

1991, 1992.
Apostolic Tradition (*see* Church Orders)
Asterius von Amasea, *Asterius of Amasea, Homilies I–XIV*, text, introduction and notes by C. Datema, Leiden 1970.
Athanasius: *Athanase d'Alexandrie, Vie d'Antoine*, introduction, texte critique, traduction et index par G. J. M. Bartelink, SC 400, Paris 1994; Life of Antony, NPNF II 4.
Augustine: *De bono coniugali*, ed. V. J. Zycha, CSEL 41, Vienna 1900, 187–231; *Confessions*, translated Henry Chadwick, Oxford 1991; Latin text and commentary ed. J. O'Donnell, Oxford 1992 (3 vols); *De cura pro mortuis gerenda*, ed. V. J. Zycha, CSEL 41, Vienna 1900, 619–60; *S. Aureli Augustini(. . .) Epistulae*, ed. A. Goldbacher, CSEL 34/2, Prague etc. 1898; Letters, translated W. Parsons, Washington DC 1992 (6 vols); *De nuptus et concupiscentia*, ed. C. F. Vrba and J. Zycha, CSEL 42, Vienna 1902, 211–319; *Treatises on Marriage and other Subjects*, translated by C. T. Wilcox etc., Washington DC 1992; *Sancti Aurelii Augustini Retractationum Libri* II, ed. A. Mutzenbecher, CChr. SL 57, Turnhout 1984; *Sancti Aurelii Augustini in Iohannis Evangelium Tractatus CXXIV*, ed. R. Willems, CChr. SL 36, Turnhout 1954; *Tractates on the Gospel of John*, translated by J. W. Rettig, Washington DC 1992–5 (5 vols).

Basil: *On the Value of Greek Literature* (= *Admonition to the Young*), Greek and English, ed N. G. Wilson, London 1975; *Exegetic Homilies*, translated by A. C. Way, Washington DC 1992.

Canons: [see Synods]
Dio Cassius: *Roman History*, translated E. Cary, LCL, London 1914–27 (5 vols).
Church orders: Didache, in *The Apostolic Fathers*, ed. Kirsopp Lake, LCL, London 1912–13 (2 vols), Vol. 1; *The Apostolic Tradition*, ed. Gregory Dix, London 1937.
Claudian: *Claudii Claudiani carmina*, ed. J. B. Hall, Leipzig 1895; translated by M. Platnauer, LCL, London 1922 (2 vols).
Clement of Alexandria: *Clemens Alexandrinus Bd 1, Protrepticus und Paedagogus*, ed. V. O. Stählin, third revised edition by U. Treu, GCS *Clemens Alexandrinus* I, Berlin 1972; English translation in ANF 2.
(Ps.-)Clement of Rome: in *The Apostolic Fathers*, ed. Kirsopp Lake, LCL, London 1912–13 (2 vols), Vol. 1.
Codex Theodosianus: *Theodosiani Libri XVI cum Constitutionibus Sirmondianis*, ed. V. P. Krueger and T. Mommsen, Dublin and Zurich [4]1970/71 (= Berlin 1905).
Councils, Acts of: *Acta Conciliorum Oecumenicorum*, Vol. II/3/1. . ., ed.

F. Schwartz, Berlin 1962 (= ibid. 1935).

Cyprian: *Sancti Cypriani Episcopi Opera*, ed. R. Weber, M. Bévenot, M. Simonetti, C. Moreschini and G. F. Diercks, CChr. SL 3/3A/3 B, Turnhout 1972/1975/1994; *Letters*, translated from the Latin by R. B. Donna, Washington DC 1992; *Treatises*, translated from the Latin by R. J. Deferrari, Washington DC 1992.

Dadisho of Bet Qatraje: [*Treatise on Loneliness*, Syriac text and English translation], ed. A. Mingana, Woodbrooke Studies VII, Cambridge 1934, 201–47 or 70–143.

Didache: [see Church Orders].

Dio Chrysostom: *Dionis Chrysostomi Orationes*, ed. G. de Budé, BiTeu (2 vols), Leipzig 1916/1919; translated by J. W. Cohoon and H. Lamar Crosby, LCL, London 1932–51 (5 vols).

Egeria: *Égérie, Journal de Voyage (Itinéraire), Introduction, texte critique, traduction (. . .) par P. Maraval*, SC 296, Paris 1982; *The Pilgrimage of Etheria*, translated by M. L. McClure and C. L. Feltoe, London 1921.

Epiphanius of Salamis: Vol. 1, *Ancoratus and Panarion Haer. 1–33*, ed. K. Holl, GCS Epiphanius I, Leipzig 1915; *Panarion haer. 65–80, De fide*, ed. K. Holl, second revised edition by J. Dummer, GCS Epiphanius III, Berlin 1985; *The Panarion of St. Epiphanius, Bishop of Salamis*, selected passages translated by P. R. Amidon, New York and Oxford 1990.

Eunapius of Sardes: *Philostratus and Eunapius, Lives of the Sophists*, edited and translated into English by W. C. Wright, LCL, London 1968 (= 1921).

Eusebius: *Church History/On the Palestinian Martyrs*, ed. E. Schwartz, GCS Eusebius II/1–3, Leipzig 1980–9; Eusebius of Caesarea, *The Ecclesiastical History*, translated with introduction and notes by H. J. Lawlor and J. E. L. Oulton, London 1927–28 (2 vols); *On the Life of the Emperor Constantine*, ed. F. Winkelmann, GCS Eusebius I/1, Berlin, [2]1991; T*he Life of the Emperor Constantine*, in NPNF 1; *The Onomastikon of Biblical Place Names*, ed. F. Klostemann, GCS Eusebius III/1, Hildesheim 1966 (= Leipzig 1904).

Gerontius of Jerusalem: *Vie de sainte Mélanie*, ed. D. Gorce, SC 90, Paris 1962; *Das Leben der hl. Melania von Gerontius*, translated from the Greek by S. Krottenthaler, BKV 5, Kempten and Munich 1912, 445–98.

The Greek Anthology: translated by W. R. Paton, LCL, London 1916–1918 (5 vols).

Gregory of Nyssa: *Gregorii Nysseni Opera Ascetica*, ed. W. Jaeger, P. Cavarnos and V. Woods Callahan, Gregorii Nysseni Opera VIIII/1,

Leiden 1952; *Ascetical Works*, translated by V. W. Callahan, Washington DC 1992; *Gregorii Nysseni Sermones Pars II*, ed. G. Heil, J. P. Cavarnos and O. Lendle, Gregorii Nysseni Opera X/1, Leiden etc. 1990; *The Life of St Macrina*, translated by W. K. Lowther Clarke, London 1916.

Gregory the Miracle Worker: *Grégoire le Thaumaturge. Remerciements à Origène – La Lettre d'Origène à Grégoire*, ed. H. Crouzel, SC 148, Paris 1969; *Address to Origen*, translated by W. Metcalfe, London 1920.

Hippolytus: *Hippolytus Werke* 1. Band, *Exegetische und Homiletische Schriften,* ed. G. N. Bonwetsch and H. Achelis, GCS *Hippolytus* I, Leipzig 1897.

Historia Augusta: *Scriptores Historiae Augustae*, ed. E. Hohl, BiTeu (2 vols), Leipzig $^{5/3}$1971; translated by D. Magie, London 1922–32 (3 vols).

Historia Monachorum in Aegypto: Edition critique du texte Grec par A.-J. Festugière, Subsidia Hagiographica 34, Brussels 1971 (= 1961).

Iamblichus: *Pythagoras. Legende, Lehre, Lebensgestaltung,* Greek and German edition, with translation and introduction by M. von Albrecht, Bibliothek der Alten Welt. Antike und Christentum, Zürich and Stuttgart 1963; *Life of Pythagoras*, translated by T. Taylor, New York 1987.

Ignatius of Antioch: in *The Apostolic Fathers*, ed. Kirsopp Lake, LCL, London 1912–13 (2 vols), Vol. 1; ed. William R. Schoedel, Hermeneia, Minneapolis 1992.

Inscriptions: *Berliner Griechische Urkunden, Ägyptische Urkunden aus den Königlichen Museen zu Berlin*, Vols 1ff. Berlin 1895ff. ; H. Dessau (ed.), *Inscriptiones Latinae Selectae*, Vol. I, Berlin ^{3}1962; W. Dittenberger (ed.), *Orientis Graeci Inscriptiones Selectae* (2 vols), Hildesheim 1986 (= Leipzig 1903–1905); id. (ed.), *Syllogae Inscriptionum Graecarum* (4 vols), Hildesheim 1960 (= Leipzig 1915–1924); *Inscriptiones Latinae Christianae Veteres*, ed. E. Diehl (3 vols), Dublin and Zurich ^{3}1970; U. von Wilamowitz-Moellendorff, 'Alexandrinische Inschriften', in *Sitzungsberichte der königl. preussischen Akademie der Wissenschaften, philosophisch-historische Classe* 49, 1902, 1093–9; M. Picirillo, *Chiese e mosaici di Madaba*, Studium Biblicum Franciscanum, Collectio Major 34, Jerusalem 1989.

Irenaeus of Lyons: *The Demonstration of the Apostolic Preaching*, translated by J. Armitage Robinson, London 1920; *Against the Heresies*, ANF 1.

Jerome: *Saint Jérôme, Apologie contre Rufin*, ed. P. Lardet, SC 303, Paris 1983; [Biographies of the Church Fathers] *Gli uomini illustri. De Viris*

Illustribus, ed. A. Ceresa-Castaldo, Biblioteca Patristica 12, Florence 1988; *Saint Jerôme, Lettres, Tome I*, texte établi et traduit par J. Labourt, Collection des Universités de France, Paris 1949; *Tome II*, texte établi et traduit par J. Labourt, Paris 1951; *Select Letters*, translated by F. A. Wright, LCL, London 1933.

John Chrysostom: *Jean Chrysostome, Sur le sacerdoce (Dialogue et Homelie)*, ed. A.-M. Malingrey, SC 272, Paris 1980; *On the Priesthood*, translated by T. A. Moxon, London 1907; *Jean Chrysostome, La Virginité*, ed. H. Musurillo, SC 125, Paris 1966; *Catecheses Baptismales. Taufkatechesen*, translated with an introduction by J. Kaczynski, FChr 6/1–2, Vienna 1992; *Commentary on St Matthew*, NPNF I, 10; *Commentaries on Acts and Romans*, NPNF I, 11; *Commentary on First and Second Corinthians,* NPNF I, 12.

John Stobaeus: *Johannes Stobaei Anthologium*, ed. V. C. Wachsmuth and O. Hense (5 vols.), Dublin and Zurich 1974 (= Berlin 1884–1923).

Josephus Flavius: *Flavii Iosephi Opera*, ed. B. Niese, Vol. IV . . . *Vita*, Berlin 1940; *Works*, translated by H. StJ. Thackeray, LCL, London 1926–1965 (9 vols: *Vita*, vol. 1).

Julian, called the Apostate: *Iuliani Imperatoris librorum contra Christianos quae supersunt*, ed. C. I. Neumann, Scriptorum Graecorum qui Christianam impugnaverunt religionem 3, Leipzig 1880; *Works*, translated by W. C. Wright, LCL, London 1913–23 (3 vols).

Julius Africanus: J.-R. Vieillefond, *Les 'Cestes' de Julius Africanus*, Publications de l'Institut Français de Florence, Ière série, no. 20, Florence and Paris 1970; F. C. R. Thee, *Julius Africanus and the Early Christian View of Magic*, Hermeneutische Untersuchungen zur Theologie 19, Tübingen 1984.

Justin: *Die ältesten Apologeten*, texts with brief introductions, ed. E. J. Goodspeed, Göttingen 1984 (= 1914); *Complete Writings*, translated by T. B. Falls, Washington, DC 1992; *The Dialogue with Trypho*, translated by A. Lukyn Williams, London 1930.

Lactantius: *De la mort des persécuteurs* (= On the Deaths of the Persecutors), edited and translated into French with a commentary by J. Moreau, SC 39, Paris 1954; *De mortibus persecutorum*, translated by J. L. Creed, Oxford 1984; other works in ANF 7.

Latin Panegyrics: C. E. V. Nixon and B. S. Rodgers (eds), *In Praise of Later Roman Emperors. The Panegyrici Latini.* Introduction, translation and historical commentary with the Latin text of R. A. B. Mynors, Berkeley etc. 1994.

Letters on Virginity: H. Duensing, 'Die dem Klemens von Rom zugeschriebenen Briefe über die Jungfraulichkeit', *Zeitschrift für Kirchengeschichte* 63, 1950–1951, 166–88; *Sancti Patris Clementis*

Romani Epistolae Binae De Virginitate Syriacae. . ., ed J. T. Beelen, Leuven 1856.

Lucian: *Luciani Opera*, ed. M. D. Macleod (4 vols), Scriptorum Classicorum Bibliotheca Oxoniensis, Oxford 1972–1987; *Works*, translated by A. M. Harmon, LCL, London 1913–36 (5 vols); *The Syrian Goddess*, translated by H. A. Strong, London 1913.

Magical papyri: *Papyri Graecae Magicae. Die griechischen Zauberpapyri*, edited with a translation by K. Preisendanz (2 vols), Berlin and Leipzig 1928/1931; H.-D. Betz, *Greek Magical Papyri in Translation, including the Demotic Spells*, Chicago 1992.

Marianus: *Vita Procli*, ed. I. F. Boissonade, Leipzig 1814 = Amsterdam 1966; *The Life of Proclus or Concerning Happiness by Marianus of Samana*, translated by K. S. Guthrie, Grand Rapids 1986.

Mark the Deacon: *Marc le diacre, Vie de Porphyre. Évèque de Gaza*, edited with French translation and commentary by H. Grégoire and M. -A. Kruger, Collection Byzantine, Paris 1930; *The Life of Porphyry, Bishop of Gaza*, translated by G. F. Hill, Oxford 1913.

Marriage contract: H. A. Sanders, 'A Roman Marriage Contract', in *Transactions and Proceedings of the American Philological Association* 43, 1938, 104–16.

Martyrdom of Polycarp: in *The Apostolic Fathers*, ed. Kirsopp Lake, LCL, London 1912–13 (2 vols), Vol. 1.

Melito of Sardes: *Melito of Sardis, On Pascha and fragments*. Texts and translations by S. G. Hall, Oxford Early Christian Texts, Oxford 1979.

Methodius (of Olympus): *Werke*, ed. C. N. Bonwetsch, CICS, Leipzig 1917; *Symposium: A Treatise on Chastity*, translated by H. Musurillo, Mahwah, NJ 1958.

Origen/Rufinus: *Origène, Commentaire sur le Cantique des Cantiques*, ed. L. Brésard and H. Crouzel, SC 375, Paris 1991; *Song of Songs: Commentary and Homilies*, translated by N. P. Lawson, Mahwah, NJ 1956; *Homilien zum Hexateuch in Rufins Übersetzung*, ed. W. A. Baehrens 2. Teil, *Die Homilien zu Numeri, Josua und Judices*, GCS Origen VII, Leipzig 1921; *Die Schrift vom Martyrium. Buch I–IV gegen Celsus*, ed. P. Koetschau, GCS Origen I, Leipzig 1899/ *Buch V–VIII gegen Celsus, Die Schrift vom Gebet*, GCS Origen II, Leipzig 1899; *Des Origenes acht Bucher gegen Celsus*, translated from the Greek by P. Koetschau, BKV 52, Munich 1926; C. Jenkins (ed.), 'Origen on I Corinthians', *Journal of Theological Studies* 9, 1901, 231–47, 353–72, 500–14; *Matthäuserklarung I: Die griechisch erhaltenen Tomoi*, ed. F. Klostermann, GCS Origen X, Leipzig 1935; *Der Kommentar zum Evangelium nach Mattäus*, introduction, translation and notes by H. J.

Vogt, 1. Teil, Bibliothek der Griechischen Literatur 18, Stuttgart 1983; *Contra Celsum*, translated with introduction and notes by Henry Chadwick, Cambridge 1953; *Exhortation to Martyrdom, Prayer and Selected Works*, edited and translated by Rowan Greer, Mahwah, NJ 1979.

Orosius: *Orosio, Le Storie contro i Pagani* (2 vols), ed. A. Lippold, Scrittori Greci e Latini, 1976; *Seven books of History against the Pagans*, translated by I. W. Raymond, New York 1936.

Pachomius: *The Life of Pachomius (Vita Prima Graeca)*, translated by A. N. Athanassakis, Texts and Translations 7. Early Christian Literature Series 2, 1975 (with Greek text by F. Halkin).

Palladius: *The Lausiac History of Palladius, Vol. II, The Greek Text*, edited with introductions and notes by C. Butler, Texts and Studies VI/2, Cambridge 1904; *The Lausiac History*, translated W. Lowther Clarke, London 1918.

Papyri: *Veröffentlichungen aus der Heidelberger Papyrussammlung I: Die Septuagintapapyri und andere altchristliche Texte*, ed. A. Deissmann, Heidelberg 1905; C. Wessely, *Les plus anciens monuments du Christianisme, écrits sur papyrus*, Patrologia Orientalis IV/2 or XVIII/3, Paris 1906 or 1924.

Passio Sanctarum Perpetuae et Felicitatis: Vol. I ed. C. I. M. I. van Beek, Nijmegen 1936; Latin text and English translation in H. Musurillo, *The Acts of the Christian Martyrs*, Oxford 1972, 106–31.

Paul, Acts of: *Acta Apostolorum Apocrypha*, ed. R. A. Lipsius, Vol. 1, Darmstadt 1959 (= Leipzig 1891), 235–69; *New Testament Apocrypha*, Vol. 2, ed. W. Schneemelcher and R. McL. Wilson, Louisvillle, Ky and Cambridge 1992, 213–70.

Persian Acts of Martyrs: P. Bedjan (ed.), *Acta martyrum et sanctorum* (7 vols), Paris 1890–97; *Ausgewählte Akten persischer Märtyrer*, translated from the Syriac by O. Braun, BKV 22, Kempten and Munich 1915.

Philo of Alexandria, *Opera quae supersunt*, ed. L. Cohn/P. Wendland (6 vols), Berlin 1962 (= ibid. 1896–1915); Philo von Alexandria, *Works*, translated by F. H. Colson and G. H. Whitaker, LCL, London 1929–62 (10 vols: *On the Contemplative Life* is in Vol. 9).

Pilgrim of Piacenza: *Itinera Hierosolymitana Saeculi III–VIII*, ed. P. Geyer, CSEL 39, Prague etc. 1898, 159–91; H. Donner, *Pilgerfahrt ins Heilige Land. Die ältesten Berichte christlicher Palästinapilger (4.–7. Jahrhundert)*, Stuttgart 1979, 240–314.

Plato: *Letters*, Greek text in *Opera* 5. ii, ed. J. Burnet, Oxford 1913; translation in *Thirteen Epistles*, introduced with translation and notes by L. A. Post, Oxford 1925.

Pliny the Elder: *Natural History*, translated by H. Rackham, LCL, London

1938–1962 (10 vols).

Pliny the Younger: *Letters*, translated by W. Melmoth, revised W. M. L. Hutchinson, LCL, London 1913 (2 vols).

Plutarch: *Lives*, translated by B. Perrin, LCL, London 1914–26 (11 vols); *Moralia*, translated by F. C. Babbitt et al., LCL, London 1927–76 (16 vols).

Porphyry: 'Gegen die Christen', ed. A. von Harnack, in id., *Kleine Schriften zur Alten Kirche, Band. II: Berliner Akademieschriften 1908–1930*, Opuscula IX/2, Leipzig 1980, 362–474; *Life of Plotinus*, in Plotinus, *Enneads* Vol. 1, translated by Stephen Mackenna, LCL, London 1917; *Select Works*, translated by T. Taylor, London 1994.

Prudentius: *Prudence, Tome III Psychomachie. Contre Symmaque*, edited with a translation by M. Lavarenne, Collection des Universités de France, Paris 1948; Tome IV, *Le Livre des Couronnes (Peristephanon Liber). Dittochaeon. Épilogue*, edited with a translation by M. Lavarenne, Collection des Universités de France, Paris 1951; *Works*, translated by H. J. Thomson, LCL, London 1949–53 (2 vols).

Quintilian: *Institutio Oratoria*, translated by H. E. Butler, LCL, London 1921–22 (4 vols).

Seneca: *Epistulae Morales*, translated by R. M. Gummere, LCL, London 1917–25 (3 vols); *Moral Essays*, translated by J. W. Basore, LCL, London 1928–35 (3 vols).

Socrates Scholasticus: *Socrates, Church History*, ed. C. C. Hansen, GCS, Berlin 1995; *Socrates, Sozomen: Church Historians*, NPNF 2.

Sozomen: *Sozomène, Histoire Ecclésiastique, Livres I–II*, Greek text edited by J. Bidez, SC 306, Paris 1983.

Suetonius: *C. Suetoni Tranquilli Opera Vol. 1, De Vita Caesarum Libri VIII*, ed. M. Ihm, BiTeu, Stuttgart 1978 (= Leipzig 1908); *Works*, translated by J. C. Rolfe, LCL, London 1914 (2 vols).

Sulpicius Severus: *Libri qui supersunt*, ed. C. Halm, CSEL 1, Vienna 1865; writings translated in NPNF II, 11.

Symeon Stylites: *Syriac Life*, translated by F. Lent in *Journal of the American Oriental Society* 35, 1915–17, 103–98.

Symmachus: *Der Streit um den Victoriaaltar. Die dritte Relatio des Symmachus und die Briefe 17,18 und 57 des Mailander Bischofs Ambrosius*. Introduction, text and translation by R. Klein, Texte zur Forschung 7, Darmstadt 1972.

Synods: *The Decrees and Canons of the Seven Ecumenical Councils*, NPNF II 14; P. Joannou, *Fonti. Fascicolo IX, Discipline générale antique (IIe–IXe s.)*, I/I *Les canons de conciles oecuméniques*, Grottaferrata 1962; II *Les canons des Pères grecs*, Grottaferrata 1962 [no critical texts].

Syriac Didascalia: *The Didascalia Apostolorum in Syriac*, ed. A. Vööbus (2 vols), Corpus Scriptorum Christianorum Orientalium 401/407 Series Syri 175/179, Leuven 1979; *Die ältesten Quellen des orientalischen Kirchenrechts, 2. Buch: Die syrische Didaskalia*, translated into German with a commentary by H. Achelis and J. Flemming, Texte und Untersuchungen 25/2, Leipzig 1904.

Tatian: translation of works in ANF 2.

Tertullian: *Quinti Septimi Florentis Tertulliani Opera. Pars I Opera Catholica, Adv. Marcionem, Pars II Opera Montanistica,* CChr. SL 1. 2, Turnhout 1954; English translation of works in ANF 3 and 4.

Theodore of Mopsuestia: *Les homélies catéchétiques de Théodore de Mopsueste. Reproduction phototypique. . .*, translation, introduction and index by R. Tonneau in collaboration with R. Devreesse, Studi e Testi 145, Modena 1981 (= Vatican City 1949); *Theodor von Mopsuestia, Katechetische Homilien*, translated into German with an introduction by P. Bruns, FChr 17/1–2, Freiburg etc. 1994/1995; *Theodori Episcopi Mopsuesteni in epistolas B. Pauli commentarii*, ed. H. B. Swete (2 vols), Cambridge 1880/1882.

Theodoret of Cyrrhus: Théodoret de Cyr, *Thérapeutique des maladies helléniques* (= Healing of the Greek Sicknesses), ed. P. Canivet (2 vols), SC 57, Paris 1958; *Theodorets Kirchengeschichte*, ed. L. Parmentier, third edition ed. F. Scheidweiler and G. C. Hansen (GCS), Berlin 1998; Theodoret de Cyr, *Histoire de moines de Syrie*, ed. P. Canivet and A. Leroy-Molinghen, SC 234/25, Paris 1977/1979; *Des Bischofs Theodoret von Cyrus Mönchsgeschichte*, translated into German from the Greek by K. Gutberlet, BKV 50, Munich 1926; *Des Bischofs Theodoret von Cyrus Kirchengeschichte,* translated into German from the Greek by A. Seider, BKV 51, Munich 1926.

Theophilus of Antioch: *Theophili Antiocheni ad Autolycurn*, ed. M. Marcovich, Patristische Texte und Studien 44, Berlin/New York 1995; *Trois livres à Autolycus. Texte grec établi par G. Bardy*, translation into French by J. Sender, SC, Paris 1948.

Zeno of Verona: *Sanctus Zeno Veronensis Tractatus*, ed. B. Löfstedt, CChr. SL 22, Turnout 1971; *Des hl. Bischofs Zeno von Verona Traktate (Predigten und Ansprachen),* translated from the Latin by A. Bigelmaier, BKV, Munich 1934.

Select Bibliography

No entry is given here for lexicon articles relevant to the topic from the great lexicons (e. g. *Reallexikon für Antike und Christentum*, Stuttgart 1950ff.; *Pauly-Wissowas Realencyclopädie der classischen Altertumswissenschaft*, Stuttgart 1893–1980; *Theologische Realenzyklopädie*, Berlin and New York 1977ff.; *Reallexikon der byzantinischen Kunst*, Stuttgart 1966ff.; *Dictionnaire d'Archéologie Chrétienne et de Liturgie*, Paris 1903–1953, even if grateful use has been made of them.

Aland, Kurt: *Über den Glaubenswechsel in der Geschichte des Christentums,* Theologische Bibliothek Töpelmann 5, Berlin 1961.

Albrecht, Ruth: *Das Leben der heiligen Makrina auf dem Hintergrund der Thekla-Traditionen. Studien zu den Ursprüngen des weiblichen Mönchtums im 4. Jahrhundert in Kleinasien*, Forschungen zur Kirchen- und Dogmengeschichte 38, Göttingen 1986.

Alföldy, Geza: *Die Krise des Römischen Reiches. Geschichte, Geschichtsschreibung und Geschichtsbetrachtung. Ausgewählte Beiträge,* Heidelberger althistorische Beiträge und epigraphische Studien 5, Stuttgart 1989.

Andresen, Carl: *Die Kirchen der alten Christenheit*, Religionen der Menschheit 29,1/2, Stuttgart 1971.

Bardy, Gustave: *Menschen werden Christen. Das Drama der Bekehrung in den ersten Jahrhunderten*, Freiburg 1988 (= Paris 1949).

Bauer, Walter: *Orthodoxy and Heresy in Earliest Christianity*, Philadelphia and London 1967, ET of *Rechtgläubigkeit und Ketzerei im ältesten Christentum*, Beiträge zur historischen Theologie 10, Tübingen ²1964.

Bendix, Reinhard: 'Umbildungen des persönlichen Charismas. Eine Anwendung von Max Webers Charismabegriff auf das Frühchristentum', in *M. Webers Sicht des antiken Christentums*, ed. Wolfgang Schluchter, stw 548, Frankfurt am Main 1985, 404–43.

Bibliotheca Hagiographica Orientalis: edd. socii Bollandiani, Subsidia Hagiographica 10, Brussels 1970 (= 1910).

Bornkamm, Günther: 'Baptism and New Life in Paul (Romans 6)', in *Early Christian Experience*, New York and London 1969, 71–86: partial ET of *Das Ende des Gesetzes. Paulusstudien*, Beiträge zur evangelischen Theologie 16, Munchen 1952.

Bouley, A.: *From Freedom to Formula. The Evolution of the Eucharistic Prayer from Oral Improvisation to Written Texts,* Studies in Christian Antiquity 21, Washington 1981.

Brown, Peter: *Society and the Holy in Late Antiquity*, London 1982; *The Cult of the Saints*, Chicago and London 1981; *The Body and Society: Men, Women and Sexual Renunciation in Early Christianity*, New York and London 1988.

Calder, William M.: 'Leaves from an Anatolian Notebook', *Bulletin of the John Rylands Library*, Manchester 13, 1929, 254–71.

Campenhausen, Hans Freiherr von: *The Formation of the Christian Bible*, Philadelphia and London 1972; *Ecclesiastical Office and Spiritual Power in the Church of the First Three Centuries*, London 1969; *Tradition and Life in the Church*, London 1968.

Courtois, Christian: *Les Vandales et l'Afrique*, Paris 1955.

Dassmann, Ernst: *Ämter und Dienste in den frühchristlichen Gemeinden*, Hereditas. Studien zur Alten Kirchengeschichte 8, Bonn 1994.

Deichmann, Friedrich Wilhelm: *Einführung in die christliche Archäologie,* Darmstadt 1983.

Deissmann, Adolf: *Light from the Ancient East*, London [2]1927

Dodds, Eric Robertson: *Pagans and Christians in an Age of Anxiety*, Cambridge 1965.

Dörries, Hermann: 'Erneuerung des kirchlichen Amts im vierten Jahrhundert', in B. Moeller and G. Ruhbach (eds), *Bleibendes im Wandel der Kirchengeschichte. Kirchenhistorische Studien*, Tübingen 1973, 1–46.

Downey, Glanville: *Antioch in the Age of Theodosius the Great*, Norman 1962.

Effenberger, Arne: *Frühchristliche Kunst und Kultur. Von den Anfängen bis zum 7. Jahrhundert*, Leipzig 1987.

Elert, Werner: *Abendmahl und Kirchengemeinschaft in der alten Kirche hauptsächlich des Ostens*, Berlin 1954.

Fox, Robin Lane: *Pagans and Christians in the Mediterranean World from the Second Century AD to the Conversion of Constantine*, London [2]1988.

Frank, Karl Suso: *Geschichte des christlichen Mönchtums*, Darmstadt [5]1993.

Frankfurt Catalogue 1984: *Spätantike und frühes Christentum. Ausstellung im Liebighaus, Museum alter Plastik, Frankfurt am M. 16. 12. 1983 bis 11. 3. 1984*, Frankfurt am Main 1983.

Froehlich, Karlfried: *Biblical Interpretation in the Early Church*, Philadelphia 1984.

Frohnes, Heinzgünter and Knorr, Uwe W. (eds): *Kirchengeschichte als Missionsgeschichte, Bd. 1: Die Alte Kirche*, Munich 1974.

Fuhrmann, Manfred: *Rom in der Spätantike*, Munich and Zurich 1994.

Gamble, Harry Y. : *Books and Readers in the Earlv Church. A History of Early Christian Texts*, New Haven und London 1995.

Grant, Robert M. : *Early Christianity and Society*, London 1978.

Gribomont, Jean: *Saint Basile. Évangile et église. Mélanges*, Spiritualité orientale et vie monastique 36/37, Begrolles-en-Mauges 1984.

Gülzow, Henneke: 'Soziale Gegebenheiten der altkirchlichen Mission', in H. Frohnes and U. W. Knorr (eds), *Kirchengeschichte als Missionsgeschichte* I [see above], 189–226.

Guillaumont, Antoine: *Aux Origines du Monachisme Chrétien. Pour une phénoménologie du monachisme*, Spiritualité Orientale 30, Begrolles en Mauges 1979.

Guyot, Peter and Klein, Richard: *Das frühe Christentum bis zum Ende der Verfolgungen. Eine Dokumentation*, Texte zur Forschung 60/62, Darmstadt 1993/1994 [Sources, translation and commentary].

Hahn, Johannes: *Gewalt und religiöser Konflikt. Studien zu den Auseinandersetzungen zwischen Christen, Heiden und Juden im Osten des römischen Reiches in der Spätantike*, typescript Habilitationsschrift, Heidelberg 1992/1993.

Hanssens, Jean Michel: *La Liturgie d'Hippolyte. Ses documents – son titulaire – ses origines et son caractère*, Orientalia Christiana Analecta 155, Rome [2]1952

Harnack, Adolf von: *Entstehung und Entwickelung der Kirchenverfassung und des Kirchenrechts in den ersten zwei Jahrhunderten*, Darmstadt 1990 (= Leipzig 1910); *Die Mission und Ausbreitung des Christentums in den ersten drei Jahrhunderten*, Wiesbaden 1981 (= Leipzig [4]1924); *Über den privaten Gebrauch der heiligen Schriften in der Alten Kirche*, Beiträge zur Einleitung in das Neue Testament V, Leipzig 1912.

Hengel, Martin: *Property and Riches in the Early Church*, London and Philadelphia 1974; *Die Evangelienüberschriften*, Sitzungsberichte der Heidelberger Akademie der Wissenschaften, Philosophisch-Historische Klasse Heft 3/1984, Heidelberg 1984; *The Charismatic Leader and His Followers*, Studies of the NT and Its World, Edinburgh 1989.

Heussi, Karl: *Der Ursprung des Mönchtums*, Aalen 1981 (= Tübingen

1936).

Holl, Karl: *Gesammelte Aufsätze zur Kirchengeschichte, Bd. II: Der Osten, Bd. III: Der Westen*, Darmstadt 1964 (= Tübingen 1928).

Huber, Wolfgang: *Passa und Ostern. Untersuchungen zur Osterfeier in der alten Kirche*, Beihefte zur Zeitschrift für die neutestamentliche Wissenschaft 35, Berlin 1969.

Jensen, Anne: *Gottes selbstbewusste Töchter. Frauenemanzipation im frühen Christentum?*, Freiburg etc. 1992.

Jeremias, Joachim: *Heiligengräber in Jesu Umwelt. . . Eine Untersuchung zur Volksreligion der Zeit Jesu*, Göttingen 1958; *Infant Baptism in the First Four Centuries*, London 1960.

Kelly, John Norman Davidson: *Golden Mouth. The Story of John Chrysostom — Ascetic, Preacher, Bishop*, London 1995.

Klengel, Horst: *Syrien zwischen Alexander und Mohammed. Denkmale aus Antike und frühem Christentum*, Leipzig 1986.

Kretschmar, Georg: 'Die Geschichte des Taufgottesdienstes in der Alten Kirche', in K. F. Müller and W. Blankenburg (eds.), *Leiturgia V*, Kassel 1970, 1–348.

Lampe, Peter: *Die stadtrömischen Christen in den ersten beiden Jahrhunderten. Untersuchungen zur Sozialgeschichte*, WUNT 2. R. 18, Tübingen [2]1989.

Lohse, Bernhard: *Das Passafest der Quartadecimaner*, Beiträge zur Förderung der christlichen Theologie 11/54, Gütersloh 1953.

Loisy, Alfred: *The Gospel and the Church*, London 1904.

MacMullen, Ramsay: *Christianizing the Roman Empire (A. D. 100–400)*, New Haven and London 1984.

Maier, Jean-Louis: *Le Dossier du Donatisme, Bd. I: Des origines à la mort de Constance 11(303–361)*, Texte und Untersuchungen 134, Berlin 1987.

Maraval, Pierre: *Lieux saints et pélérinages d'Orient. Histoire et géographie des origines à la conquête arabe*, Paris 1985.

Markschies, Christoph (with A. Böhlig): *Gnosis und Manichäismus*, Beihefte zur Zeitschrift für die neutestamentliche Wissenschaft und die Kunde der älteren Kirche 72, Berlin/New York 1994; 'Die platonische Metapher vom "inneren Menschen": Eine Brücke zwischen antiker Philosophie und altchristlicher Theologie', *Zeitschrift fur Kirchengeschichte* 105, 1994, 1–17; 'Platons König oder Vater Jesu Christi? Drei Beispiele für die Rezeption eines griechischen Gottesepithetons bei den Christen in den ersten Jahrhunderten', in M. Hengel and A. M.

Schwemer (eds.), *Königsherrschaft Gottes und himmlischer Kult*, WUNT 55, Tübingen 1991, 385–439.

Martin, Jochen and Quint, Barbara (eds): *Christentum und antike Gesellschaft*, Wege der Forschung 649, Darmstadt 1990 (collection of articles).

Merkelbach, Reinhold: *Mithras*, Königstein im Taunus 1984.

Metzger, Bruce M. : *The Canon of the New Testament*, Oxford 1987.

Milan catalogue: *Milano capitale dell'impero romano 286–402 d. c. Milano – Palazzo Reale 24 gennaio – 22 aprile 1990*, Milan 1990.

Niebergall, Alfred: *Ehe und Eheschliessung in der Bibel und in der Geschichte der Alten Kirche,* posthumously edited by A. M. Ritter, Marburger Theologische Studien 18, Marburg 1985.

Peterson, Erik: *Frühkirche, Judentum und Gnosis. Studien und Untersuchungen*, Darmstadt 1982 (= Freiburg 1959).

Praet, Danny: 'Explaining the Christianization of the Roman Empire. Older Theories and Recent Developments', *Sacris Erudiri* 33, 1992–1993, 1–119.

Rahner, Hugo: *Greek Myths and Christian Mystery*, New York 1971.

Ritter, Adolf Martin: *Charisma und Caritas. Aufsätze zur Geschichte der Alten Kirche*, ed. A. Dörfler-Dierken etc., Göttingen 1993.

Rousseau, Philip: *Basil of Caesarea*, Berkeley etc. 1994.

Schöllgen, Georg: *Ecclesia Sordida? Zur Frage der sozialen Schichtung frühchristlicher Gemeinden am Beispiel Karthagos zur Zeit Tertullians*, Jahrbuch für Antike und Christentum, Ergänzungsband 12, Münster 1984; 'Monepiskopat und monarchischer Episkopat. Eine Bemerkung zur Terminologie', *Zeitschrift für die neutestamentliche Wissenschaft* 77, 1986, 146–51.

Tchalenko, Georges: *Eglises de Village de la Syrie du Nord, Planches*, Paris 1979, Album, ibid. 1980.

Theissen, Gerd: *The First Followers of Jesus*, London 1978.

Thraede, Klaus: 'Soziales Verhalten und Wohlfahrtspflege in der griechisch-römischen Antike (späte Republik und frühe Kaiserzeit)', in G. K. Schäfer and T. Strohm (eds.), *Diakonie – biblische Grundlagen und Orientierungen*, Veröffentlichungen des diakoniewissenschaftlichen Instituts an der Universität Heidelberg 2, Heidelberg 1990, 4–63.

Troeltsch, Ernst: *The Social Teachings of the Christian Churches* (2 vols), London 1930.

Trombley, Frank R. : *Hellenic Religion and Christianization c.370–529*,

Religions in the Graeco-Roman World 115/1–2, Leiden etc. 1993/1994.
Turner, Victor and Edith: *Image and Pilgrimage in Christian Culture. Anthropological Perspectives*, Oxford 1978.

Veyne, Paul (ed.): *A History of Private Life, 1. From Pagan Rome to Byzantium*, Cambridge, Mass. 1987.
Vittinghoff, Friedrich: *Civitas Romana. Stadt und politisch-soziale Integration im Imperium Romanum der Kaiserzeit,* Stuttgart 1994.

Weber, Max: *Wirtschaft und Gesellschaft*, Band I, Cologne 1964.
Wengst, Klaus: *Pax Romana. Claim and Reality*, London 1987.
Wilken, Robert L. : *The Christians as the Romans Saw Them*, New Haven 1978.
Wischmeyer, Wolfgang: *Griechische und lateinische Inschriften zur Sozialgeschichte der Alten Kirche*, Texte zur Kirchen- und Theologiegeschichte 28, Gütersloh 1982; *Von Golgatha zum Ponte Molle. Studien zur Sozialgeschichte der Kirche im dritten Jahrhundert*, Forschungen zur Kirchen- und Dogmengeschichte 49, Göttingen 1992.

Zahn, Theodor von: *Skizzen aus dem Leben der Alten Kirche*, Erlangen and Leipzig 1894.

Chronological table

30 (?)	Crucifixion of Jesus
54–68	Nero emperor
64	Nero persecutes the Christians
70	Destruction of Jerusalem
81–96	Domitian emperor
98–117	Trajan emperor
115(?)	Arrest of Ignatius, Bishop of Antioch
160 (?)	Tertullian born in Carthage, died after 220
161–180	Marcus Aurelius emperor
c.165	The emperor Justin executed in Rome
177/78	Irenaeus becomes Bishop of Lyons
190/191	High point of the dispute over the date of Easter
193–211	Septimius Severus emperor
before 215	Death of Clement of Alexandria
235–238	Maximin Thrax emperor
249–251	Decius emperor
250/251	Decius persecutes the Christians
253–260	Valerian emperor
254	Death of Origen
257/258	Valerian persecutes the Christians
258	Execution of Cyprian, Bishop of Carthage
c.270	Death of Gregory Thaumaturgus, Bishop of Neocaesarea
270–275	Aurelian emperor
284–305	Diocletian emperor
303–313	Diocletian persecution of Christians
305–311	Galerian emperor (Caesar 293–305, Augustus 305–311)
313	Edict of Milan
324	Constantine sole ruler
325	First imperial council in Nicaea
337	Death of the emperor Constantine
337–361	Constantius II emperor
339	Death of Eusebius, Bishop of Caesarea in Palestine

346	Death of Pachomius
354–430	Augustine, from *c*.396 Bishop of Hippo
356	Death of Antony
360–363	Julian 'the Apostate' emperor
378	Death of the emperor Valens in the battle of Adrianopolis
379	Death of Basil, from 370 Bishop of Caesarea in Cappadocia
379–395	Theodosius emperor
380	Edict *cunctos populos* of Emperor Theodosius
c.390	Death of Gregory of Nazianzus, Bishop of Constantinople 379–381
397	Death of Ambrose, from 374 Bishop of Milan
c.405	Death of Prudentius
407	Death of John Chrysostom, from 397 Bishop of Constantinople
c.410	Death of Asterius, Bishop of Amasea
410	Conquest of Rome by the West Goths
459	Death of Simeon Stylites

List of Illustrations

Index of Persons

Index of Places

Subject Index

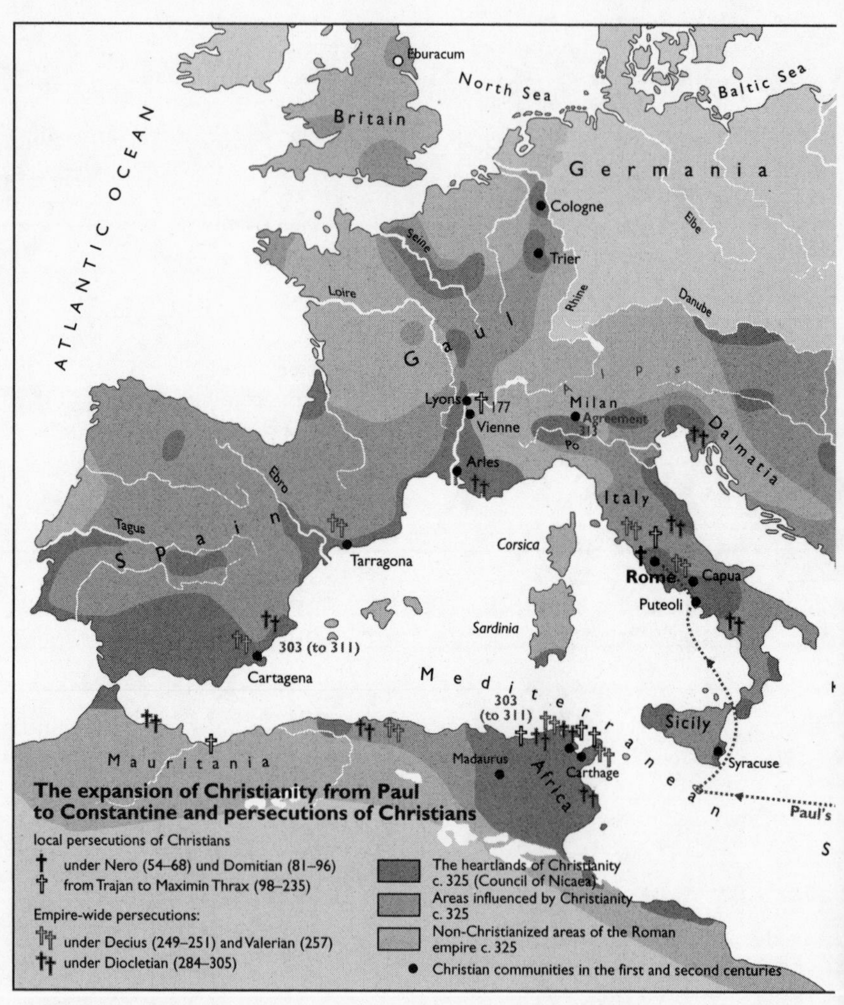

The expansion of Christianity from Paul to Constantine and persecutions of Christians

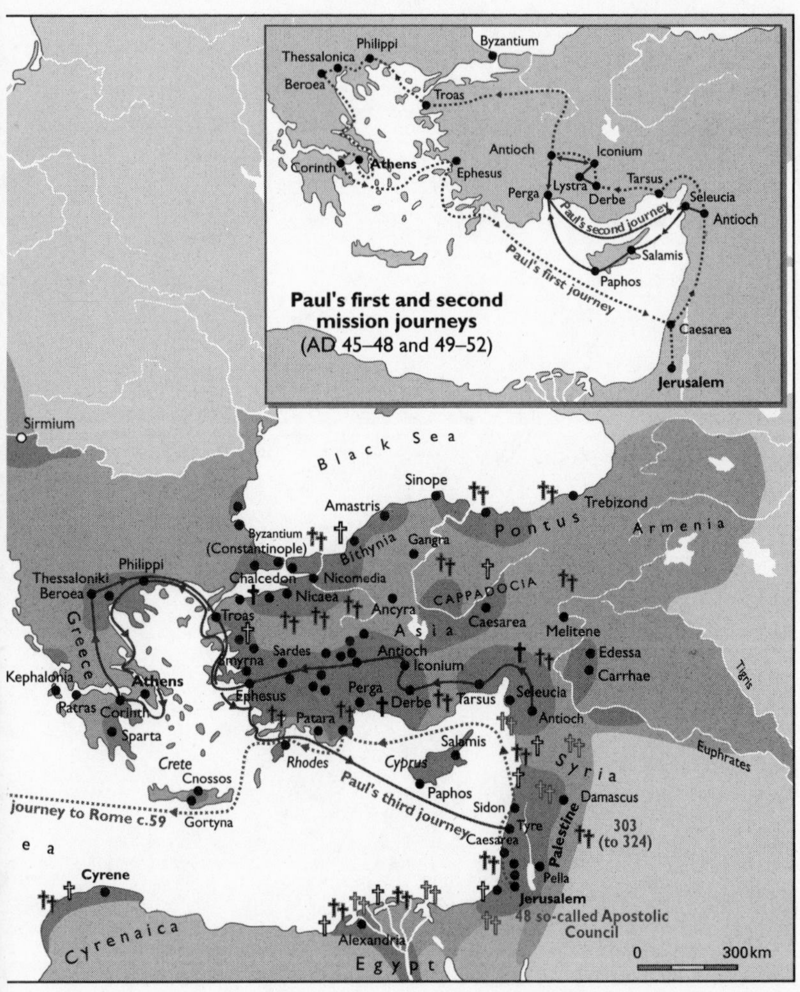

Paul's first and second mission journeys
(AD 45–48 and 49–52)
Philippi
Byzantium
Thessalonica
Beroea
Troas
Antioch
Iconium
Corinth
Athens
Ephesus
Tarsus
Perga
Lystra
Derbe
Seleucia
Antioch
Paul's second journey
Salamis
Paphos
Paul's first journey
Caesarea
Jerusalem
Sirmium
Black Sea
Sinope
Amastris
Trebizond
Pontus
Armenia
Byzantium
(Constantinople)
Bithynia
Gangra
Chalcedon
Nicomedia
Thessaloniki
Philippi
Beroea
Nicaea
CAPPADOCIA
Ancyra
Greece
Troas
Caesarea
Asia
Melitene
Sardes
Antioch
Edessa
Smyrna
Iconium
Carrhae
Kephalonia
Athens
Tigris
Ephesus
Perga
Derbe
Tarsus
Seleucia
Patras
Corinth
Patara
Antioch
Sparta
Salamis
Rhodes
Cyprus
Syria
Euphrates
Crete
Cnossos
Paphos
Damascus
Paul's third journey
Sidon
journey to Rome c.59
Gortyna
Tyre
Palestine
303
(to 324)
Caesarea
Cyrene
Pella
Jerusalem
48 so-called Apostolic Council
Cyrenaica
Alexandria
Egypt
0
300km